Contents

Acknowledgements   viii

EDERLEZI: Burn It Down   1

INTRODUCTION: In a Poor Town…   6

SERBIA   15
MAHALA BLUES 1: On, From and Upon Garbage   28
GUČA: The Rave That Time Forgot   42
ŠABAN BAJRAMOVIĆ: A Great Consumer of Life   52
BOBAN MARKOVIĆ: I Bring Sevdah   68

LANGO DROM (The Long Journey)   80

MACEDONIA   85
ESMA REDŽEPOVA: We Are Guests on This Earth   98
ELVIS HUNA: I Had to Steal Her   112
FERUS MUSTAFOV: Little Big Man   122
NAAT VELIOV: Have Trumpet, Will Travel   132
MAHALA BLUES 2: Good Music, Good Culture, Good People   146

O PORRAJMOS (The Great Devouring)   160

ROMANIA   167
FULGERICĂ: Slave to the Accordion   180
TARAF DE HAÏDOUKS: You Don't Learn This Job, You Steal It   188
MAHALA BLUES 3: Who is Killing Balkan Music?   204
FANFARE CIOCĂRLIA: Brass On Fire   214

TEHARA BRISIND DELA (The Rain May Come Tomorrow)   231

BULGARIA   235
JONY ILIEV: The Fate of the Gypsies   248
AZIS: The Brightest Smile in Town   260
MAHALA BLUES 4: The Saddest Place On Earth   274

EPILOGUE: Sometimes the Bear Gets You...   294

SELECT BIBLIOGRAPHY   297
SELECT DISCOGRAPHY   302
SELECT FILMOGRAPHY   308

PRINCES AMONGST MEN

Journeys with Gypsy Musicians

✦

Garth Cartwright

A complete record for this book can be obtained
from the British Library on request

The right of Garth Cartwright to be identified as the author
of this work has been asserted by him in accordance
with the Copyright, Designs and Patents Act 1988

Copyright © 2005 by Garth Cartwright

First published in 2005 by Serpent's Tail,
4 Blackstock Mews, London N4 2BT
website: www.serpentstail.com

Designed and typeset at Neuadd Bwll, Llanwrtyd Wells

Printed by Mackays of Chatham plc

10 9 8 7 6 5 4 3 2 1

To Esma Redžepova and Aung San Suu Kyi, soul rebels, natural mystics

The Gypsy Queen: Esma Redžepova and Ensemble Teodosievski

Acknowledgements

A book like this couldn't be written without the contributions of many people in many places. Along the way I've experienced great generosity and help from countless individuals who have all angled to make the journey smoother, communications easier. Foremost, I must offer praise and thanks to the Gypsy musicians, their families and friends – without such openness and willingness to talk to a strange Gadje in their midst no book would exist. Beyond this community I'm in debt to all who follow: Doug Rogers (who said 'you've got to write a book'), John Williams (who said 'I'll get you a deal'), Pete Ayrton (who said 'let's make a deal'), Nick Nasev (whose knowledge and enthusiasm shine throughout the text), Henry Ernst (an honourable travelling companion), Bojan Djordević, Boris Mitić, Ilija Stanković, Ivana Teofilovska, Michel Winter, Stephane Karo, Kim Burton, Helmut Neumann, David Katz, Dušan Bijanić, Karpa Stevanov, Selena Rakočević, Jovana Lukić, Rumiana Kotseva, Igor Andreevski, Krisi Naumovski, Vera Giese, Dragi Šestić, Mihai and Doina Serban, Bogdan and Dani, Ian Anderson@fRoots, Michelle Rosaus, David Jones, Bryn Ormrod, Miles Evans, Danielle Richards, Sanya Johnson, Jon Walton, Carol Silverman, Svanibor Pettan, Alexander Sclater, Jean Trouillet (Network), Sophie and Matze (Piranha), Robert Hackman, Yingzhao Liu, Conrad Heine. To friends international: many blessings. Finally, to the Roma people of this earth, 'Zhan le Devlesa tai sastimasa – Go with God and in good health.'

No thanks to Austrian Air – don't fly 'em.

For more information and images relating to this book go to www.journeyswithgypsies.com.

Let the Gypsies come and blossom.
We miss them.
They can help us by irritating our fixed orders.
They are what we pretend to be; they are the true Europeans.
They do not know any borders.

Günter Grass

Livin' like a Gypsy,
honey, it ain't easy
tryin' to be free

Aerosmith, 'Mama Kin'

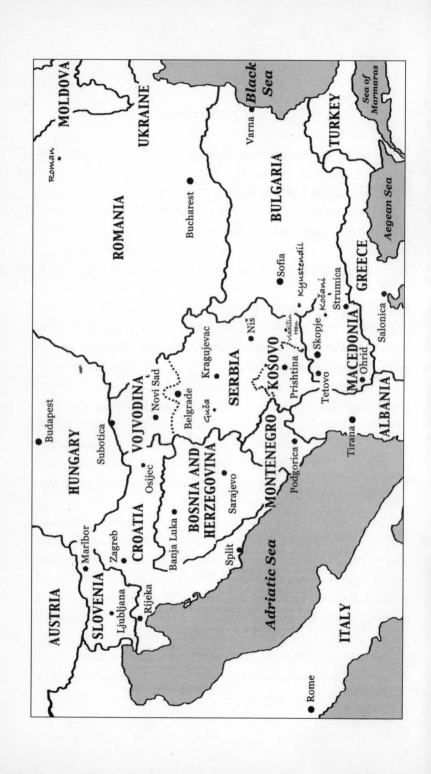

Ederlezi:

Burn It Down

Darkness slips across the mahala. As the sun's rays fade across the troubled West Balkan Peninsula the mahala is reverential. Sun Sun Sun. No one chants, no one actually says anything, but I'm conscious of an eerie sensation that at once we are all worshippers. As if to enforce this all around me the Roma are quiet. Now there's an oxymoron, quiet Gypsies. But it's true. Heat and brightness held the day and now their slow dissolve has captured everyone's attention. The mahala remains silent, lost in a splish splash of thoughts – tonight's festivities, rains that never arrived, crops beginning to curl, Roma beauties glimpsed in the plaza, Jony singing for us today, Kosovo, where the sun hides and no Roma dare show their dark faces, the impossibility of escaping poverty in this godforsaken place: Gypsy curses? The curse of being born a Gypsy!

There is something both beautiful and ominous about the Balkan twilight. I've crisscrossed this peninsula on countless journeys and always feel a slight hesitation as the sun disappears. Maybe I've watched too many vampire movies, heard too many tales of haïdouks robbing travellers, but – and I'm guilty of conjecture here – but the scent of blood often appears to ride the early evening air. A scent I recall accompanied the on-rush of darkness when, a decade ago, I wandered rural Mississippi in search of blues oracles. And as the last of the afternoon sizzle gives way to this, the most primal of nights, I sense sangre.

The light fades. A Lada, chemical orange in colour, splutters into the main plaza. No one moves too fast, the air still heavy with the day's heat. Mongrels so mangy they resemble hyenas remain splayed, motionless, soaking up the warmth trapped in the plaza's tatty tarmac. The mood is rich and listless, everyone enjoying the unnaturally warm ambience. Surrounded by mountains, the ancient spa town of Kyustendil entertains extreme Balkan climates – freezing in winter, boiling in summer – yet today is only May 5th and already afternoon temperatures are busting the mid-30 mark.

Not that the heat has dampened energy levels. Nothing less than the wrath of God could stop Kyustendil's mahala dwellers taking to the streets to party. Tomorrow, May 6th, is the day of the Gypsies, one they can mark as their own. St George's Day. Ederlezi in Romani. Gergyovden in Bulgarian. Djurdjevdan in Serbian. Gjurgjovden in Macedonian. Hidrellez in Turkish. George is the catch-all saint for the Balkans yet to the Roma, why, he's theirs. As Passover is to Jews and Christmas to Christians, Ederlezi is to the Roma. Yet Ederlezi is perhaps more akin to Thanksgiving in the USA, a hymn to a community's survival. And on the evening of May 5th Roma communities across the Balkans rise and come out to play.

Jony Iliev, Gypsy song icon and ghetto prince, grew up on the dirt streets of this mahala. As do most of the men born here who possess a marketable skill and/or ambition, Jony fled for brighter lights, bigger cities. A decade gone, he returns only occasionally, visiting his mother and brother and the two children he fathered before Sofia's barren concrete terrain lured him north. Returning for Ederlezi he's arrived in style: putting on a free concert in the square for the mahala dwellers, giving out awards to the children who have excelled at school, wandering through the mahala's medieval back streets – 'the ghetto', Jony calls it – embracing old friends, a magnet to urchins who follow screeching and laughing in Jony's wake.

Jony pats the head of a kid caked in dust, yelping for attention, and smiles. 'Mingra manus (my people),' he says and looks a little pained. 'Too much poverty, but what can I do?' he adds. Jony and his seven brothers sang and played their way out of this very ghetto, working before he hit puberty, a wedding singer rocking mahalas across Bulgaria's southwest territory. He was good, a gifted child, people would touch him just for luck. Even now they reach out to him. 'Jony!' they shout. 'Jony!'

This evening, having fulfilled all duties, Jony joins the festivities surrounding his nephew Alex's engagement party. The shriek of a clarinet cuts the air and here they come, a heaving mass of dancers spinning and turning, a moving, omnivorous circle that – hands linked, feet kicking – begins to resemble a giant, tangled centipede. This is it, the horo danced to a trio of accordion, clarinet and bass drum, Gypsy joy in motion. Alex's fiancée, Macarena, hair hennaed a brilliant crimson, is dressed in beige linen skirt and blouse which well-wishers pin fat wads of lev notes to. The dancers snake into the square, scattering yelping dogs and squealing children.

Jony's band regroup, help bring the noise, firing electricity into a temperate night sky. Listen to it build – elemental, unamplified instruments creating resonance surely similar to that which accompanied the Roma as they wandered west, crossing the wastelands of Balochistan and Persia, venturing into Armenia and Byzantium, versus saxophone, electric guitar, drum kit, keyboards, the hi-tech pulse of the Europe they ended up resident in – yet, of course, there is no sound clash; all these musicians, apprenticed at weddings, believe in the dance.

The whole day so far has been one of active celebration – Jony singing, awards, children's activities, even the heat feels like a gift from St George – and the horo dancing in the square keeps the mahala's temperature rising. After two hours the spinning slows, loses its centre, unravels. All those who can squeeze into the café owned by Chico, Jony's older brother and father to Alex, in the corner of the square. Here plates of salad, cheeses and cold sausage are shared amongst the festive gathering to a soundtrack of chalga, the hard

Oriental electronic music of Bulgaria's Gypsies. Infants are put on tables and encouraged to shake to the beat. Chico's a devout Seventh Day Adventist, a man whose blood knows no impurities, but this being Ederlezi and an engagement, the ultimate double header of celebrations, means the Pirinsko Pivo (ale) and rakija (brandy) flow like heavenly waters.

A chill breeze carries down from the still snowy Osogovo mountains circling Kyustendil to the east, raising goose pimples, firming nipples. Across the square a youth takes this as a signal to douse a tractor tyre in petrol. A match is tossed with casual glee. Dig the hisssss! A latex necklace erupts into flame, dense plumes of black smoke pour forth and bitter burning rubber invades nostrils and mouth. 'Gypsies can't party without fire,' says Chico, stoic after years of witnessing the mahala's toxic avengers. 'And a used tyre, it's easy to come by and will burn longer than wood.' Gypsies. Fire. Like bread and butter, politicians and lies, you sense they instinctively go together. But in Kyustendil no one is dancing around the fire to flamenco accompaniment. No caravans are parked near. No preening males with cruel, handsome mouths play bristling guitars. Those who gather around the rubber inferno, some spitting mouthfuls of rakija or petrol on the tyre, are the scorched of this earth, Roma youths who stagger, blasted on cheap liquor and glue, pupils swollen, eyes bulging, facial burn wounds, so high they're blind, a blank blank blank generation, the Gypsy zombies have come out to play.

The witching hour and Kyustendil erupts. Leaping out of doorways, entire neighbourhoods dance across alleys and towards the plaza. Trios of musicians are everywhere, summoning the spirits of Asian ancestors, channelled by a clarinet's harsh, reedy shriek, the music calling across generations, borders, cultures, right back to somewhere west of the River Ganges and south of the Hindu Kush. And what sounds: sounds without words but speaking to all revellers of bloodlines – how many roads, how many tears, have we left behind? – a loose, whooping joy overwhelming the mahala.

Except for the zombies. They stagger yet can't fall, stare but don't see, oblivious to the beginning of Ederlezi and all it suggests – the rebirth of nature, the start of summer, the bringing of good luck and good health to those who wish for it – the salvation on offer. Jony and Chico are deep in the night, feeling their way through, riding the wave of Roma joy. But whenever another tyre crackles, hisses and explodes into toxic flame, they withdraw a little, uneasy amongst the abandoned, aware the ghetto feeds on its own and blood is in the air. 'Sometimes,' says Chico as he peers through smouldering fumes, 'sometimes I think we should burn it all down.'

INTRODUCTION:
In a Poor Town...

All the beauty that's ever been, it's moving inside that music. The voice the wind had in Africa, the blues, and the spirituals, and the remembering, and the waiting, and the suffering, and the looking at the sky watching the dark come down – that's all inside the music.
　　　　　　　　　　　　　– Sidney Bechet, Treat It Gentle

Folk Devils/Moral Panics

Darting amongst congested traffic...tanned teak brown from the August sun...wiping windscreens with gold-toothed smiles then proffering an outstretched palm...the Gypsies move easily, seemingly oblivious to the tense congestion around them, occupying a south-east London traffic junction, marking out territory, performing the squeegee hustle. The women, dressed in long, heavily patterned skirts, headscarves and aprons – indicating Romanian origins – are the most active, bouncing on their heels, laughing. The men, shirt-sleeves rolled up and trilbies cocked at an angle, are more interested in pursuing sedentary pleasures: smoking cigarettes and girl-watching. Cars crawl past, drivers wearing the London motoring mask – brow furrowed, lips curled – refusing eye contact. Or swear and spit at the squeegees. Only too familiar with this behaviour the Gypsies step back, shrug, wait for

Nineteenth-century
Romani man

Felix Kantitz, *Donau Bulgarien und der Balhen*

more benevolent vehicles. When I pull up on my bicycle we share a bemused look. 'Patjival o manus an' la vi anda gav xaljardo,' I say. 'A righteous man will profit even in a poor town.' Or it would be if my pronunciation wasn't so poor and recall of Romani even worse. Most likely I uttered something sounding more gibberish than proverb. The sisters – they have to be sisters, corners of their mouths curling to the left, opaque beauty and Orient eyes – laugh. Gadje dilo. Crazy stranger. The lights change. I'm off. The Roma remain, exotica amongst exhaust fumes.

That Balkan Roma can be found in south-east London at the dawn of the twenty-first century is no cause for surprise. Southwark's traditionally been a dumping ground for the poor and dispossessed and as London councils struggled to house refugees throughout the 1990s the ruined North Peckham estate played host to a vast ethnic mosaic. Alongside Jamaicans, Nigerians and Vietnamese came those fleeing the disintegration of Yugoslavia, Somalia, Sierra Leone. And then the Gypsies arrived. Supposedly so many that by spring

2000 the Sun, the Express, the Evening Standard and the Daily Mail all featured shrill front pages warning readers a Gypsy invasion of England was under way. These headlines were recycled in early 2004 when the tabloids realised that the new EU member states' accession date was May and Roma in Poland and Slovakia could well decide to spend summer in England. Was this media-driven climate of fear and loathing so different from when their Roma ancestors first landed here in the late fifteenth century? Considering the anti-Egyptian legislation passed during the reigns of Henry VIII and the first Queen Beth, I'd guess not.

Being a Peckham estate dweller my new neighbours fired my interest – who are these people? Where exactly do they come from? Why do they carry themselves with such pride? Having repeatedly crisscrossed the former Eastern Bloc, backpacking and chasing an elfin Czech beauty, I was conscious of the Roma – dark-skinned/brightly clothed – yet never encountered them individually. They didn't appear to be employed in shops or hotels or on trains or planes; a visible yet socially invisible presence. Asking East European acquaintances about their nations' Roma resulted, too often, in a litany of invective. 'The Gypsies are dirty and dangerous,' the Czech elf told me. 'Have you ever met one?' I enquired. 'Noooooo,' she replied. 'But I know.' This book then is rooted in my desire also to *know*.

Where to start? The only Gypsies I'd ever encountered were in movies, books and music, characters often as rooted in reality as leprechauns or Golems. Thus Gypsy women are always cast as tempestuous beauties: the indomitable Ava Gardner in The Barefoot Contessa, Bizet's Carmen, two babes fighting alongside (and bedding) James Bond in From Russia With Love, Curtis Mayfield's campfire dancing Gypsy Woman, Caravaggio's palm-reading/pick-pocketing hustler, John Singer Sargent's scarlet temptress and Otto Muller's tan, naked beauties. If the women were hot the men lived way, way outside the law. Virginia Woolf described them as savages. D. H. Lawrence as noble savages. Cher's Gypsies, Tramps and Thieves was Woolfian while Van Morrison's 'Gypsy Queen' (moon above, road below, woody glens etc.) chose a Lawrencian outlook. Hippies and alt.lifestylers fêted Gypsies as romantic outlaws. Jimi Hendrix wrote songs and named a band after them. All of which had me pondering – could any people possibly possess more bohemian cool? Also – beyond acting as mythic touchstones, what was the Gypsy existence?

To answer these questions I dived into the Balkans. One extremely steep learning curve lay ahead.

Unclean Powers

The curve, initially, involved overcoming three omnipresent clichés. Firstly, the slur that Gypsies are 'dirty and dangerous'; vindictive politicians and media organisations continue to stoke this centuries-old fear, one rooted in the same loathing of the 'other' that once branded Jews vermin. While today only the violently deranged revert to anti-Semitisms, Gypsy-bashing has never faded. Next, the cliché presenting flamenco musicians and their dance troupes as absolutely the last word in wild, sweaty 'Gypsy passion'. Yes, Joaquin Cortes fills those tight leather pants well but one pouting icon does not represent a people. Finally, what the Slavs called 'nečiste sile' – unclean powers…magic. Roma contact with the spirit world has long been emphasised and with the rise in US TV/movies focusing on the supernatural Gypsies make for delectable necromancers.

How to break through such entrenched clichés? Music. Music has always been the Roma area of absolute excellence, as essential as human speech and just as precious. The twentieth century's love affair with American music – and Europe's catastrophic wars and divisions – sidelined a great deal of Gypsy music. Yet the few who broke through helped reshape modern music: Django Reinhardt, raised in a caravan in Belgium, was recognised as

Django Reinhardt

Photo: ©Warner Jazz France

Europe's first truly outstanding jazz musician. Joe Zawinul, born to an Austrian Roma family and from age six playing Gypsy music on accordion with the family band, went on to collaborate with Cannonball Adderley and Miles Davis, so extending jazz's sonic borders. Camaron de la Isla's titanic howl provided flamenco with a haunted, visionary voice.

'We don't live for tomorrow,' says Macedonian trumpet legend Naat Veliov. 'We live for today. And it shows in our playing – we put everything in, the heart and the soul. To make music is our happiness and we love to share our happiness.'

Tsingani. Egyptian. Cingano. Gypsy. Cikan. Sipsiwn. Cigani. Zigeuner. Gitano. Cingene. Yiftos. 'So many names they call us,' says Macedonian diva Esma Redžepova, 'we who know ourselves as Roma.' Rom/Roma is Sanskrit for 'man' or 'husband' and was adopted as the official form of reference at 1971's First World Romani Congress. Musicians are often referred to, both by themselves and others, as Gypsies; understandably as the music continues to be marketed as 'Gypsy' in an affirmative manner.

To be a musician amongst the Roma is trade and calling, an initiation begun in childhood, one carrying forth a community's beliefs and concerns. As with West Africa's griots the musicians are primarily entertainers, artisans, yet the alchemic possibilities of music – its ability to move sober listeners – finds exalted musicians regarded as allied with spirit forces.

'Living for song and with song I sometimes feel I touch the sky,' notes Esma. 'Other times I feel I'm on the brink of a terrible precipice. What saved me from falling? My love for singing. Song guards one against all evils.'

And the Roma are all too familiar with evil forces: from Vlad Dracul to Corneliu Vadim Tudor, Balkan slave traders to Hitler's SS, they have constantly encountered Europeans intent on oppressing, exploiting, even exterminating them. Thus their great singers wail a dark, raging blues; Džansever's low, masculine moan speaks plenty about human anguish; Nicolae Neacşu's toothless decrying of Ceauşescu's cruelty is harsh as a blunt razor shave; Esma Redžepova's volatile vocal was described to me by a Macedonian Roma as 'the voice of village Gypsies and all the suffering we have known'.

Suffering. The music of the Roma, its eerie intensity and savage resonance, arises from this hurt, music offering a form of soul-making, and, possibly, redemption. Well, that's my take on an extremely foreign music, one capable of...engagement... connection...Not that there's anything new in Gadje infatuation with Gypsy music. For centuries music has been the way Roma have carried forth their culture, myths and language. Formidable musical talent has led European society to often embrace the gifted few. After the Berlin Wall fell this began again.

By the early 1990s Balkan Roma had featured in acclaimed films by Yugoslav and French directors while the West's world music circuit embraced all manner of Gypsy music...wobbly rhythms, creaking violins, exploding brass...here was music full of living colour, sounds conceived in a forgotten Asia, shaped by the bitter European experience and sung in a tongue few can translate.

This tongue would act as siren, luring me east, into Roma villages and mahalas. Mahala is Turkish for 'neighbourhood' and across the Balkans mahala signifies 'poor part of town', y'know, the Gypsy ghetto. These were journeys of revelation, both joyous and extremely sad – the Roma possess a great lust for life yet to encounter such noble people reduced to living in slums and shanty towns offers little hope for better tomorrows.

The Roma wish to be heard – why else raise their voices so loud in song? These voices, in song and conversation, shaped this book. Not that it's always easy to write accurately on a people who have few written records. Their beliefs, claims, chronologies can vary across the region, shifting size and colour, blending myth and fact. Jamaica's Rastafarians talk of 'overstanding' and that fluid concept's worth keeping in mind when dealing with a people who have often had little more than an instinctive creativity to help their communities survive. For close to millennia the Roma have formed Europe's largest minority yet remain the continent's 'invisible nation', forever marginalised, often little more than footnotes to persecution. If history is written by the victors then the Roma only ever win at music. Which is why I've focused on musicians: let their kings and queens, Europe's musical royalty, sing their stories.

'I find it [Gypsy music] difficult to describe but there is no Gypsy existence without music,' says Chico Iliev. 'We have such a heavy life and if we didn't have the music we would kill ourselves. The music is our medicine. Our opium.'

Let's Call The Children Home

Hard travel, uneasy integration, the constant struggle to survive, establish a margin of freedom and, of course, celebration times:

these are the qualities of Gypsy song. Gypsy musicians may tour the West's most esteemed concert halls yet back in the Balkans their music remains communal property, created and played on the streets. Witnessing Macedonia's Sudahan Rušid blow clarinet through a cranked-up PA on a Skopje street I imagine New Orleans at the dawn of the twentieth century. Back then trumpet player extraordinaire Buddy Bolden would say, 'Let's call the children home' before he began squeezing out sparks. Much as Sudahan fires up a wedding party, his reedy, Arabic-flavoured clarinet acting as Pied Piper to all within hearing.

This ability to invite everyone to the dance remains central to Gypsy music, an organic welcoming absent from too much of our society. Indeed, in an increasingly homogenised/regulated Europe Gypsy music and culture convey secret histories; the enigma and wisdom of these people remain little understood. Who gives credence to the Roma having reshaped Europe in their image and sound? Imagination. Beauty. Expression. Migration.

The Roma laid a foundation for a non-aggressive, culturally open movement many in the West now emulate. Paradoxically, a people celebrated for their freedom are today profoundly un-free; trapped by poverty, visa laws and discrimination, many Roma inhabit a shadow Europe. And in this shadow Europe music is often the only way out. I'm often asked why Western nations so soaked in hip and hype respond to illiterate Gypsy musicians dressed in slacks and nylon shirts. One word: *spirit*. Spirit draws audiences from Japan to Mexico, New York to Berlin. *Let's call the children home.*

I chose Serbia and Macedonia, Bulgaria and Romania, for their rich reservoirs of Gypsy music. Across the centuries these nations have formed a bridge between east and west: many civilisations, cultures, armies and religions have intersected here – the traces of their presence being especially strong in the music, music which blooms in brilliant colours across the Balkans, music shaped and spread by the Roma, the seeds they planted producing extraordinary fruit, one that survives all manner of war, oppression and regime. Today around 50 per cent of Europe's Roma live in the Balkans.

As my nominated nations rarely attract attention in the West – and if they do it's usually for the worst reasons – this means the cultures the Roma exist amongst are rarely understood. And living in the Balkans, a territory now a byword for senseless wars (*Collins English Dictionary* defines 'balkanise' as 'to divide into warring states'), the musicians become tainted. Primitives. Fuelled by apocalyptic ethnic animosities. Stretching across time immemorial. Well, that's the standard Western line.

Now here's the rub: for centuries the Balkans found different ethnicities and cultures living alongside one another (admittedly, not always easily) and sharing many things, none more so than music. The rise of singular nationalism – fuelled initially by nineteenth-century west European romantics who championed an idealised Greek state – has had horrendous effects on the Balkans with stateless Roma (and pre-Israel Jews) being buffeted and shredded by wild, violent currents.

The collapse of East European communism and the Yugoslav wars have generated many texts yet the writers who pass through the Balkan wastelands and killing fields never appear to ask about the Roma. They're referenced as local colour or an emblem of suffering vis-à-vis Kosovo. But to actually converse with? Their role in history is reduced to a silent, supporting cast. And the Roma know this – nobody's listening – so feeding a sense of exclusion. Let their voices rise, is my intention. If I've done right by these Balkan sorcerers of sound then I'll have encouraged the reader to listen. So pass the rakija, get back in the saddle…till the paint peels and the wheels fall off.

SERBIA

'Welcome To Serbia, Europe's Premier Pariah State' reads the sign in Belgrade Airport's arrivals hall. Matter o'fact, it don't. But considering the deflation of Serbia's reputation – once centre for the world's most equitable attempt at pan-national state socialism, now home to a people whose most popular politicians are on trial for war crimes – the sign might as well do. Indeed, the airport's tatty furnishings and resigned service suggest a toll taken on the nation since President Tito's death in 1980.

Step through and into hot July sun. All appears mute, even the taxi drivers can barely register the effort to signal for a cab. Heat. Dust. Silence. At the start of Goran Paskaljević's bitter 1998 portrait of Belgrade, *Cabaret Balkan*, the taxi driver addresses his passenger with the question, 'What brings you back to the asshole of Europe?' As ever, we all have our reasons. Belgrade today isn't the inferno it was last decade but three survival rules still apply for Serbia.

1: Keep drinking.

2: Don't talk politics.

3: Keep drinking.

The airport bus, like the terminal, has seen better days. Farmland. A smattering of suburbs. Then New Belgrade appears. New Belgrade fits its name: nothing here can be older than two score and ten. Initially resembling a monochrome movie set, the prevailing architectural design recalls a child's kit-set: hard rectangles with edges chopped off, concrete mushrooms, structures employing unwieldy step patterns. And acre after acre of housing estates; weather-stained tower blocks standing in formation like so many mutant corn rows, industrial housing built to contain the village-to-city influx that trickled into a flood through the 1960s. Should be familiar with the fortress effect by now, Belgrade being a regular crossroads in my Balkan wanderings, but this cityscape still burns the eye.

Belgrade (Beograd) stands for 'white city', a laurel I'm sure certain Serb nationalists have caressed. Rumbling through these avenues of sensory brutalism, though, I feel 'grey city' would be a more appropriate handle. Recently Tirana, the capital of Albania, was transformed from crumbly Stalinist hues to a rainbow of colours due to the city's mayor's determination to make the metropolis a more enticing place. Serbs will grind teeth at the suggestion they could learn from Albanians yet a slap of paint wouldn't hurt New Belgrade.

Then, suddenly, all is beautiful. The bus crosses Brankov Bridge, over the Sava River's emerald waters. The Sava's a tributary of the

Danube – Belgrade was founded by Celts 2,300 years ago on a bluff overlooking the confluence of the two rivers – and they lend the city a flowing, watery soul.

Old Belgrade could, indeed, also use a paint job. Still, it possesses the rolling, winding, impenetrable flavour so essential to a city's character. Ramshackle street markets sell Turkish and Chinese junk, tiny bakeries proffer sweet and sour pastries, people hustle, people bustle. Hotels aren't too plentiful in Belgrade – tourism in Serbia remains something of an oxymoron – but the Old Town offers a few Tito-era edifices both inexpensive and habitable. Hotel Prag, with its huge ashtrays, narrow rooms and air of permanent disaffection, suits my mood. Drop backpack and contemplate initial moves.

Gene Pitney once sang of being twenty-four hours from Tulsa. Add a few extra hours on and change the destination to Guča, central Serbia, and Pitney's baroque ballad just about describes me. Tomorrow I'll connect with Karpa, a friend of a friend from the northern city of Novi Sad, who's going to act as driver and translator for my journey south. But today, hey, time to reacquaint myself with Belgrade.

Passing a street full of chic bars and cafés, all blaring the Fashion TV channel, I enquire as to where I am. 'Silicon Valley,' comes the reply from a bored waiter. I'm dumbfounded, there being no sign of a Balkan computer industry. 'We call it that because the girls with the silicon chests come here looking for a rich husband,' says the waiter, only slightly arching an eyebrow. Serb humour. Not bad.

Bypassing Silicon Valley, I connect with Selena. We initially met in northern Romania, checking traditional music festivities. Selena's an ethno-musicologist and, she notes, if nothing else Serbia remains a good place to ply her trade, village culture and music-making as ritual still existing in many pockets of this agrarian nation. We take a beer in one of central Belgrade's outdoor cafés. Immediately, Roma kids surround me, begging, barefoot ragamuffins with a cheeky look in their eye. Idite! (Go away!)

Course they don't, instead a particularly artful dodger hones in and – bam! – fast as a bull terrier on a royal corgi he's appropriated cigarettes and lighter. A sign from the gods saying time to quit smoking? Sure. But if there's one thing I know about the Balkans it is they're the wrong place to relinquish bad habits.

Selena laughs at the cigarettes' exodus and reminisces on the Milošević era when sanctions and hyper-inflation meant even trying to find tobacco was a desperate endeavour. Things are better now, Selena says, not quite normal but more positive. Then she reflects: 'I visited Sarajevo a little while ago and I went into a shop and tried to buy cigarettes. The man behind the counter, he could tell by my accent that I'm a Serb, refused to sell to me. I realise we Serbs are collectively guilty but, please, don't judge me as individually having blood on my hands. Will things ever be normal? Will the hatreds heal? I don't know.'

We stroll into Kneza Mihaila, the commercial heart of Belgrade, a creamy, marbled boulevard housing designer boutiques and fabulous ice cream parlours. It's reminiscent of Austria or Italy, understandably so, the Danube acting as dividing line between the Balkans and Central Europe. Shuffle up Kneza Mihaila to the Kalemagdan Citadel, this former fortress is Belgrade's prime park, offering much green space, funfairs, museums, tombs and dramatic views across the city. People ramble, children play, lovers embrace, troupes folk dance in full costume…the atmosphere's beatific. Yet there's lots of war junk: tanks, rocket launchers, missiles, bombs… much contributed by NATO. Considering the fortress now hosts a military museum I guess these munitions are what they couldn't fit inside. Still, they lend an ugly face to a beautiful space and, surely, Serbs have experienced enough war fetishism to last decades. Go figure: Vojislav Šešelj, leader of the Serbian Radical Party, achieved the largest vote in the December '03 Serbian elections. Šešelj is a fascist on trial at The Hague for war crimes. His platform: more war (Croatia, Kosovo, Bosnia). His role model: Hitler.

'It's sad that so many people vote for Šešelj,' says Selena. 'They're obviously clinging to a desperate nationalism when what Serbia needs is someone who can bring the nation into Europe rather than keeping it isolated and aggressive.'

Supporters of Šešelj and The Hague's most infamous occupant, Slobodan Milošević, trade in fermenting self-pity, playing on a siege mentality where 426 years of Ottoman rule – the Serb kingdom's defeat at the Battle of Kosovo in 1389 still rankles, a Slav Vietnam – and the brutality of German occupiers during the two world wars mark Serbs out as forever victims of foreign powers. Thus much rewriting of history and a refusal to accept responsibility for the wretched wars of the 1990s: blame Croats or Bosniaks, swear reports of concentration and rape camps are Western lies. The slaughter of non-combatants in Kosovo? Albanians are primitive, they reason, barely human. And the dissolution of Yugoslavia? A NATO conspiracy.

Now, I've no love for NATO but those who refuse to comprehend how the criminal actions of Milošević and his cronies – including a vicious and obsequious Serb media – compounded the faults of a decaying one-party system, so tearing apart what was once the most liberal and cosmopolitan East European state, induced wars that killed hundreds of thousands and left Serbia bankrupt and backward, well... Serb nationalism is wretchedly pathetic, reminiscent of Millwall FC's slogan, 'No one likes us, we don't care.'

Selena may be fluent in the ethnic music(s) of the Balkans yet she's equally versed in pop and jazz. Considering most of my Western contemporaries are scared of any non-English-language music I wonder if her tastes are diverse only because of her job. No, she says, offering a sad smile, Yugoslavia echoed to the sound of all kinds of music. All kinds. And then my beautiful friend leaves to collect her infant son while I ponder why music should be such a potent creative endeavour across the Balkans.

Tito, wise to music's international appeal, used the traditional music of the region to build cross-cultural bridges. In Yugoslavia folklore was the state-sanctioned soundtrack, music in keeping with the ideology of 'Brotherhood and Unity'. Thus Slovenians sang Kosovar Albanian songs while Serbs performed Croat dances. Ciganska (Gypsy) music, untainted by nationalism, received plenty of airplay. After Tito's death nationalist rhetoric began infecting music; Belgrade's Gypsy music community took note – Ljiljana Petrović migrated to Germany and became a cleaner, Šaban Bajromović retired to Niš, Esma Redžepova fled back to Macedonia, Aca Sisić stopped playing altogether. At the same time a Belgrade-led musical revolution – turbo-folk – swept the Balkans, an aural virus, producing a Serb superstar: Ceca.

Turbo-folk mixed Serb folk song with increasingly slick sounds from Turkey, Egypt and pre-revolution Iran. In doing so turbo-folk created an effective local alternative to Western pop/rock. Profoundly shallow, turbo-folk's big fun. And in Svetlana 'Ceca' Veličković, a peasant girl from south Serbia who first tasted stardom aged fourteen in 1987, turbo-folk found its queen. Ceca possessed the looks and body (both cosmetically perfected) and tough, personified desire necessary to rule. But a turbo-folk queen needs a king: when, in 1995, Ceca married career-criminal-turned-warlord Željko 'Arkan' Ražnatović, they gave Serbia a hellish Posh and Becks.

While Sarajevo burned and Kosovo boiled, Ceca became an icon of the Serb state. Her dark, almost masculine, features, ever-expanding bosom and marriage to a man of extreme violence cast Ceca closer to the bloodstained Balkan goddess of ancient lore than, say, the banal celebrity Madonna personifies. That she first achieved fame singing at a folk festival on the hill overlooking Sarajevo, the same hill Bosnian Serb paramilitaries would a few years later use to bombard Sarajevo's citizens, and moved easily amongst some of Europe's deadliest men, a chorus of Balkan Furies, suggests both Ceca's dark and powerful stardom and how popular culture across former Yugoslavia was infected during the insanity.

I wonder if this pretty, vacant woman ever considered that the demise of the Yugoslav ideal – Balkan brotherhood and unity – was a tragedy? With Arkan at her side, doubtful. It was a slow, messy death; Tito's state had long been corrupted economically (at the time of the Prez's death the foreign debt was $20 billion), so leading to hyperinflation and great insecurity. Slobodan Milošević, who in 1986 became head of the Serbian League of Communists, played on nationalist sentiment to guarantee his power: he exploited the fear of Albanians that runs throughout the Balkans and made great play of differences between Christian and Muslim, Serb and Croat, when little genuinely existed. His brutal manoeuvring allowed ultra-nationalists to gain serious power in Serbia (and so too in Croatia) and bred a class of employee more criminal than civil. By the early 1990s Serbia's symbiosis of government, organised crime and security forces was one area in which it led the world.

The ever-smiling, ever-charming Arkan being a perfect example. Arkan lived the life of a Mafia don cum mercenary general while holding a seat in Serbia's parliament representing Kosovo (his paramilitary Tigers made themselves known to the region's Albanian residents). Rich from the spoils of war and crime, he campaigned with a silver crucifix: protector of Orthodoxy. Ceca sang at his political rallies, oblivious to her husband's indictment by The Hague for war crimes. Arkan was gunned down in the lobby of Belgrade's Intercontinental Hotel in 2000; the list of possible assassins is very long. Ceca survived Arkan to be jailed for four months in 2003 as a suspect in the assassination of reforming Serb Prime Minister Zoran Djindjić. When arrested, her mansion bristled with weaponry and gangsters. Freed, she remains a Serb superstar, her every movement an Event.

Haunted by Ceca and the potent Balkan pop voodoo she conjures, her songs – 'Kukavica' (Coward), addressing her ex-Bosnian lover; 'Ličiš Na Moga Oca' (You Look Like My Father), talking about how Arkan is a father figure to her; 'Isuse' (Jesus), a prayer for strength in fighting Islam – on a loop in my skull, I opt to take a taxi to Dedinje,

Let it all hang out…
Ceca

© PGP RTS

an upmarket suburb where stands the mansion Arkan and Ceca built. My driver offers a broken English gesture-guide to the 'hood: there's Milošević's mansion, here's Red Star Belgrade's football stadium and that one is – I know, cut him off before he can say it, I know. Beneath a grey, humid Belgrade sky I confront Ceca's castle. As it should be: a turbo-mansion, four storeys of mirrored glass windows and ornate neo-classical design, proudly/aggressively vulgar. Arkan's rise to glory began as head of the Red Star Supporters Club, turning terrace hooligans into paramilitaries, so building his fortified crib next to all he held sacred. If walls could whisper, damn, imagine the tales this house would tell.

I get out. Stand on the pavement. Stare. Some people go to Beverly Hills, me, I rubberneck in Belgrade. As my journey begins I'm paying weird homage outside the house some would say Balkan music ends at. Feel him before I see him: glowering through shades, shell suit, shaven head, stocky like Tyson, a 90s relic and f'sure a gentleman, a real charmer. No sightseeing? The taxi driver's gesturing for me to get back in the cab. Ain't like I'm going to interview Ceca. Though that could be interesting. But for now a close encounter with this remnant of the 'Delije' (Arkan's Knights) is enough. No need for me to make a mess on this clean street. Get in the cab.

Back in muggy central Belgrade I've still got an evening to kill. Phone call here, phone call there. People are on holiday. Preoccupied. Finally I manage to contact Aca Šišić, a man considered by some to be the finest traditional violinist of the Tito era. It had been suggested to me that Aca was Ciganin (Gypsy). But when, on a previous visit, I broached this with Aca he spluttered, turned pink, red, a shade of purple, and damn near exploded. Worried I'd be the hack who gives Aca, sixty-seven and comfortably corpulent, a heart attack, I apologised profusely for the unintended slight. This visit I'm determined to keep the G-word silent.

Aca lives amongst the tower blocks in New Belgrade. A tram and then a taxi deposits me at the base of his building. Broken glass. Graffiti. Refuse. The lift wobbles and creaks. Aca's violin skills, fabulous as they are, obviously never got him anywhere near Ceca's suburb. Aca's at the door, ever-welcoming, offering a broad smile and Turkish coffee so thick, so concentrated, I feel a heart murmur coming on. Kickback, listen to him talk, his life story being deep Balkan blues.

'My fathers and grandfathers were violinists. All the men in my family are violinists. The legend of the family was during the time when the Austrian Empire controlled Serbia one of my ancestors tried to escape but they caught him. They were going to shoot him so he said, "When you bury me just bring me my violin" and the sergeant said, "You are a musician? You can live!"'

Aca chuckles. His small flat is crowded with photos of grandchildren, his younger self with violin, and images of Orthodox saints. Mica, Aca's wife of forty-eight years, bustles around, silent but smiling. 'I owe everything to Mica,' says Aca. 'All my colleagues, they're divorced but not me. Mica's my right hand, she understood my life, she was my manager and secretary. Tito knew of her. He'd say to me, "How's your Mica, your secret policeman?"' Aca and Mica laugh at the memory, happy people. 'Human respect and tolerance is the secret of a good marriage,' says Aca when I ask what makes love last. What a nice man. And what an amazing musician.

'I started to play violin as a small child. I grew up in Brenovitz [near Belgrade] in a family that spoke Romanian as a first language. I never had a small violin. I always had a big one. It was funny to see. At five I was an attraction and started to earn money. By eight I was leading a band.'

Across the Balkans folk dancing remain a potent part of all celebrations and Aca's a dance master, the original DJ. Most popular are the formation dances (kolo/oro/horo/čoček); at any given opportunity inhabitants will jump up, clasp hands, form a circle and begin to skip and hop. The anti-clockwise movement follows an asymmetrical rhythm, everyone holding hands and moving as one, a unified, happy world until the music finishes. This circle was smashed during the Second World War when the Nazis occupied Yugoslavia, murdering and murdering and murdering. As a tot Aca was placed on tanks and told to fiddle for the fascists, undoubtedly a terrifying experience. And to speak of war wipes Aca's smile.

'My uncle was the best violin player in the family – he was murdered by the Germans in a concentration camp because they saw him as a Gypsy. The professors of music in Brenovitz, they were also murdered by the Germans. Same reason. We're not Gypsy. We have this kind of skin but we are not Gypsies.'

As Aca speaks a Romanian dialect I wonder if he is Vlach. 'No,' he answers. Though I'm sure last time I visited he said he was. The Vlach being a small ethnic group scattered across the Balkans who speak a language closely resembling Romanian. In Hungary Vlach simply means 'Romanian-speaking Gypsy',

Magyar Vlach being descended from Romanian Roma slaves
who fled to Hungary in the nineteenth century. To be honest, Aca
looks more Slav than Roma yet Mica is dark and photos of their
grandchildren reveal gorgeous tots who, with their inky black hair
and big brown eyes, again look Roma. Perhaps the terror rained
on his community from 1941 to 1945 finds Aca shutting out any
suggestion of minority ethnicity. Understandably: 6.4 per cent
of Yugoslavia's 1941 population died during the Second World
War, the Roma second only to Jews in terms of devastation with
31.4 per cent murdered. At Jasenovac's infamous concentration
camp – a place so brutal only Pol Pot's killing fields match it
for murderous primitivism – Croatia's fascist Ustasha regime
slaughtered more than ten thousand Roma.

'I had a very rough road to fame as I had to work hard to buy
shoes, notebooks, help my parents. In the middle of summer I was
in a village twenty kilometres from Brenovitz and the temperatures
were very high and I had to stand in the middle of a field and play
violin for those harvesting. By playing all day I would earn twenty
kilos of corn to make bread. And then with the violin and the big
bag I'd walk home. My father never said, "Oh, my son, you made
that with your hard work". I will never forget that. My father never
helped me. Sometimes he hindered me. He had a stick like this
[indicates a cane] and he would hit me over the fingers. I learned
a lot from his mistakes. Now when I have a pupil and he makes
mistakes I say, "It will be all right, my son".'

A local star from an early age – 'there was no celebration or
feast that they wouldn't call me, Little Aca! They'd carry me to
the festivals!' – Aca never tired of learning new ways of making
music. Initially playing restaurants and kafanas (honky tonks), he
became a member of the TV Folklore Orchestra, playing for Tito
and touring the world.

'I have a big joy in me and I have my own style, my own
profundity. And in my joy and happiness the world received me

Mr Magic Violin...
Aca Šišić

Photo: Garth Cartwright

with open arms. No money can pay what I experienced touring! Mexico was the best – on every corner was a violinist and I felt like one of them. In Costa Rica the conductor came after the concert to check my hands saying, "What is this? Is it a magic violin?" And we crisscrossed Europe. Many times. For Tito I was a prince. I played for Tito for twenty years. They were good times under Tito, people lived well, there was no hatred. For Milošević I was nothing and I avoided playing for him. I was afraid they would call me to play and I could see he was not a good man.'

Aca sat out the 1990s in his fifth-floor flat. 'I thought my fame would last a hundred years,' he says of the wilderness years. The phone never rang, no one but his wife to play to; for a man whose life has been dedicated to making people dance the isolation was an unnatural punishment. Post-Milošević, there's a growing respect for the traditional music of Yugoslavia: Aca again plays concerts and in 2004 director Emir Kusturica employed him to play on the soundtrack of *Life Is A Miracle*.

'I even have a small part in the film. Kusturica liked my playing so much he offered me free time in the recording studio. Young people are now coming to see me and they love how I play, they stand and dance and want me to play all night and I have to beg them to let me go. I'm old now, I can only play for an hour.'

Aca's content to chat all night but I determine to give him and Mica their space. Ever the gentleman, Aca insists on calling a taxi and accompanying me out. Journey under way, I realise we're close to the Intercontinental Hotel and direct the driver there; the Intercontinental is one of the few places in Belgrade with an ATM: the collapse of the Yugoslav banking system and the international sanctions that followed Serbia's wars shut down much of the financial network.

Entering the Intercontinental involves stepping into a time warp – bright carpets, shiny leather sofas, tubular lighting, marble, chrome and glass foyer – so steeped in 70s chintz Burt Reynolds could be holding court. Searching for the ATM, I realise this is a historic site: Arkan's last stand. Got to check it out. A bored receptionist, obviously familiar with the request, points towards the Rotisserie restaurant. There's no trace of the resulting carnage from when four men with sub-machine guns opened fired on the Great Patriot, no iconic bullet holes. But, indeed, a fitting killing ground for a Balkan beast.

Arkan or Aca? Serb devils or Serb angels? The bogeyman who terrorised the region or the fiddler who generations danced to? I know what Serbia I'm in search of but, running through the Balkans, one can never be too sure exactly who one might encounter. Money in my pocket, I step back into Belgrade's humid night. Notice my heart's beating hard – result of Aca's coffee or palpitations at what lies ahead? – journey's under way, everything's coming in sight.

Mahala Blues 1:
On, From and Upon Garbage

Survival = Anger x Imagination. Imagination is the only weapon on the reservation.

Sherman Alexie,
Imagining the Reservation

Wake early to find yesterday's mugginess having ripened into pressure-cooker heat. My room's too tiny to contemplate hiding in so I venture out. Sticky. Karpa arrives this evening. Journey south begins tomorrow. Managed to book two interviews for the afternoon. But I've a morning to kill. Breakfast first and then we will see. Serbia's ongoing economic crisis means there are few food vendors. Silicon Valley offers overpriced cafés and restaurants. A monumental McDonald's dominates the centre of the city. Occasional kiosks dispense munchies but experience suggests they're not the wisest places to buy hot-weather food from. Finally stumble across a small bakery-café. Order coffee and burek. Coffee's thimble-sized, sugary and muddy – Turkey's legacy still dictating much of the Balkan diet – while the burek...damn, it's disgusting: sir (crumbly sour cheese), meso (mince) and yoghurt packed in a greasy, tough filo pastry. Force it down and feel carbohydrates sitting like plutonium in my gut. Jesus, why do I put myself through this? Back in the Balkans and, straight away, struggling to adjust to the diet. How will I cope with the climate? Step outside. 10am. Already a furnace.

Mahala child

Photo: Garth Cartwright

Milošević's Belgrade found the Serb capital on the verge of meltdown. Indeed, NATO's 1999 bombing campaign has left flattened cinder-block buildings across Belgrade, monuments to the inflammatory Serb nationalists who set Yugoslavia on fire. Today Belgrade again feels as if at meltdown, haunted weather settling across the city. Heat. Dust. Within minutes I'm leaking sweat like a squeezed lemon. Still, I'm here for the summer so time to, as noted, adjust. As taxis tend to overcharge – the stupider the driver the more you can guarantee he will open a palm and mouth 'Euros! Euros!' – I stick to trams, trams that rattle, grind and hiss, spraying black grit as they snake across the city. Wander amongst street markets ripe with fruit from local orchards, breathe deep, the scent of watermelon and peach decongesting the air. Girls dressed in turbo-gear strut down boulevards, they mightn't have much but what they got they're gonna show. Weary workers sweep streets, load lorries, faces sour and unsatisfied. Stroll along the Sava and note shady bars on moored boats abounding with the Ray-Ban royalty, those pink-cheeked possessors of 'the new wealth'.

Ironies and paradoxes abound which, I guess, for me is part of Serbia's appeal. Some Serbs are still given to muttering about historic subjection to the Ottomans yet Turkey is now the favoured holiday destination – confirmed when Ceca, passport returned, announced that's where she's taking the kids for summer 2004 – and for such an avowedly European nation the West is often viewed with intense suspicion. Thing is, I like the Serbs. Severe gestures of loyalty and friendship often accompany meetings, greetings, conversations. Less arrogant than their neighbours in Croatia (equally capable of mad-bad nationalism), they remain a warm, welcoming people. Warm, welcoming and handsome: 'swarthy' was invented to describe a certain male Serb type, all brooding, sanguine features, heavy lids, a constant stream of cigarette smoke and curses flowing. If hunting for Robert Mitchum lookalikes, then head to Serbia. While the girls are stunning, so good-looking they glow.

But the climate…It's not even mid-afternoon and the heat's already unbearable, I need shelter…no wonder the Balkans occasionally go amok…*this humidity*…comparable to being engulfed by a wet electric blanket…New Belgrade's spooky industrial cityscape appears to throb and distort…even former paramilitaries, a mutant breed of man and pit bull, look exasperated. Roll up at Selena's and request access to her air conditioning. Selena, whose quiet, chiselled beauty is a million miles from turbo-folk's brazen voluptuaries, looks at the humid mess on her doorstep and lets me in. I moan about burek for breakfast and Selena, who advocates macrobiotic food, suggests changing to a brown rice and cabbage juice diet. Thanks but…

Composure regained, Selena plays me a CD of Kosovar Roma

tallava music. My jaw hits the floor. As they say in hip-hop circles: *this is the shit*. Camps of Kosovar Roma refugees are now scattered around Belgrade's outskirts, lives emptied out by injustice, and Selena notes how the inhabitants weave religious beliefs as easily as they do musical styles, celebrating Allah and Christ without any seeming incongruity, capable of praise songs to both Serb and Albanian icons. Is there, I wonder, much of a tallava scene in Belgrade? Selena thinks not. 'The new tallava recordings now appear to be made in Germany.'

Eventually time to face the humidity again. Selena directs me to the required bus, a vehicle obviously first set to work when Tito was still breathing. First port of call: Živojin Mitrović aka 'Jiri', the founder of Roma Heart, an organisation dedicated to educating disadvantaged Roma children. Roma Heart exists on the outskirts of east Belgrade, a region where the city finishes, leaving in its wake bungalows, local industry, allotments, shanty housing thrown together by those squeezed out of elsewhere, but no sign of a school.

I've clear instructions as to where to get off but once on foot there's no sign of street names, no real sense of direction. Passing traffic coats me in diesel fumes and dust. Mongrels circle me, growling. Even the chickens appear to cackle at me. Trekking around this scalding nowhereville is punishing. Begin to envision crows as vultures, drifting in circles, hungry for my salty flesh. Finally I call Jiri and find Roma Heart's situated only metres from where I stand. Stumbling into an anonymous building I'm immediately surrounded by Roma kids laughing joyously at the disoriented Gadje. Jiri appears smiling, his skin a brilliant mahogany sheen, very Indian in appearance. We enter his office. A fan blows. The Lord is merciful.

'For twenty years I lived like other people. I grew up in an assimilated area of Belgrade – our family and one other family were the only Roma. I got a degree, became a policeman and then heard of a four-year-old Roma girl who was eaten by dogs. I went to the mahala and I remember entering one house and there were two rooms. The first room was shared by a woman washing clothes and a horse. The other room had the entire family sitting on the floor. I asked the husband, "Why?" He replied, "I have twelve children who eat bread. The horse earns me bread." So I try to change the situation and it has been ten years of struggle: these people do not know their rights – to education, housing, health, hygiene. All of us can go to primary school – it's free – but you must pay every day for the bus to school and back, pay to eat something, pay for shoes and clothes. That stops a lot of Roma sending their children to school, they feel ashamed that they lack the money.'

Around Belgrade, suggests Jiri, there are 153 Roma settlements, many having only two or three hundred people. And 96 of these settlements are illegal, literally squatted communities, the mahala as slum, shanty town. Serbia's invisible nation is tucked away on wasteland and mud flats, alongside railway lines and garbage dumps.

'Sometimes Roma live like in the sixteenth century, no electricity, no water supply. You can't integrate into society because of this and it encourages prejudice. We receive no help from the state, only from NGOs but soon they will be removing from Serbia so where do we look to find a new solution? Maybe the World Bank – perhaps they could help us try and start enterprises, encourage the economic situation. But our biggest problem remains education and many Roma face discrimination in schools from teachers, pupils and the parents of pupils. Then they say, "Gypsies don't want to go to school. They don't want to learn." The big example is Roma refugees in Germany and England. There the kids go to school and learn and live well.'

Serbia's last census suggested 108,000 Roma citizens. Jiri snorts at this, claims 850,000, tens of thousands of Kosovar Roma refugees swelling numbers. Many of the refugees speak Romani and Albanian, not Serbian, so compounding their estrangement.

Unrecognised as a national minority means little provision in state social policies; anyway, Jiri's more concerned with saving those at the bottom than extracting promises from politicians. Yugoslavia's wars and the end of Eastern European communism have, he says, facilitated a downward spiral for the Roma.

'Democracy here means everyone grabbing what they can. As we lack political power we get only crumbs. Many more Gypsies have found themselves forced into extreme poverty. Gypsy ghettoes became synonymous with shanty towns, often built around rubbish tips where people scavenge to survive. We Gypsies have become synonymous with garbage. We live on, from and upon garbage.'

Yet across Belgrade I also see Roma professionals – in McDonald's, shopping, doing office jobs – those like Jiri who've escaped the mahalas. In much of Eastern Europe, especially Romania and the Czech and Slovak Republics, even such tiny gestures of everyday existence as using shopping malls and churches are largely off-limits to the Roma, the threat of skinhead violence combined with the silent contempt of the masses forcing them to remain shadow dwellers. Serbia, for all its mad nationalists and chaos, is more accommodating.

Appropriately, a Yugoslav film helped open the international market for Balkan Gypsy musicians: 1989's *Dom Za Vesanje* ('The Hanging House'; for the West retitled *Time Of The Gypsies*) was filmed in Macedonia by Bosnian Serb Emir Kusturica. Wowing the Cannes Film Festival (Best Director), *Time Of The Gypsies* became a major art-house hit. Inspired by a December 1985 Reuters report concerning the arrest of a gang who had been stealing children from Yugoslav Roma families and selling them to Westerners otherwise unable to adopt, the film follows Perhan, a poor but honourable young Roma, tempted to Italy by Ahmed, a Roma Fagin. Children are smuggled – to be sold or turned into beggars/thieves – and wealthy Italy is grim in contrast to Perhan's poverty-stricken mahala. Much magic goes

Zumrita Jakupović takes off

Phot: Garth Cartwright

on here, both natural (weddings, music, community) and that of 'nečiste sile'.

Time Of The Gypsies is epic and vivid, comic and tragic, cognisant of Roma lore and bristling with character slur. I took the Czech elf to see it. On exiting the cinema she said, 'I told you they were dirty and dangerous!' Roma remain divided about the film. Some loathe it for perpetuating negative stereotypes. Others suggest it tells uncomfortable truths. The soundtrack by Bosnia's Goran Bregović is pure Balkan baroque, the work of a master thief: for the film's atmospheric theme, 'Ederlezi', Bregović adapted an ancient Macedonian Gypsy song, piling on effects until the tune haunts, firstly, the film and then the viewer. Today 'Ederlezi' stands as the most famous Balkan tune since the theme to *Zorba the Greek*.

Gypsies have long proved profitable for Yugoslav cinema; 1967's *Skupljači Perja* ('Feather Collectors' – released in the West as *I Even Met Happy Gypsies*) won Palme d'Or at Cannes and was nominated for an Oscar. Shot during a Serbian winter in muted, murky browns, *Happy Gypsies* revolves around ramblin', gamblin' man Bora and his desire for Tisa, who's fleeing extreme physical abuse from both Gypsy and Gadje; I once watched *Happy Gypsies* with Yingzhao, a Chinese friend, who asked, 'Are Gypsies always so brutal?' The answer's 'No', which suggests the film's spiritual dearth, an inability to complement visual riches with anything but base human emotions. Savage and nihilistic, *Happy Gypsies* ranks amongst European cinema's most desperate films.

Desperate and unforgettable: *Happy Gypsies* put contemporary Roma culture on screen and introduced 'Djelem, Djelem', a song widely regarded as oracle, lore, amongst Balkan Gypsies. I've heard countless interpretations of 'Djelem, Djelem' but never really understood the song's full meaning. The most recent effort is by a young Belgrade band called Kal – a Romani word suggesting both 'blackness' and 'future'. Kal's version of 'Djelem, Djelem' favours a lush Latin flavour, moody and reflective in handling. Appropriate, as I'm moody and reflective, having been caught without a ticket on the bus returning from Roma Heart. The two inspectors came on like they learned technique at Keraterm concentration camp; the substantial fine would easily have paid several taxi fares. Doh!

Back in New Belgrade I drift amongst the ruins of socialist dreams, searching for Kal's leader, a man called Dragan. Notice the chorus of Oynx's Street Niggez, all moronic gangsta rap threat, carefully stencilled in large silver lettering across a wall. Someone went to a lot of trouble to do this. Why? There is no Afro community here. And New Belgrade may be a grim urban desert, a real palookaville, but to associate it with black America's ghettoes…homeboy, get real. The only ethnic minority making its presence visible is the Chinese, Milošević having cultivated close ties with China, thus Cantonese restaurants, casinos, even a shopping centre, exist here.

I find Dragan in a New Belgrade housing estate. One not too different from my Peckham residence: broken glass, graffiti everywhere, yet homely too. Dragan Ristić, thirty-one, is witty, friendly, bristling with energy and a little suspicious: 'There's still lots of secret police in Serbia,' he says, eyeing my tape recorder. Kal, he announces, play traditional Gypsy music from Central Serbia, the stuff that once roared out of kafanas across Yugoslavia. Dragan's transformed a bedroom into a recording studio and a young Roma woman, Zumrita Jakupović, is laying down a vocal when I arrive. 'I found her in the mahala, a real ghetto,' he says. 'She's sung all her life but this will be the first time she's been recorded.' Dragan, trained as a theatre director, dislikes the word 'Gypsy' ('it's pejorative') yet is willing to use it on the cover of Kal CDs ('for sales purposes'). Political correctness crossed with a hustler instinct: Kal surely have a good future.

Dragan and his brother Dušan (a painter and Kal member) run Amala Summer School, where, for two weeks every summer, international students can come and study Roma language, culture and music. The brothers, sons of a teacher and a market trader, belong to the Roma middle class. 'We're neither living in the mahala or completely accepted by the Gadje,' says Dragan of their position. 'Not the easiest place to be.'

Kal's self-titled debut album is a back-to-roots move that should prove popular in the West, no turbo-folk inflections here. Their next album promises to be more varied; Dragan plays me a song recorded with Rambo Amadeus, the Montenegrin rock satirist, and suggests Manu Chao as role-model.

'I like the way he [Manu] is eclectic, mixing up different sounds while keeping the music organic and entertaining. Kal's music is rooted in the traditional music of the Central Serbian Roma, a music that's almost died out now. Šaban Bajramović is the last great artist performing anything like it. A lot of Serbs don't consider this good music because they're enthralled by whatever comes out of the West. They associate Gypsy music with kafanas, which can be rough places.'

Blues and jazz, I note, came out of extremely tough black American watering holes. Dragan agrees but adds Americans are now proud of blues and jazz. Lots of Serbs aren't too sure if they should like Gypsy music. Anyway, he says, don't think I live in the past. I go to raves, use computers, aim to take Roma culture into the twenty-first century.

Dragan earns his living translating human rights documents into Romani. Like Jiri, he and Dušan represent the success of Tito's vision. Zumrita and the other members of Kal have had less access to education so, conversely, reflect the failure of that vision. Dragan, I say, show off your skills: turn 'Djelem, Djelem' into English.

'Djelem, Djelem'

Djelem, djelem, lungone dromensa	I was wandering on the long roads
Maladilem baxtale Romenca	I met happy Roma
Djelem, djelem, lungone dromensa	I was wandering on the long roads
Maladilem baxtale Romenca	I met happy Roma
A Romale, a chavalen,	Oh Romas, oh youths
A Romale, a chavalen	Oh Romas, oh youths
A Romale, katar tumen aven	Oh Romas, where do you come from
E caxrenca baxtale dromenca?	With your tents along lucky roads?
Vi man sas ekue bari familiya	I too also had a family
Murdads las e kali legiya	They were murdered by the black legion
Aven manca sa lumiake Roma	Come with me, Roma of the world
Kai putajle e Romane droma	You who opened Roma roads
Ake vryama, ushti Rom akana	The time has come, stand up, Roma
Ame hutasa misto kai kerasa	If we rise we will succeed
A Romale, a chavale,	Oh Romas, oh youths
A Romale, a chavale	Oh Romas, oh youths

'Djelem, Djelem' appears to have existed as the wind, forever in Gypsy consciousness, and various claims have been made as to who was composer. What's certain is *Happy Gypsies* helped make the song famous and, at the First World Romani Congress in London in 1971, representatives from more than twenty countries gathered and 'Djelem, Djelem' was adopted as the Roma anthem (Esma Redžepova sang it to the Congress). A flag – green (earth) and blue (sky and the eternal spirit) embellished with a red sixteen-spoke chakra (movement) – was affirmed. Who were the song's murderous black legion? Dragan believes they were Croatian fascists, their psychotic offspring still employing this name.

'Serbs are generally quite accepting of us,' notes Dragan. 'My current girlfriend is Serb. I'm not crazy on how the Serbs try and run the government but I don't have many real criticisms of them. The end of Yugoslav identity and the new nationalism have made the Roma face up to the fact that we are seen as Gypsies, that we are Roma. Maybe we'll be able to build something from here. Ironic, huh?'

Better ironic than the killing joke which nationalism has inflicted across much of former Yugoslavia. Belgrade feels (is) fragmented, a city unsure of how to knit the needs of its many citizens together, and returning to the city's centre I try to grasp Serbia's divided soul – progressive versus reactionary, love opposed to hate, open rather than closed – aware I'll never truly understand. I mean, why hang on to Kosovo: impoverished, illiterate and seething with Albanians who hate Serbs and Roma? Leave it as a NATO base, a failed state, write it off, move on. Few Serbs will even entertain such thoughts. 1389 and all that.

'The Roma have suffered more than anyone else in Kosovo,' Dragan had said when I mentioned the protectorate. 'They have no government to look after them. What Milošević did to the Albanians was bad but what the Albanians have done with

NATO's help is equally wrong. This country's a mess. People don't understand concepts of democracy.'

Return to my hotel and Karpa's there. By all accounts Karpa possesses something of Neal Cassady's talent for cars and women. A good partner, then, to ride the highway south with. I suggest we go in search of a kafana near the Central Train Station that may host live music. Karpa's not exactly enthusiastic – 'It could be rough,' he says – but I'm insistent, needing to experience one. One kafana is, Karpa suggests, probably enough.

Situated less than two kilometres from Kneza Mihaila's polished luxury, Central Station exists in an older, more dilapidated Belgrade. Traffic's aggressive, roads potholed, surrounding hotels unsavoury. A dank green space is nicknamed Pussy Park due to it hosting the passing sex trade. Central Station possesses weary majesty, a slow authority, recalling the days when trains for and from destinations across all of the mighty Socialist Federative Republic of Yugoslavia started or ended here. What events this building has witnessed, what migrations it's helped launch, what tales it could tell. But a forlorn vibe engulfs it, stranded by history and the neighbouring coach station – now the public's transport of choice. Grey men in blue JŽ uniforms are everywhere but few appear to be doing much work. Smoking. Joking. Sleeping on stools. Balkan railway stations, I love 'em.

Nothing surrounding suggests a Balkan juke joint. Karpa stops a local who, upon hearing said request, looks at us strangely then issues directions. 'Cigansko prenoćište,' he says as if issuing warnings. Gypsy hostel. And it is: the kafana's built out of a room in a house, no more than twenty square metres. Music–noise–smoke overwhelms as we enter. Damn, this is one funky shack. In the corner a five-piece Gypsy band – bass, drums, keyboards, guitar/accordion and singer – crank out a tough, soulful groove. There's several tables, a small bar, more smoke than air and everyone, both Serb and Roma, is dangerously drunk. The swarthy singer appears capable of smoking/drinking/singing all at once, gold teeth gleaming in the light. We order beers with rakija (the region's potent grape brandy) chasers. So cheap I order another round straight off. And let's show some respect: drinks for the band. Feel the tension easing in my shoulders, Balkan spirit settling in. Karpa starts laughing. Turns out the band are performing 'becari' (improvised songs), lyrics laden with innuendo, to loud cheers. *Honky tonkin'!*

A seriously drunk Serb – heavily bearded, eyes glowing, a real Rasputin – staggers up, demands the microphone. Trouble? Uh-uh, he simply wants to celebrate his daughter's birthday. And – oh no! – Rasputin wants to sing. He tries but can't quite perform. The Gypsy vocalist starts singing the song. 'Da! Da! Da!' exclaims Rasputin, repeating the words, stuffing money into the Gypsy's shirt pocket as he staggers through a rendition of 'I Just Called to Say I Love You' so awful it quietens the room. Rasputin sways – if he lets go of the microphone he'll fall – drools, he's crying or leaking membrane, paralytic, blasted, trashed, croaking out the chorus then nodding, lost in tearful drunken reverie. Ordeal over, he's helped back to a table. The band kick into 'Kamerav, Kamerav' (I Am Dying, I Am Dying) and the kafana erupts, dancing on tables, howling from chairs, hardcore, gut-busting Gypsy soul music. More beer! More rakija!

Hours skip by, the night degenerating into weird Balkan mania. I'm drinking steadily yet, compared to those around me, seem to be in slow motion. The kafana's stuffed with men intent upon using alcohol as amnesia, liquor absolving the frustration and uncertainty of being a Serb in the twenty-first century. Tell me what it's all about? It's all about getting out. Karpa starts reminiscing about the days when he could travel to Berlin for concerts. Now even Hungary demands a visa off Serbs. He's unemployed, as are many, Serbia's shattered economy offering few opportunities. By harvesting crops on his family's land during the summer he earns a little, this return to subsistence economics taking hold across much of former Yugoslavia. No irony then in *Only Fools And Horses'* popularity here, Serbia now reduced to a nation of Trotters.

A crashing noise. Rasputin tried to stand, forgot how to, and – Timber! – fell across a table, so meeting the floor. Silence. Begin to wonder if he's still alive. I mean, I like a drink or three but in this kafana people are chugging volume, drinking as dementia, hungry for ruin. Note a rare decoration: skull and crossbones emblem, symbol of the Chetniks and Arkan's paramilitaries, nicotine yellow and curling at the edges, left, I guess, by a nationalist drinker. Yet here, in Cigansko prenoćište, a venue existing for extreme binge drinking, it acts as Grim Reaper, a reminder of fragile mortality. Rasputin twitches. Begins to rise. Calls for rakija. Starts clawing ash from his beard. His friends laugh and curse and pour beer on him. And…what's this? He wants to sing again. I head for the door.

Outside. Air, fill lungs with air. Ears with silence. Escape the madness and breathe again. Relief, baby, relief. To the east I glimpse the first light of a pale Balkan dawn. Best get some sleep, a little calm, gather senses. In a few hours we head into Central Serbia, towards a small town that hosts the pagan daddy of all music festivals, the mad Gypsy brass blowout: Guča.

Guča:

The Rave That Time Forgot

Look! Look! There are blue and purple horses...a house
made of dawn . . .
　　　　　　N. Scott Momaday, *House Made Of Dawn*

Trumpets shred the air. Mutant kettle drums lay down a rumbling sonic boom. Chaos erupts around me...Friday afternoon and the main street – and there are few streets in Guča, a central Serbian village with a population hovering around 2,500 – heaves with revellers. I hate crowds. And noise. Many of my worst experiences have occurred at raves and rock festivals. Notting Hill Carnival? My definition of hell. So I'm questioning exactly what I'm doing in Guča, surrounded by steaming Serbs seemingly intent on achieving some form of transcendence. Or of passing out in the gutter. And it's not going to stop until midnight, Sunday. Take a very deep breath. One heavy weekend, no trimmings, 'bout to be served up.

Guča hosts the biggest three-day musical celebration in the Balkans. To the musicians who participate here Guča's the high summit of Balkan brass: orkestars from across Serbia come to play non-stop, earn plenty of sweaty dinars, take future bookings and, maybe, be called to compete for the penultimate brass honour, the Golden Trumpet. To the quarter million Serbs who turn up, Guča is, quite simply, the wildest party of the summer. To the town's inhabitants the gathering represents pure chaos and an annual payday. And to outsiders, well, Guča's sonic odyssey, a seventy-two-hour struggle for the soul of the new Serbian nation.

Blow, man, blow: Guča kicks off

Guča's hidden deep in Serbia's heartland, a land of rolling hills, thick forest, emerald lakes, farmsteads, cottages, quaint hamlets. Here people farm, raise families, wonder why stuffy, pompous men in Belgrade and Zagreb chose to launch fussy, unfinished wars when all that ever truly changes is the seasons. Nostalgia for Titoism is, I imagine, strong here, the greying population containing those who recall the brutality of fascism and the way Tito brought order, built roads and schools, ensured none went hungry. Milošević's era was turbo-folk, turbo-war, turbo-inflation. Bullshit bullshit bullshit.

As we rolled towards Guča I observed the region's residents: faces suggesting a certain toughness of form, character informed by the silence of rural life, moving to a rhythm dictated by nature and Orthodox cosmology. Mop my forehead and pretend I'm a peasant. Why not? The Dragačevo region has abundant rustic charm: mud/dung brick dwellings with wonky, smoking chimneys, neatly stacked firewood, cavernous hold-alls woven from branches and filled with maize, soil the colour of merlot, little vineyards crawling up embankments, people existing in unhurried motion – a real South London fantasy – maybe one day I'll retire here, be a gentleman peasant, pay the locals to bring in the harvest while I sit, smoke and sip rakija in the tranquil sunshine. And then we arrived in Guča and it spelt an end to silence.

Heatpeoplenoise: it all blends into shimmering cacophony. Guča 2003 represents the thirty-second year Balkan brass has reigned supreme across the town. Not that it was always like this. Not that it was ever expected to be like this. Officially called Dragačevski Sabor Trubača, the festival was created to keep the brass orkestar tradition alive. Tito's Yugoslavia was big on all things folkloric and some sharp-eared apparatchik, noting how the steady flow of humanity from rural to urban locations was depleting brass bands, came up with the idea of the festival/competition.

Initially a low-key event, following the huge success of Emir Kusturica's films featuring Goran Bregović's arrangements of Balkan brass – *Time Of The Gypsies, Underground, Arizona Dream* – orkestars began supplanting rock and rave as Serb party music. And to be in Guča's main street on Friday afternoon feels like stepping on to a Kusturica set: brass orkestars blast out of tents, bars, alleys, spilling on to streets, marching in formation, forcing their way through crowds pumping-pumping-pumping. Damn, these men can play! Sucking in humid air and blowing out great blocks of sound, stiff backed and gimlet eyed, brass dervishes, a musical force so potent it's physical. And everywhere people are dancing. Beefy blokes turn bright pink, stepping to the knees-up, knees-up pattern males everywhere do as dance, holding plastic pints of beer high, screeching with stupefied satisfaction. Their girlfriends, outfitted in push-up bras, tight pants and midriff-flexing tops, dance a dainty kolo, smiling the smile that comes with an awareness of the male as the stupider of the species.

Guča's saturnalian atmosphere attracts plenty of knuckleheads, most of whom run stalls displaying knifes designed for gutting pigs and people. Or else they proffer a selection of T-shirts, key rings, mugs and framed portraits featuring Radovan Karadžić and Ratko Mladić – those foul practitioners of genocide across Bosnia – and Chetnik leader Draža Mihailović. The latter's also presented as an Orthodox religious icon. Tainted love? Sorry, I don't pray that way. Milošević's hangdog features are occasionally represented but as he turned a quest for Greater Serbia into the reality of Greatly Diminished Serbia he lacks any vulgar 'heroism' or iconic status.

War criminals…weapons…ominous vibes? Uh-uh. The streets heave with merry human traffic, completely absent is any sense of threat. That the pure products of Serbia go crazy, buzzing on nationalist myths, to the sound of Gypsy musicians, true internationalists, makes for some paradox. A few even try and comprehend, Guča being about release rather than rationalism… Throughout the day and into the night it continues, dancing and drinking and drinking and dancing, the atmosphere tangy with grilled meat, urine, sweat, putrefying garbage. People exist as a blur, physical graffiti, lost in the brass trance, dancing. No one does the Funky Chicken. Or the Mashed Potato. Or break dances. Or body pops. Such frantic, free-spirited music. Yet such polite dancing. The Balkans never cease to amaze me. One by one exhaustion and cold fell players and dancers until those few left standing exhibit the red-eyed mysticism that accompanies travellers on the road to excess, a certain pagan wisdom encountered with the chill light of dawn.

Having sifted much rumour and lore, I've boiled down the brass orkestar creation myth so it follows a certain chronological development. Initial form was provided by Austrian court influence at the beginning of the nineteenth century. The Ottoman army belatedly followed, forming its own brass ensembles: mehter. The Janissary army dissolved the mehters in 1839 so leading to large ensembles fragmenting into smaller configurations, orkestars. These transferred their service to local patrons, travelling to play for outdoor gatherings (weddings, funerals, circumcisions and sobors:

picnics held on saints' days). The Roma, always highly regarded by the Ottomans for their prowess on wind and string instruments, would surely have been in brass bands from the beginning, adding funky dissonance. The orkestars proved popular across southern Serbia, eastern and Aegean (now northern Greece) Macedonia, west Bulgaria. Serbia remains the brass powerhouse and Guča's where the heavyweights come to battle, an OK Corral of brass blasts.

Everywhere awnings are rolled out and instant restaurants created. Here orkestars enter, surround a table, blast. If the table's occupiers want music they start pasting dinars on musicians' foreheads and trumpets and the sound accelerates. When the table's attention drifts the orkestar moves on. This, more than winning the Golden Trumpet, is what counts: a good Guča means musicians return home with fistfuls of dinars.

Competition for the dons, the men who rule the tables, is fierce: under an awning I witness a Gypsy orkestar and a Serb orkestar battle. The Gypsies curl out high, shrieking Oriental notes across fast čoček rhythms while the Serbs play a strident march. Both orkestars spit the sharpest solos possible, trying to steal the table's attention, oblivious to the waiters forcing their way through, determined to get more meat and alcohol to those seated. The Serbs hold the furthest end of the table while the Gypsies concentrate on two young women who leap up to dance in between musicians, waiters and chairs, moving like so much denim-clad jelly to the hard, zig-zagging beat, shakin' that ass, shakin' that ass. Neither orkestar gives an inch, backs facing, musical wrestling, no surrender.

Guča's official festival is split into three parts: Friday's opening concert, Saturday night celebrations and Sunday's competition. Friday's concerts are held at the entrance to the official Guča Festival building. This event features previous winners, each orkestar getting to play three tunes while folk dancers, all kitted out in bright knitting patterns, dance kolos and oros in front of a hyped-up audience. Some wag once said the only things one shouldn't try are incest and folk dancing; obviously, he never saw Serb girls dancing. The orkestars display dynamics but the music gets formulaic, tied to convention. Patience: later this evening Boban Marković Orkestar will play. To paraphrase Mingus on Charlie Parker: if Boban was a gunslinger there'd be a lot of dead cowboys.

Boban Marković's won Guča so often that, this year, he's not even competing. Instead, the King has returned to play for his people and when they announce Boban Marković Orkestar will be on next I feel excitement, an almost electric charge, move through the crowd. This is special, something to savour. I see Boban, standing by the PA, taking his last draw on a cigarette, nodding to himself then stepping on stage, twelve-piece orkestar following. While the other orkestars have been dressed identically (slacks and short-sleeved shirt being the uniform), Boban, all long, unruly hair, dresses as jazz and rock musicians are supposed to. And then there's Marko, Boban's fifteen-year-old, trumpet-rockin' son, this golden youth, hip and nonchalant, wearing a bright white drape coat, pure Gypsy flash. Boban nods to Marko and the kid hits the opening notes. It's slow, a dreamy instrumental, uncomfortably familiar. A Serb shouts 'Titanic! Titanic.' And, damn, it's 'Theme from Titanic'. I start laughing, not cos it's the *Titanic* theme, more at Marko, so young yet such a hustler, already aware how to play the public. But, of course, this is Gypsy business and TV and movie themes are often worked into orkestar repertoires; *Dallas* being a wedding favourite. As the 'Theme' fades Boban presses trumpet to lips, hits a long high note, an improbably yearning sound, and the orkestar swing in, begin to blast and Guča…Guča erupts.

Youths start moshing, leaping off chairs, the gonzo Gypsy intensity of the brass groove – howling, feral solos – creating Friday night fever. This ain't no disco…or is it? The orkestar are dropping sonic bombs, everywhere Serbs are dancing, mouths agape with joy and wonder, rock kids headbanging, others dancing čoček – the dance of the Gypsies – shaking hips on the rhythm breaks, cheering Boban's guttural Romani chants, a tidal wave of music washing across us all in a rub-a-dub Gypsy style. The music rages, defiant and proud, in the humid Balkan night. At the dawn of the twenty-first century no other music on the planet kicks quite so hard, offers such primal funk, as a Gypsy brass band. Funkyfunkyfunky – yeeeeh!

Boban's orkestar work like this: a goc (bass drum) and dobos (snare) keep a booming pulse while tenor horns and bass tubas pump fat'n'greasy brass rhythms. Boban and Marko swap solos, building spiralling patterns of notes, pushing forth strange, angular sounds, harsh and beautiful, music of spirit, of flight, stuff that goes way back, pre-Roma, pre-Slav, back to the Celts' mournful melodies which stayed alive through shepherd and village song, music which travelled across Asia with Boban's ancestors, mysterious music which absorbs all and builds something new yet still has strong ties with its ancient roots.

A century ago music with a corresponding spirit arose out of New Orleans and went on to set the world on fire: do subliminal connections exist, I wonder, between these Gypsy brass magicians and New Orleans' jazz pioneers? Tens of thousands of Balkan Roma migrated to the US during the nineteenth century and some of them would have been carrying clarinets, trumpets, zurlas, kavals, gocs, tapans, cimbaloms, tamburas, pan pipes, cobzas, the tools of their livelihood, sacred instruments that allowed an illiterate people to speak in several tongues. In the US the Roma would have lived – as they did in the Balkans – in the poor part of town, cheek by jowl with another people who knew too much about slavery and discrimination and used brass and string instruments to express the soul of a man.

Could Gypsy musicians have helped pioneer early jazz? Well, damn, why not? Sidney Bechet writes of the streets of New Orleans, at the dawn of the twentieth century, hosting 'bucking contests' where 'one band, it would come right up in front of the other and play at it, and the first band it would play right back, until finally one just had to give in...And that band was best that played the best *together*. No matter what kind of music it was, if the band could keep it together, that made it the best. That band would know its numbers and know its foundation and it would know *itself* (italics Bechet). Which, to me, sounds totally Guča, very Gypsy.

Legend has Miles Davis, in Belgrade when Yugoslavia could still host major jazz festivals, being played a recording of a Gypsy brass orkestar. Miles, astonished, replies, 'I didn't know a trumpet could sound like that.' Maybe his forefathers did; maybe the retuning of brass instruments invoked by African Americans in New Orleans came with a little help from a people who'd also have been considered 'colored' (or, maybe, 'Creole'). It's been written that there are Afro-Roma communities in Louisiana, dating back to the nineteenth century. Speculation is a fine thing but I've no facts to back me. None at all. More importantly, at the turn of the twenty-first century Balkan brass demolishes contemporary US and European (Scandinavian nu-jazz? C'mon) efforts.

Boban's orkestar rage for ninety minutes, pumping non-stop raw Romani funk, a sound both liberating and exhausting. They finish and I flee, seeking relief from the brass madness. Heading into darkness I find, on the festival's outskirts, 430 kilos of buffalo slowly roasting on a spit; handlers occasionally spray this fleshy colossus with beer, the smell of sizzling beef carrying across the field, my imagination running wild, visions of olde Europe leaping amongst flames. The day's heat has faded and a valley chill pushes many towards the fire. It's here I meet Ilija Stanković, Guča's promoter. Ilija has nothing to do with the competitions, instead he's focused on building Guča from a regional phenomenon into an international event. PA. Promotion. Facilities. Respect for musicians. Experience gained working in the German music industry giving him an understanding of how to take things forward. Guča's future, says Ilija, involves world brass: New

Ekrem

Photo: Garth Cartwright

Orleans, Italian, German, Macedonian, Romanian. TV rights, a DVD, sell the festival to the West's world music audience. Ilija has Big Ideas. He sees Balkan brass hypnotising the West's slothful pop kids in the same way it has played pied piper to Serb youth. Ilija is, depending on whom I talk to, either Guča's saviour or Satan.

Ilija introduces me to his charge, Ekrem Sajdić. Ekrem's a trumpet player from southern Serbia whose *Rivers of Happiness* album ranks amongst the very finest of Balkan brass offerings. Ekrem's band consists of a dozen old friends, men like him with sunburned features and a quiet, rural stoicism. Ekrem struggles to describe his music – 'It's all about the sound of the trumpets,' he states of the weeping horns. 'The others simply don't have this sound. It's honest, sad and deep. It's everything that we have.'

Rivers of Happiness finds Ekrem joined by Serb jazz trumpet player Duško Gojković. Neither musician was aware of the other's work before Ilija brought them together, resulting in a striking feed between Gypsy brass and jazz.

'We used to listen to some jazz music when we were young,' says Ekrem. 'We don't know everything but we know globally what it is about. We play our old music and like them we improvise, we play in the free style. The first time we met Duško was the first time we had played with a jazz musician and it was a natural chemistry. After we finish playing I say to him, "You are one of ours now!"'

Ilija explains how each band has a sound and it's this sound, not phenomenal technique, which defines the orkestars. Orkestar after orkestar has built on the traditional tunes, each adding their own signature. 'Brass music – it's a ritual,' says Ilija. 'It has the strength of ritual. You can't make up or sell the ritual.'

Under a silvery Saturday moon the strength of this ritual becomes clear. At 11.30pm the packed local football stadium becomes a temple of brass, a PA pumping the heaped horns with a force recalling dub reggae sound systems, music to wade through. The largest sector of the crowd is youths between fifteen and twenty-five, cranked up really (really) high on wild solos and cocek rhythms. Above their heads huge flags, both Serb and the Chetnik skull and crossbones, are trawled, back and forth, forth and back. 'Nationalism's the ideology of the banal,' wrote noted Yugoslav author Danilo Kiš. Yet as Ilija observed, 'Serb nationalism is a sleeping dragon, one that could easily be awakened.'

And so they party, the hills echoing the sound of music, dancing in circles through the crowd, kicking up dust clouds, dancing to good Balkan bands, dismayed by a very poor American orkestar who break the one and only rule: got to be funky! Buddy Bolden's spirit is in the air, calling the children home. A Serb beauty, soaked in dust and sweat, dances furious cocek rhythms, her eyes burning through the muck, smile never leaving her lips, goddess at the rave that time forgot. Only metres away a skull and crossbones arcs through the air, waved to the booming rhythm of a big goc drum, scything back and forth, forth and back, hungry for prey.

ŠABAN BAJRAMOVIĆ:
A Great Consumer of Life

You know the Gypsy woman told me
You your mother's bad luck child
Well you havin' a good time now
But that'll be trouble after while
                    Muddy Waters, 'Gypsy Woman'

Niš hovers in the distance, shimmering beneath a big Balkan sun, heat waves and dust clouds blurring and morphing municipal borders, an urban hallucination rolling across the plains and rising to meet the Svrljiške Mountains. City on fire. And, if memory holds true, not for the first time. Karpa keeps his foot to the floor, an unspectacular 90 kilometres an hour being all his rusty Escort can be pushed to, as we laugh the soft, narcotic laughter of travellers who know something good, yes, something fine, awaits. It's been a long morning, leaving Guča in the pre-dawn mist, weaving through central Serbia's lush, rustic landscape before connecting with the E75, the main highway that runs to Thessaloniki in Aegean Macedonia. Karpa crossed himself as we set off and murmured, 'God help me that all will be all right' and, considering the way Serbs overtake, I sensed a wise and rational gesture. Beyond the occasional Balkan bomber seemingly intent on clearing the slow lane of all other traffic the E75 flows smoothly, the motorway surrounded by deluxe service stations, tidy towns and fertile farmland. Serbia once was, and perhaps still is, a wealthy East

The Lizard King: Šaban

European nation, my wanderings around north and central Serbia rarely suggesting the economic and social battering this nation has experienced over the past fifteen years. Then Niš is upon us.

Pancake-flat and built on a grid system, canyons of concrete tower blocks spreading towards the horizon, Niš is, undoubtedly, a workers' city; functional, provincial, diligent, a city constructed by blood, sweat and tears. We pass Roma adults sifting skips for anything worth recycling, loading materials on to horse and cart. 'Welcome,' says Karpa, 'to southern Serbia.'

Inhabited since pre-Roman times, Niš has no hint of historic majesty. Instead, the city's ambience is that of a dusty, weary frontier town, ragged round the edges and a little forlorn. Which is appropriate as Niš is the gateway to Serbia's south, a region whose impossibly bleak saga is chronicled through too many wars and not enough peace: from Roman armies to NATO cluster bombs, this city has suffered. Thus the ebb tide of history has left only sanguinary traces, Niš hosting one of East Europe's last surviving cenotaphs. I've a strange fascination for these monuments to death,

a personal favourite being the Sedlec Ossuary church interior in
Kutná Hora, Czech Republic. The Czech church is decorated with
human skeletons, a skull and bones chandelier resembling the kind
of Grand Guignol décor Hannibal Lecter would savour. Serbia's
contribution to this grimly humorous architectural domain is Niš's
Ćele Kula (Tower of Skulls), a macabre monument erected by the
Ottomans after a failed uprising in 1809. The Duke of Rešava led
the revolt but quickly found his Serbian forces being crushed by a
superior Turkish army. Desperately rushing Turkish defences, the
Duke fired into their powder magazine. *Boom! Boom! Out go the
lights!* That one shot detonated a mini-Hiroshima, killing 4,000
Serbs and 10,000 Turks. This unwitting application of scorched
earth policy may explain Niš's absence of historic edifices. Those
who survived must have surveyed a cityscape of unimaginable
ruination. The Ottomans slaughtered whatever Serb resistance
remained, beheading and scalping corpses. Ćele Kula was thus
created by embedding skull after skull after skull, a tower of
doom.

I'm tempted to go explore but Karpa, who, when called up by
the Serbian army, told them, 'Sure I'll join. Just as soon as you draft
Milošević's son Marko into my platoon,' is not interested in seeing
another reminder to past tyranny. As Serb nationalists play upon
historic injustice dished out by the Ottomans – during the Bosnian
genocide Muslim Slavs were referred to as 'Turks' so to excuse the
carnage Milošević/Tudjman and cronies were wreaking – and our
journey involves music, that most international and healing of arts,
I agree. Let us find the man who would be King.

Niš may not be pretty but it knows how to feed a fella. Lunch
is pljeskavica, a huge rectangle of spicy, grilled hamburger. I order
a shopska salad that Karpa looks upon with horror – *vegetables?*
– and, appetite sated, we do what all good citizens of Niš do: go
to work. Karpa phones the man they call the Gypsy King, Šaban
(pronounced 'Sha-ban') Bajramović, and collects what turns out to

be some pretty wayward instructions. After thirty minutes spent circling inner-city estates and traffic intersections we're finally directed towards an older area of the city where the concrete jungle thins and small houses crop up. I've one question buzzing around my mind: will Šaban talk to us? There's good reason for doubting he will – and everyone in Belgrade has suggested he won't – as just weeks before he demanded cash for questions from a BBC TV crew. Being one of life's optimists and having interviewed Šaban in Amsterdam, January 2002, I'm hoping he remembers me and will, ya know, chat a while.

'During all these shitty times, all these sad times, when we have so little,' says Karpa as he navigates, 'I believe we Serbs have learned from the Gypsies. How to live on so little and yet to live.' Interesting theory but, of more immediate importance, do Karpa's generation recognise Šaban? 'We listen more to rock but of course we respect Šaban. He's the King.' Turning right into a narrow street dominated by low-level houses I count the numbers down. 30–28–26– OK, there's Šaban standing in his front yard. For a man routinely acknowledged by everyone and anyone with an interest in Gypsy music as the King of Balkan Gypsy song, Šaban lives in a surprisingly modest grey fibre-glass bungalow. The entire outside area is concreted and only a pigeon hutch suggests Šaban makes any use of the area. These birds, I'm aware, have become his obsession; he's even written a song ('Gledam Ja Golubove') about them.

At a glance Šaban could be everypensioner, dressed in slacks, cotton shirt, nylon jacket, sensible shoes, glasses. Look again: the Lizard King stands in front of us, leathery skin, gnarled features, black eyes, thick lips curled into something resembling a sneer… Damn, this cat is something else, surely ruler of some weird domain hidden from official histories, brooding and emanating dark powers like a character from Robert E. Howard's pulp phantasmagorias. He nods, beckoning us forward, a true Balkan prince. We shake hands and Karpa asks Šaban if he remembers me from Amsterdam. Da. I present him with a copy of the *fRoots* magazine featuring the 2002 interview. He thumbs it then indicates towards a plastic table and chairs in front of the house. So far, so good.

Šaban appears unchanged from our Amsterdam encounter. No, hold that, he is showing increasing signs of wear. Grey ends peak through his dyed black hair. A skin irritation has left his hands blotchy and behind thick glasses his left eye looks rheumy. At sixty-seven Šaban's big, battered brown face resembles, as Americans say, forty miles of bad road. Not that he was ever a pin-up for moderation and clean living: knife scars crisscross his cheeks and faded jailhouse tattoos are evident on his lower arms. Šaban's friendly if cautious, checking Karpa, then me, trying to define who we are, what exactly we want. Everyone breaks out cigarettes, the signal a Balkan meeting has begun. Šaban smokes Red Marlboros, the cigarette of choice for Gypsy icons. He lights one, draws deep, and his satisfaction is evident as he exhales, the Virginia tobacco tasting of America. Of success. Karpa and I smoke Serbian cigarettes, their dry, cheap tobacco reinforcing the rich aroma of the Marlboro, its scent of victory.

Karpa explains why we're here, what my book's about. Šaban nods. No problem. He's more relaxed than in Amsterdam. There he played a disquietingly formal classical music venue and, obviously, wanted to get the fuck out of that icy city, badgering the record company to get him a ticket to Düsseldorf where a daughter lives. Today, at home, he's in a mellow mood. He brings up the BBC's aborted visit, noting they turned up with a lot of expensive equipment but couldn't find any euros for Papa.

'I said "Excuse me, I am not prepared for this. And you are here to make something commercial. That, gentlemen, is gonna cost you. Don't be angry, I just want what is mine."'

Outrageous, I say. Total lack of respect. 'Da,' says Šaban, 'assholes.' A child peaks through the curtain. One of yours?

'One of my grandchildren. I have twelve! I've four daughters and one of them and her daughter lives with us.'

A woman appears, obviously Šaban's daughter, and serves Turkish coffee. Šaban nods, lights another cigarette, and orders her to the shops. She returns with a large plastic bottle of imitation Fanta. Why Balkan Roma so love this sugary drain clearer I don't know but Šaban obviously feels the table's incomplete without.

What, I wonder, are his memories of growing up in Niš?

'My mother was singing nice and we heard a lot of pop music from Mexico and Spain and Italy. And there were always parties and Gypsy parties always have music.'

Is he ever playing concerts here?

'No. The occasional wedding but generally if I'm to play a wedding it's in Spain or France.'

I heard he recently sang in Belgrade.

'Right. With Novica Zdravković. He's the brother of Toma Zdravković who was a very esteemed Serbian singer. He died in '91 or '92 and it was a farewell concert, a memory concert. He had good songs, was a chanson singer. I gave him three or four songs I wrote and with them I helped raise him to success. We were good friends.'

In Amsterdam he mentioned hoping to write a book about Roma people.

'Yes, I am writing a book about them, from the beginning of time, from the time when the world was created, because Roma people don't know their origin. Some people say we are from Italy because of the city Roma! I prefer the name Cigani or Gypsy. Others say our origin is in Spain. And some Gypsies, they believe this, they don't know that their origins are the Punjab in India.'

The Punjab. OK. I recall a photo of Šaban and Indira Gandhi shaking hands.

'That was a long time ago. 1960-something. Yeah, it was good to go there, the energy in their blood was great. Our problem, us

Gypsies, is we don't have an alphabet. All Gypsies use the alphabet of the country where they live.'

But these days you can buy a Romani dictionary?

'Yeah, but those are made up words. There is a legend that says a horse ate the Gypsies' alphabet and that's why we are wandering.'

Šaban speaks softly, chuckles often, his voice mellifluous, smooth as when he sings. And when he does sing few can touch him, the calm, confident delivery, sometimes murmuring, other times declaiming, such a beautifully bruised voice, always knowing, always soulful. If eloquent suffering has a sound then it's Šaban. Consider all the Šaban I've listened to, cheap cassettes, burnt CDs, scratched vinyl, no matter how thin the sound his majestic tenor rides through, the Godfather of Gypsy soul. And here he is, in the sun, the sorcerer's stone of so much Balkan music. Perfect. Your voice, how did you develop it?

'As a youth I walked past a house where someone was picking out notes on a piano. I thought, "that's an A", and walked on. Then I stopped, realised, "Boy, you've perfect pitch".'

And today, you're still singing well?

'Better than ever. Like wine with age.'

Karpa and Šaban start talking football and Šaban compares himself to Diego Maradona ('Papa is the greatest,' he says). It's not a bad comparison, two extremely gifted wild things whose talent and desire to burn brightly meant they dominated their respective genres. They then start talking Serb football teams and Europe's premier league...Zzzzzzzzz. I tune out and weigh up Šaban's achievements, the music that made him Gypsy song's greatest champion.

Born April 16, 1936, Šaban's childhood was interrupted by the Nazi invasion – a concentration camp was built outside Niš and the area's Roma ruthlessly murdered. A Gypsy song from the war goes:

Give me, God
two big wings
that I may fly
to kill a German.
To take from him the great keys
and to open the Niš camp
(translation Grattan Puxon)

Did Šaban ever sing said lament? I don't doubt it for his parents'
death forced Šaban on to the streets and into a desperate existence,
a boy amongst monsters. Surviving the war he ran errands, shined
shoes, laboured, hustled, played football very, very well and sang
at Roma festivities. Conscripted into the Yugoslav army aged
eighteen, Šaban found military discipline anathema so went AWOL
in search of his girlfriend: correspondence being impossible
– Šaban was illiterate. Blues pianist Otis Spann once sang, 'Twenty-
six letters in the alphabet an' I can't even spell my name,' and to
Šaban Bajramović, the Roma ragamuffin, the white man's world
was an equally hostile place. Tito's Yugoslavia, still paranoid of
Soviet invasion, showed no mercy towards deserters and a military
court sentenced Šaban to three and a half years. He told the judge
they'd never hold him. Sentence was upped: five years.

Šaban spent a year of his sentence on Goli Otok (barren island),
the Yugoslav Alcatraz. Filled with political dissidents and hardened
criminals, Goli Otok froze in winter and roasted in summer, an
environment so savage the island's now considered Tito's gulag.
Why Šaban was dumped here, a youth amongst the wretched on
a prison island in the Adriatic, I'm unsure. Possibly he was made
an example to all conscripts and Roma. Yet today Šaban carries no
bitterness, instead claiming prison was his university of life: here
he learned to read and write, met professional musicians, sang in
the prison orchestra, was goalkeeper for the prison's football team
– they nicknamed him the Black Panther due to his prowess. Once

freed he took to singing in kafanas, at weddings and feasts; his liquid voice and elegiac songs quickly marked him as the Roma chronicler, a street poet of Gypsy love and combat.

In 1964 Šaban released his first record, 'Pelno Me Sam' (I Am Imprisoned), an original composition. The song's protagonist begs his mother to get him out of jail so he can see his daughter get married. This is it, the deep Gypsy blues. During the 1960s and 70s Šaban would be to Balkan Roma what James Brown was to African Americans, a musician who carried great cultural weight. Understandably, who else was singing in Romani, 'Hey, another beating from the police'? Hailed as the king of Nove Romske Pesme – New Romani Song – legend has Yugoslav Roma respecting Tito the most, Šaban second and then, after ten empty places, once again Šaban.

Fronting The Black Mambas, Šaban had his teeth capped with gold, drank and gambled heavily and, as his star rose, grew wilder, missing gigs, wrecking cars, raising all kinds of holy hell, a Balkan Jerry Lee Lewis. 'Šaban is a great singer,' Esma Redžepova once told me, 'but I can't admire him because he is so unreliable and that gives us Roma a bad name.' Aca Šišić refused to work with Šaban again after being employed to play on an album, calling him 'unprofessional'. Nicknamed 'No Show Šaban', he was banned from Yugoslav state TV for failing to appear on programmes he'd been booked for. A similar lackadaisical approach to live performance meant he might turn up and deliver the concert of your life. But if cards or women or other tribulations distracted then so be it. Šaban, with his gold teeth and swarthy skin and Muslim name, represented Gypsy Fury – lawless, wild, a force of nature – playing by his own rules, music flowing out of him. Today, says Šaban, he's released 20 albums, 50 singles and written 760 songs.

'Life inspires me to write songs. My inspiration is life because I am a great consumer of life! I spend [money] but I like to earn [money] too. If you don't earn, you can't spend. Everything goes around. I've never desired for some fortune in my life, I didn't have dreams to become rich, just to live normal.'

Šaban also claims he's never been paid in full for his recordings. Yet his love of dice and cards surely swallowed many royalties. Legend has Šaban, flush with success, entering Niš's mahala driving a white Mercedes, wearing a white suit, accompanied by two bodyguards. Invited to sit in on a game of poker he accepts, plays through the night until, at dawn, he leaves without money, Mercedes or bodyguards. Wonder if he still wore the suit? I ask Karpa to recite the tale. Šaban listens, grins, laughs loudly.

'Well,' he says, looking both proud and slightly annoyed, 'it's true I love to gamble. But that story isn't so true. People have spread a lot of bad stories about me.'

Šaban lights a cigarette, eyes narrow, checking us again, the weary, brooding nature of his songs notable in the way he commands the table, for sure a tough old hombre. Fixing me with his one good eye, a Gypsy Cyclops, I feel the weight of his gaze. Again he chuckles, grins that grin, and we laugh. About nothing. About everything. About a King who never wanted for more than a bungalow and pigeons and the respect that comes with singing the Balkan blues.

As the 1970s got under way Šaban confirmed his dominance of the Balkan music scene with classic song after classic song. These were Yugoslavia's fat years, the nation awash on a seemingly limitless supply of 'loans', everyone living well, Tito ageing and loosening his grip, the whole world appearing to love this unique non-aligned state, the likes of Lepa Brena pioneering what would become known as turbo-folk, everything getting slicker, easier, yet Šaban's booming voice and charged sound conveyed hard times and high times, the Gypsy soul experience. Keepin' it real? Šaban was gangsta before the term existed. His look was classic 70s macho, an Asiatic Charles Bronson, mean moustache and leathers, the Lizard King of this sensual, fragile nation.

'At the beginning they told me I am Charles Aznavour as I was singing his songs very well. Then they compared me to Frank Sinatra, who is also good, but he doesn't have…he is a good actor, but…Šaban Šaulić is absolutely the best Yugoslav singer. For foreign singers, Elvis Presley, the best in the world.'

As with Sinatra and Presley, Šaban's been co-opted by Yugoslav cinema, if in a more circuitous manner: Goran Bregović's hugely popular scores for Emir Kusturica's films borrow heavily from certain Šaban hits. In December 2000 Claude Cahn, a lawyer for the European Roma Rights Centre, visited Šaban in Niš and offered to act as Šaban's legal representative against Bregović to recover publishing royalties – the controversy surrounding Bregović's 'adaptation' of 'folk songs' into original material having raged throughout the last decade.

Bregović was guitarist/leader of popular 1970s Sarajevo prog-rock band Bijelo Dugme (White Button). Bregović's talent for adapting and arranging Balkan folk music asserted itself when Kusturica employed him to create soundtracks. Cahn notes that where we take folk songs to be something of anonymous authorship sung by peasants since time immemorial, Bregović borrows complete songs written by the likes of Šaban. The third track on *Underground*'s soundtrack is called 'Mesečina'. The original melody is from 'Djeli Mara', one of Šaban's most famous songs. Bregović plays all kinds of tricks with the tune – drum machines, overdubbed horns etc. – to create an epic slice of cartoon Wagner. Nowhere is Šaban acknowledged as author. Cahn laid out his case to Šaban, who agreed this was correct but remembered signing things, documents that probably paid him a set fee for the use of his music. Had he kept copies of them? No chance.

'They took my song,' Šaban told me after the Amsterdam concert. 'I probably signed things away. I was going to sue Bregović but taking him to court in Serbia…what a mess. So I don't bother. I forgive him.'

Šaban on sale:
Serbian 1970s hit cassette

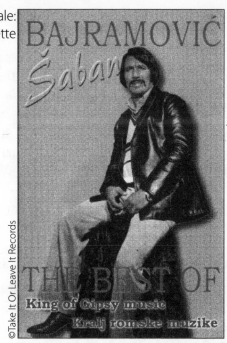

Forgive he did. Šaban sang three songs on Bregović's 2002 album *Tales and Songs From Weddings and Funerals*. The album finds Šaban in good, playful voice and Bregović, who often recycles his tunes across several albums, is in inspired form. Admittedly, Bregović's not capable of creating anything but Balkan-lite yet sometimes that's no bad thing. The only pity is that Bregović has not hired Šaban to be part of his touring orchestra: his concerts synthesise a pick'n'mix of the region's folk flavours into vivid spectacle, one that's proved immensely successful internationally. OK, it's a Balkan minstrel show, grandiose and soulless – Bregović's compositions bearing the same relation to Gypsy music that Led Zeppelin's did to blues – but the music's verve and epic scale remain impressive.

Kusturica, having split with Bregović after *Underground*, composed his own score (big mistake) for 1997's *Black Cat, White*

Cat. Here he attempted to repay old debts by employing Šaban to sing the theme tune. Šaban took the job but has no love for Emir.

'He's winning all these awards in the film world but he's only showing the black side of Gypsy culture. It's much easier to show the begging, the stealing. But he doesn't show the Gypsies who go to work in the factory every day, the good ones. It's easier to work with scum. He's like Bregović, he puts things upside down. He shows the worst side of Gypsies.'

Šaban speaks more highly of 1987's *Andjeo Čuvar* (Guardian Angel; director Goran Paskaljević), a film about the illegal trade in Roma children, in which he sings the theme song and acts.

'The French Academy elected the song I sing in it as one of the hundred best original songs in film history,' he says. The 1997 Macedonian film *Gipsy Magic* (director Stole Popov) found Šaban cast as a mahala don. The very mention of the film causes him to yelp.

'I wish I had never had anything to do with it. It's an insult to my people.'

The film Šaban rates highest amongst Yugoslav cinema's myriad attempts at Gypsy subjects is *I Even Met Happy Gypsies*.

'That film is the one that has shown real Gypsy life. What Kusturica is doing, it is imagination, fake. We are humiliated, the Gypsies, in these films. Skupljači Perja shows our situation.'

Initially signed to Radio Belgrade's label, in the 1980s Šaban joined Ljubljana Radio-Television, the Slovenian label, allowing him to record albums with a greater sense of space, demonstrate his soul-jazz phrasing. And then Yugoslavia fell apart and Šaban all but vanished.

'I have very nice memories of Yugoslavia. It was a golden age and I got to sing for Tito. Then it all went to shit, the politics, the music. I stopped making a lot of music because whatever you released the bootleggers copied it and sold it for one euro.'

Šaban kept his head down in Niš, still venturing into Germany to sing at weddings and Yugoslav restaurants, releasing cassettes to be sold in Central European markets catering to the Yugoslav Diaspora. Largely forgotten – a rumour spread that he'd died in poverty – he then scored the biggest hit of his career in 1997 with 'Kasandra'. The song celebrated Cassandra, the title character of a Venezuelan soap opera that was a TV phenomenon across Serbia, Bulgaria and Macedonia. So much so a Bulgarian woman worked the Belgrade markets telling impatient Serb fans what forthcoming episodes held, Bulgaria having screened the series and experienced the mania first.

The series followed the beautiful Gypsy Cassandra's forbidden love for Randu, her macho Latin lover. Across the Balkans many Roma children born in 1997/98 were named after Cassandra and Randu. Fittingly, the Balkan celebrity event of 1997 involved the stars of *Cassandra* visiting Serbia. Fans jammed the streets, thousands gathering outside the Venezuelans' hotel to sing Šaban's song. Šaban met Cassandra and photos of the two of them appeared in newspapers and even on the cover of a TV listings magazine. Šaban's very proud of this.

'You see, whatever features Gypsies does well in the world. *Cassandra* was the most popular TV programme ever and Kusturica's films about Gypsies pick up the awards in Cannes. The world loves us!'

Indeed, world music audiences would have loved the wild Gypsy King had Šaban shown any inclination to make an impression on audiences beyond the Balkans. In 1999 Bosnian producer Dragi Šeštić tracked Šaban down and persuaded him to make an album for the Dutch World Connection label. Backed by fine Bosnian band Mostar Sevdah Reunion, Dragi cut Šaban singing fifteen glorious tunes.

'How easy he was to record,' recalls Dragi. 'Never makes a mistake, always pitch perfect, great energy.'

The resulting album, *A Gypsy Legend*, is superb. Šabán played the aforementioned Amsterdam concert then went on to rock Frankfurt.

'I started singing and all the Gypsies in the crowd got up and started dancing and then all the Germans got up and began dancing. I couldn't believe it! Two thousand people! Imagine,' says Šaban, laughing, 'Hitler must be spinning in his grave!'

The next concert, in Zagreb, sold out instantly, Croatians overcoming a diet of coarse nationalism to see the Godfather of Gypsy soul. Then Šaban went AWOL, a pensioner yet still wild, still reckless. Apparently a Yugoslav restaurant in Düsseldorf made him an offer to sing and Šaban, being Šaban, accepted. Dragi finally persuaded Šaban's wife and daughter to pressure Šaban into appearing for the Zagreb concert. Šaban turned up at the last minute, less than happy about having to give up his restaurant gig.

'I had to say to him after that concert "you are a genius but I cannot work with you any longer, you are giving me a heart attack,"' says Dragi.

I tell Šaban Dragi sends his regards (true) and Šaban looks dismayed. 'Dragi? He never calls me. Why doesn't he call me?' He then claims World Connection sold 100,000 copies of *A Gypsy Legend* yet he's not seen 'a single dinar'. 'More like 3,000,' mutters label boss Albert Nijmolen. 'Šaban could have been a big star with Western audiences if he wanted to. But he's too unreliable for people to book.'

Dragi's name has quietened Šaban. He sits, lost in thought, reflecting on good times, bad times, wasted opportunities, so much lost (including the gold teeth: 'too much alcohol'), my questions forcing him to remember, to make whole again, all that he's lived through: the Roma orphan wandering a ruined Yugoslavia, belly aching with hunger pains, hiding from fascists, scavenging for food; the will to survive Goli Otok and its myriad cruelties; the fear of the written word and then the mastery of it; the power of song, a power that's freed him from poverty, allowed him to stand tall against all the authorities who dared penalise and beat him, led him to be embraced by Tito and Indira Gandhi; fame's dizzy high; all the madness that besieges when it's you, you who are anointed King…the King of Europe's invisible nation.

'Nobody is taking care of Gypsies in Europe,' says Šaban, his big, battered face furrowed with sorrow. 'People like us musicians but don't want to deal with ordinary Gypsies. Don't want to bring them in off the street or take the musicians to academies. They ignore us.'

In front of me an old man speaks bitter truth, no laughter, no music, in his throat. Šaban looks frail, disillusioned. For your people, I offer, these are cruel times.

'I'm a little cold,' says Šaban. 'I go inside now.'

Boban Marković:
I Bring Sevdah

Religion is music, the breath of the flute is the path to
enlightenment, a sermon is better made with sounds
                                        – Zen Fuke aphorism

Onwards we roll, past Niš's dusty borders and into a Serbia where
history is ancient and fresh, dry as the infinite bones buried across
this land and scabby as wounds not yet healed. Open up and bleed?
Not this evening, thanks. The highway's smooth, built with EU
money to carry traffic towards Athens for Greece's fateful Olympics.
And then on not so good highway, broken tarmac, little cracks
threatening to become big craters. Same road but we're entering
the deep south so the funds have dried up or been siphoned off.
Then again, this could be a primitive form of Morse code to let
travellers know they are nearing the former Yugoslav Republic
of Macedonia and the once Socialist Autonomous Province of
Kosovo. Macedonia is straight ahead, only a couple of hours away,
a tensely peaceful place. Kosovo involves turning right and signs
still hang in the air, giving directions for the road to nowhere; the
border's closed now, slammed shut by retreating Serb soldiers in
June 1999 after Milošević recalled them, fleeing a land flayed by a
decade of repression and months of carnage. As the troops crossed
back into Serbia the Kosovar Albanians returned, NATO having
won the war for them, vengeance in mind, employing the same
terror tactics as Milošević's stooges had used to ethnically cleanse

Cigarettes and coffee blues: Boban Marković

Photo: Garth Cartwright

Kosovo's resident Serb and Roma population. Hatred breeds hatred. Seventy-two hours ago an Albanian gunman opened fire on Kosovar Serb children as they played in a river, killing two and wounding several. NATO, having now secured Kosovo as a protectorate (i.e. strategic base), no longer deigns to pretend human rights issues are important. Pity about the pogroms, the likes of Tony Blair say. But that's war, baby.

All around us the land stretches, infinite flat, dry hectares, arable but surely not very fertile. Rows of crops lend an eerie sensation to the countryside, seemingly empty of human presence; only occasional petrol stations and farmsteads in the distance suggest anyone lives around here. Damned by history's misfortunes, southern Serbia has been systematically depopulated, the recent withdrawal north of troops perhaps picking up panicking people on the way, locals fleeing the imagined Albanian forces of darkness. Karpa shivers, tightens his grip on the steering wheel.

We pass a sign for Žitoradja, hometown to Ceca and a place that will surely become the Serbian Graceland. Ceca's fame helped her father become Mayor of Žitoradja. Legend has it he was illiterate. Which is perfect, Ceca being the ultimate peasant fantasy made malleable flesh. I'm tempted to tell Karpa to turn off, let's go check Žitoradja, see if they have a statue of the divine diva in the centre of town – she having already been subject to much sculpting, I'm sure they could model a monument with a plastic surgeon's scalpel – but it means heading west and the light is already beginning to soften and thin.

Onwards, Karpa answering politely at police checkpoints; onwards, through too much sun-bleached nothingness; onwards, skipping the city of Leškovac; onwards, with a chill wind ripping across the plains, sending a tiny tornado of dust across the highway, a Kosovar wind, says Karpa, one that brings no good tidings. Karpa, wise to the nationalist lie, can only shake his head and wonder what bitter spirits fuel the Albanian psyche. Serb villages in this part of Serbia, he notes, suffer occasional terror attacks. And if we, in his battered Escort with Novi Sad number plates, crossed into Kosovo violent death would soon overtake us. 'Even being this close to Kosovo, it feels ominous,' he says. 'It's open season on Serbs. The hatred down there is extreme.' Lean out of the window and breathe deeply, certain the scent of blood will flavour the evening's arrival. Then the road starts to slope, to drift into valleys, around us the Kukavica mountains rise as a protective border and soon we're sweeping along the banks of Južna Morava. Serbia is fresh, beautiful, safe and whole again.

Villages that once clung to the river now crawl towards the motorway offering elemental petrol–restaurant–motel complexes. A-frame chalets decorate the hills, monuments to Yugoslavia's lush era, a time when the West pumped money into Tito's seductively non-aligned state. Who could believe, says Karpa, that we could go from having it so good to what things are like now? Against the dying of the light we roll on, limpid mists rise off the river, cattle are walked back from fields, the road keeps winding, tracking the river's flow, recalling Texan bluesman Albert Collins wailing, 'The highway is like a woman/soft shoulders and dangerous curves'. You tell it, Albert. Every few kilometres there's another settlement – some tiny, others sizeable – and I begin reading off their names: Grdelica, Prevajane, Dep and, finally, Vladičin Han.

Entering Vladičin Han at twilight and I encounter immediate disappointment. Vladičin Han, this town of brass legend, bears more than a passing resemblance to Staines or Kettering, England's bleak new towns. Saturday evening yet little activity appears on the street. What was I hoping for – a secret city where everyone struts down the street to a funky brass groove? A Gypsy New Orleans? Still, Vladičin Han feels strangely silent, what with being home to Boban Marković. And Boban, as they say, is the man. But nothing suggests this as we drive around, Karpa's enquiries as to where Boban lives resulting in blank looks and shrugs. Admittedly, Vladičin Han (pop. 10,000) is not just a brass town but an industrial one too, famous for producing jams and juices. Finally a man walking his dog suggests we cross the river, the mahala being built on the opposing hill.

Good? Not exactly. Actually, all is chaos: Boban supposedly expects us (his Belgrade-based manager had OK'd with him that I turn up this evening) but when calling from Niš he never answers his mobile. And attempts here are equally futile. What to do? Returning to Belgrade is not an option; I'm heading south, next stop Macedonia. And, having met Boban in Guča, I know he's amiable. So it's unlikely he's avoiding our presence. Also, tomorrow he's off to Budapest to perform so this tight pocket of time is the only chance I have of catching him at home. But where is he? How do we find him? Karpa retreats to the area close to the river then takes decisive action by going into a local bar. I want to join him, rakija being medicine for frayed nerves. But Karpa insists this isn't about drinking. Minutes later we're moving, with the bar's manager giving directions. The bar's Boban's local and this guy's a personal friend.

Rising straight from the river, the mahala hangs on steep hillside. Where central Vladičin Han features contemporary Serbian urban styling (concrete), the mahala bears the imprint of Ottoman times. The streets are cobbled in the traditional Turkish manner of kadrma and the feeling is suddenly very, very country; houses are covered in vines, every available inch of open ground is worked, the smell of freshly turned soil invades nostrils, chickens cluck and pigs oink. I'd heard that on weekend evenings local Roma youth in southern Serbia strut the streets with their brass instruments but, no, not here. This is probably explained by the precipitous angle the Roma are forced to live upon – step back to blow a solo and you're rolling towards the bottom of town.

Pull over opposite a large white house with a big balcony, Villa Boban, and our guide leaps out, runs up to the front door and rat-a-tat-tats. The door opens and…and it's not Boban. Instead a small, plump woman wearing an apron wipes her hands and looks quizzically at us. The bar manager engages her in friendly but intense conversation. Lots of 'da da da' and gesturing follow until we get the signal to enter and Mrs Boban, for it is she, ushers us into an open plan kitchen/living room.

Boban's obviously earning well as everything looks very new. There's a wood inlay dining table and equally elegant French chairs, sofas, drinks cabinet, TV, stereo and chandelier. Several oil paintings hang on the wall, all of them featuring trumpets in a symbolic cod-Chirico manner, and sentimental statues are on tables and in corners. A collection of plastic dogs with nodding heads very much suggests the female touch. Mrs Boban fusses around her unexpected guests. Sugary orange drink is served and coffee put on the boil. Plates of sticky sweets, comparable in design if not taste to lokoum, are set down. It appears last night was the family's slava – a day's celebration of their chosen saint – which is why there's heaps of sweets. Mrs Boban encourages us to munch. The slava went on until 6am, she says, with the weary gesture of someone who's had to rise and clean the mess up.

She and Boban recently became grandparents for the first time and photos of daughter Tamara and husband are proudly presented. Tamara looks every bit the Gypsy princess – all billowing gowns and gold jewellery – and mama looks with pride upon daughter, now living in Niš, in the same way Boban is proud of Marko. And the man himself? Off conducting business in a neighbouring village. But she expects him home. Or she did; once we're all on the way to serious caffeine and sugar poisoning Mrs Boban starts dialling numbers – her husband obviously having phones for all occasions – until she finds him. Boban may well be the King of Guča, the world's foremost Gypsy trumpet player, but Mrs Marković cracks the whip when it comes to domestic duties. Visitors. A journalist. Saying Bojan cleared arrival with you. They're in my living room. Get your ass home now. Or something to that effect. She hangs up and says Boban will meet us in two hours' time in our guide's bar. Huge sighs of relief. Time for a few rakijas.

Boban Marković's playing incorporates a lyricism and technique capable of captivating jazz fans while his orkestar blast a hard Romani funk appealing to ravers of all ages. Boban may be Guča's most decorated winner but, aware of the limitations of Serbian brass stardom, he's hungry for international success. And with his son Marko possessing both trumpet talent and the dark, malleable looks associated with the likes of Enrique Iglesias, well, sky's the limit.

We settle into the bar, Vladičin Han's youth surrounding, Kylie's 'Can't Get You out of My Head' on high rotation, small town Saturday night under way. Time to reflect on the Marković oeuvre: Boban began releasing cassettes in Serbia in the early 1990s before signing to Hungary's X Produkcio for three fine albums: *Srce Cigansko* (Heart of a Gypsy), *Millenium* and *Bistra Reka*. The latter two show Boban experimenting – drum machines and strings – while still draining great, fat notes from tender, muted trumpet solos. Moving to Berlin's Piranha Records he released 2003's *Live In Belgrade*, an album that captures the flat-out, full-force impact of the Balkan brass concert experience, and 2004's *Boban/Marko*, an album full of startling brass beauty and weird resonance. Opening tune 'Balkan Fest' begins with rattling percussion, netherworld voices, horn fanfares, Boban and Marko's trumpets recalling Miles Davis's voiceless blues on Rodrigo's *Concierto De Aranjuez*, Balkan funk building like a ghostly cavalary charge before a spooked vocal from Svetlana Spajić Latinović kicks in, so creating something which sounds to these ears, after today's journey, like the soundtrack to a Roma road movie…*Uneasy Rider*…'Gimme Shelter' as brewed in Balkan badlands.

Three hours and lots of rakija pass until, finally, Karpa wanders out to phone. Yes, he's on his way. Another twenty minutes. An hour later he strides into the bar, wearing that delirious Boban smile, eyes brutally bloodshot, demanding coffee. How much time, I wonder, will I have with this guy? I mean, he looks like he's barely slept across the past week. Which, it turns out, is close to the truth. Boban's rising international reputation means he's constantly on the road. I congratulate him on his Guča performance and he shrugs.

'When I'm in Guča I feel like the King but it's not necessary for me to be there. There's lots of young players and for them it's great to be number one. Since 1981 I've gone constantly but I think I'm over with the competition. I'm making space for Marko now, let him do all the solos, he's young! Anyway, I want to make popular music, not music for ethnomusicologists.'

Boban's thirty-nine but looks a decade older. A lifetime of late nights, fuelled by nicotine, rakija and caffeine, has weathered once cherubic features. Talking rapidly, Boban's brooding and wry. Maestro, how's the wonder boy?

'He's a little tired but he's good. My father and mother say I was exactly like Marko as a child. At three years old he would play with the trumpet in the sand, would lose it and I'd have to dig for it. At seven he started to take the trumpet seriously. I trained him but wanted him to find his own way. Many people think Marko is riding on my back, people who have never heard him play trumpet, but he's there because he's good. He's a bit of a maniac for the trumpet, playing ten hours a day, and at home with three generations of us living together he's starting to drive us all a bit crazy. I had to buy him a mute. And he wants the orkestar to rehearse ten hours a day. He doesn't realise the rest of the band have families and other commitments.'

Brass madness? Yeah. Here being a musician is more than a career, it's a calling, lore, ritual, the Roma vocation.

'In school I was very bad. I chose to play the trumpet and I practised every day. My idols were the great Gypsy trumpet players but I knew that I was getting better than them. My mother's grandfather got to play for the King, for rich people, he was a fabulous musician but my father was only average and he wanted me to finish school but when he saw it was not good business he let me leave. My father taught me by singing notes to me. We didn't have a gramophone or anything like that. He'd work at night and come back very late and wake me and make me play the notes he had taught me that day. He was very hard on me but it's understandable as I was the seventh child and first son and he did this because he believed I had talent for brass. By fifteen I was earning money playing.'

Boban joins us in chugging beer with rakija chasers and soon the evening's descending into dissolute ramblings, much fun but incoherent. Still, Boban's antenna never completely withdraws and even innocent queries can be met with defensive answers. Example: has Albanian music had any influence on your playing? 'I don't talk politics!' Example: how many Roma live in this mahala? 'We're a good community and get on well with the Serbs! No drug dealers or murderers live here!' Which is interesting simply because Boban's so relaxed most of the time. Like many aspiring Roma he wants, understandably, to fit in, to be accepted – as he obviously is in Vladičin Han – so prefers to save chat for safe musical territory. I mention we spent the afternoon with Šaban. Boban lightens.

'Shabbie, he's truly the king of Roma song. I've played concerts with him and feel very lucky to have this experience although it's embarrassing to sing on the same stage as him. I'm a good singer but we don't compare. He's too great.'

We talk jazz. Boban mentions he's lifted a few tricks from Miles Davis. Yet his true love is the East.

'Turkey, that remains such a big part of our sound. And Arabic music, I like this music so much.'

Boban's first international exposure came when he and his orkestar were hired by Goran Bregović to play on the soundtracks for Kusturica's early and mid 1990s films *Arizona Dream* and *Underground*. *Underground*'s huge 1995 success – Cannes Award, art-house hit, much controversy over its portrayal of Serb history – should have launched Boban's international career. Instead, with Serbia then being an international pariah, he found himself stuck in Vladičin Han while Bregović toured the West playing a pastiche that had critics too lazy to listen to Balkan music acclaim him as a composer of genius.

'Kusturica is the big professional, a good man. Bregović…well, we worked together and the music is my idea. One part is from a Šaban song and the other part is mine. I took the winning tune from that year's Guča and played it and Bregović added his things and when the soundtrack came out he did not credit me for writing the music. This made me very angry. Bregović has asked me to do more work with him but I've established myself and don't need to work [with him]. If we do work [together] in the future it'll be on my conditions.'

'Djelem, Djelem' and 'Ederlezi': what's the story of these tunes?

'"Djelem, Djelem" is our anthem. Gypsies have been singing it for many years and whenever I play it the Gypsies all stand up, they all know it. "Ederlezi", it's also old, maybe Macedonian. Nobody knows who's stealing from whom but, anyway, all our songs are made beautiful.'

By now we're near meltdown, exhausted from the journey and oozing alcohol. Boban, realising we haven't eaten, leads us to a local sandwich shop for Serb fast food – meat, pickles, bread, sauce – then leaves us at Millenium Turist Hotel with a promise to meet for coffee with Marko at 10am. If ever an establishment were less aptly named it's this dump. The hand basin floods the floor, there's no hot water, the plaster's peeling…grunge is the word. It's no bargain (20 euros per head) but all Vladičin Han has, the Serb tourist industry still reeling from Milošević's efforts at promoting the nation.

Waking at 7am the room's uncomfortably damp. Fuck it, I'll take my chances with the elements. Walk up the hill to the mahala to clear the fog settled across my brain, air so fresh it tastes better than coffee. There's little extreme poverty here. Sure, some of the dwellings are ramshackle but none are shanties and most houses look cosy. Well, after Millenium Turist Hotel pretty much anything would. Many people keep pigs, which kills the suggestion that this area's populated by Muslim Roma. Pity swine can't digest plastic, tin and glass, as household refuse tends to get dumped, the town's refuse collectors obviously not trekking up the mahala's steep streets.

Back in central Vladičin Han I notice a memorial for two local teenagers killed by NATO's hot-rods of the apocalypse. What, I ask Karpa, is there to bomb around here? A jam factory? 'NATO

Brass boys:
Boban (right)
and buddy

Photo: Family Marković

was trying to hit a train and missed. The teenagers were in a car and the bomb hit them.' Collateral damage? A dumb bomb? God knows what those at the Pentagon call the extinguishing of children's lives. Karpa shrugs and recalls a proverb they have in the north: 'As it gets further south, all has more sorrow'. He guesses the saying relates to the days when this region was an Ottoman stronghold. Today, with the crisis in Kosovo, the proverb carries added resonance. Does it hold true for the music? In Šaban's songs, sure, there is pain. And in Macedonia the music is often marked by melancholy. But within Boban Marković's Orkestar I find journeys, exploration and celebration.

Boban and Marko appear after eleven. Gypsy time. Boban still looks shagged and takes refuge in cigarettes and coffee. Like Šaban he smokes those potent symbols of success, Red Marlboros. It's the first time I've seen Marko when he's not on stage and he's smaller and shyer than one imagines a burgeoning trumpet legend. He's amiable, sure, but only really comes alive when the café puts on the new album, *Boban/Marko*, instinctively counting out rhythms, miming solos, losing himself in the wild Balkan funk. What music do you like to listen to, Marko?

'My father.'

What about MTV?

'No, I like Serbian, Bulgarian, Turkish and Indian music.'

While touring do you miss your friends and playing football?

'Of course I do but this is my job. I have to do it.'

Marko left school young. Like father? Indeed. Boban mentioned last night how Marko's unwillingness to study at school – bad reports, phone calls from teachers – initially infuriated him. Then his wife insisted Boban listen to Marko play. The thirteen-year-old held papa's ear and the apprenticeship was soon under way.

'I had the big wish to become what I am now,' says a reflective Boban. 'I feel like I have achieved something with my life. Gypsies are good at playing music and dancing and it's well known we can't live without music. This is why when I go to America or Europe people respond – it's the universal in my music they're responding to, not just me. And when I do a concert I don't just do a job and say "good night". I bring sevdah.'

Sevdah is a Turkish expression: emotional, passionate, sensual, spicy, wild. Boban smiles at the thought of it, his eyes drift, ancient Roma musical lore in mind.

'Time is not important,' he says quietly, 'it's fluid.'

LANGO DROM
(The Long Journey)

Northern India, the arse end of what Europe's calling the first millennium, reels as warrior tribes from north-west Asia invade, fuelled by the new religion of Islam. Convert or die? Or flee. And so the migration began and a people (the Roma) were forcibly born out of war, flight, adversity. This epic exodus would come to stand as the equivalent of an oral chapter of the Vedas, a secret history whispered amongst descendants as the lango drom.

Academics argue over the exact dates the Roma began their migration yet what's now ascertained is that some time between the sixth and eleventh centuries ACE (After the Christian Era) large numbers of people from north-west India marched across West Asia into North Africa and Europe. This is extreme terrain, hostile in every sense: what can they have encountered? How did they know where they were going? What did they carry? Tools, utensils, food, wood and, yes, musical instruments. Linguists suggest the migratory groups consisted of large armies (and the retinues travelling with them) due to the number of military words still employed in Romani. As these migrations occurred over several decades, possibly centuries, communities put down roots in different places – Egypt and the Caucasus are both home to long-resident Romani-speaking communities.

For centuries it was believed these migrants had arrived in Europe from Egypt – thus the (E)Gypsies. An easy mistake: India was little more than fable – think of Christopher Columbus's misguided attempts to reach India in 1492 – while Egypt was associated with the occult and divination; when the Roma are first noted in Constantinople in 1068 it was written they were 'notorious for soothsaying and sorcery'. Moving into Europe as the Turks conquered Byzantium – initially fleeing then later accompanying Ottoman armies – certain Roma tribes claimed to be serving a seven-year banishment for the sins of their Egyptian forefathers who turned away the Blessed Virgin with the child Jesus. Having lived by their wits for several centuries they may have reasoned claiming to be penitent pilgrims was their best chance of being welcomed into these new Christian lands.

In 1422 bands of nomadic Roma displayed letters of safe-conduct from the Pope. While the Papal letters surely provided some initial cover, European attitudes soon hardened against the new arrivals – their nomadism, dark skin, foreign tongue, unconventional clothing and talent for petty theft arousing hostility. 'They travelled in bands and camped at night in the fields outside towns, for they were excessively given to thievery and feared that in the towns they would be taken prisoner,' wrote a German observer in 1435. 'Got to keep movin', got to keep movin', blues fallin' down like hail,' wailed Robert Johnson as he drifted across an unforgiving Mississippi delta. The Roma, strangers in estranged lands, may have sung of a similarly ominous flight.

Communism forced settlement on most Roma across much of East Europe. Industrialisation encouraged it but the nomads still exist. How many? No one's sure. In the UK many of the travellers who inhabit caravan parks and call themselves Gypsies are of Irish descent with no connection to the Roma at all. George Monbiot suggested, after a Sussex village threw a mock caravan with 'PIKEY' – slang for traveller – painted on it upon a November 2003 bonfire, that open hostility against travellers could be traced back to the time of Cain and Abel. Cain was a farmer, a settled person; Abel was a herder, a nomad. Cain killed Abel, the beloved of God. This hatred of freer spirits, escaping the crushing of the soul that everyday *urban existence can enforce, has grown, Monbiot suggests, with the explosion of the cities.*

As the good burghers of Sussex have shown, old intolerances die hard. Entering the twenty-first century, the Roma remain 'notorious' for crimes and acts both real and imagined. Yet if their supposed freedom is what we envy it is their musical gifts we celebrate. A payment by the Duke of Ferrara in 1469 in the Duchy of Modena (northern Italy) to a Cingano for playing a citole (a plucked stringed instrument) is an early association of Roma with music in Europe. A Hungarian census taken in 1780–83 records the main livelihoods of the Roma as smithery and other manual work; behind these came music. Across the centuries Roma have excelled as musicians – the court of Russia's Catherine the Great established them as amongst Europe's finest and most fashionable while their pre-eminence in Hungary and Spain goes unquestioned.

So they were good, maybe the best, musicians. No one denies that. But what is 'Gypsy music'? Sounds of Asian origin or simple mimicry of European music? An Oriental flavour is found in much of the music made by those residing in former Ottoman territories. But any direct link to the Pandits and Ustads, India's master musicians who teach by example, is long broken. Roma musicians have always been – and remain – innovators endowed with magpie musical ability. Just as the descendants of African slaves built modern musical styles across the Americas out of disparate sources, Roma verve, ability and imagination helped reshape European music.

Understandably, we continue to respond to Gypsy music because the vast bulk of music we make and consume in the West today is static, smug, self-conscious, unbearably craven, bereft of magic, unable to capture spirits because it is, in itself, dispirited. Even Hendrix, hoping to emulate the freedom and intensity he heard in flamenco and North African recordings (so calling his post-Experience outfit Band Of Gypsies), failed to match the bands of Gypsies I've encountered across the Balkans. Not that Hendrix got there first in emulating the

Roma: demonic violinist Niccolo Paganini played so wildly he was rumoured to have Gypsy blood while Hungarian pianist Franz Liszt boasted that he did. Early twentieth-century classical composers Béla Bártok and Zoltan Kódaly paid close attention, even making pioneering field recordings of Gypsy musicians in Transylvania.

Today, as Roma continue to move from east to west, they may still open our ears, challenge how we hear. And as with their lango drom ancestors they're forced to take to the road because violence and poverty drive them to seek shelter. Got to keep movin'...blues fallin' down like hail...

Grandmother and child reunion

MACEDONIA

*Rolling and tumbling towards the border…lightning storms perform switchbacks across the mountains…peels of thunder calling my name…*Serbia sizzles, hot August rain lashing the coach, dropping temperatures and adding turbulence as we helter skelter along roads winding from peak to valley. Kickback, wind down, absorb the furies of the old gods, how they mock us, feeble mortals packed sardine tight, descending ancient trails. Sheet lightning colours the sky. Love it. Taste the electricity in the air, feel it leap from fellow passengers' skin, ablaze in dark Balkan eyes…the atmosphere's charged, perfect conditions to exit Serbia…this road runs to the northern Greek coast, could ride it till I hit the Aegean…sometimes

I get a great notion to jump in the river and drown...maybe not right now, sticky as the evening is. Anyway, Greece is a border too far. The ancient land of Macedonia's growing closer, coming in sight.

Igor meets me at Skopje's bus station. 'Let's eat,' he says. Un hombre simpatico. 'What are you looking for in Skopje?' he asks. 'Women,' I reply. Igor cocks an eyebrow. OK, time to qualify things: primarily, I'm here to pay homage to two female singers of remarkable artistry and character. Esma Redžepova, the crowned Queen of Gypsy singers, and Džansever, princess in waiting. Or, as it would appear, in exile. Esma, I've been assured, would be here. Yet how to find Džansever?

No one seems to have a clear idea. Which is appropriate: Macedonia appears hazy at first, hidden beneath the weight of history. Yet the closer you get the more Macedonia takes surprisingly confident shape, finds beautiful form. With only two million citizens, this landlocked nation produces phenomenal music and exceptional musicians; brass bands for every occasion, singers for all events. Maybe it's in the water. Or the tomatoes. Or the rakija. Or, more likely, the Roma. Macedonia is the Balkan nation with the most integrated of Roma populations. Sure, all the problems associated with an impoverished minority are here. Yet Macedonia has made an effort. More so than Serbia and in sharp contrast to Bulgaria and Romania, both largely leaving Western NGOs to deal with 'the Gypsy problem'. In Skopje there's Roma TV and radio, Roma MPs and the Roma are enshrined in the constitution as an ethnic minority with equal rights. This sense of equality surely lends spirit to the music, a positive psychic energy to the nation.

That said, mid-summer temperatures lend lethargy, not energy, to Skopje. Paint blistered, concrete chipped (and there's a lot of concrete)...initial impressions suggest a city on the verge of falling apart. Crossing the city by foot finds me leaping at shadows, cowering beneath shrubs, anything to escape the sun's relentless glare. Belgrade? Belgrade was temperate compared to Skopje's sauna conditions. Local Roma men cruise the housing and industrial estates scattered across Skopje in horse and carts or large, adapted tricycles, trawling through skips, searching for waste cardboard to sell to recyclers. Roma children, ragged and brimming with mischief, beg at cafés around Ploštad Makedonija, offer to wash windscreens at city intersections. So far, so Serbia.

Escaping the heat I visit the Museum of Macedonia, its star attraction a collection of Orthodox icons kept in a locked room. While studying a variety of Virgins, saints and Sons of God I realise by entering this room of heavenly art I'd inadvertently stumbled upon answered prayers – effective air conditioning. The museum's other revelation being that this ancient infant of a nation is not falling apart so much as struggling against the historic tendency to tear itself apart: being at the crossroads of the Balkans rarely allows for peaceful existence.

Macedonia's moment in the sun came when Alexander the Great rose from Aegean Macedonia in the fourth century BC to conquer much of the ancient world. Since then Macedonia has been lashed by history. The Romans came, conquered and left the region to Constantinople. Slav tribes settled around the seventh century. The Roma arrived peacefully between the eleventh and thirteenth centuries. Bulgaria, Serbia and Byzantium constantly fought over the turf until the Ottomans, who, having defeated the Serbs in Kosovo in 1389, ruled for the next half millennium. Even then peace rarely lasted long. 'All life and trade died out and the Sultan's laws were disregarded,' wrote a French traveller as he passed through Macedonia's scorched territories after the war between Turkey, Austria and Russia (1787–92).

The twentieth century proved a savage one for Macedonians: five wars – two world, three Balkan – were fought across their territory and Greece, Serbia and Bulgaria all claimed Macedonia.

Pre-WWII Serbia dominated the land and banned the Macedonian language. Hitler's conquest of Yugoslavia allowed him to gift Macedonia to fascist Bulgaria; the Bulgarians' ensuing brutality has never been forgotten. Tito gave Macedonia republic status and when Yugoslavia fell apart only Macedonia, after holding a referendum in 1991, peacefully extracted itself. Lack of a large Serb populace, modest resources and good government saved Macedonia from Slobodan's savage embrace.

Still, independence wasn't going to be easy: Greece – the only EU nation to actively support Milošević's criminal administration – cried wolf and implemented an economic blockade against Macedonia, claiming the new nation had territorial imperatives on Aegean Macedonia (part of the modern Greek state since 1913). Macedonians, having no military, economic or political power, simply revived the old folk song 'May God Kill the Greek Archbishop' and offered an extended middle finger south. Albanian extremists, fired up by NATO handing them Kosovo, began employing a distorted nationalism (the fascist construct of a Greater Albania) to create a ragtag militia that threatened for several months during 2001 to tear Macedonia apart. Calm heads managed to hold the nation together but as I drift across Skopje billboards declare an amnesty for guns, hinting at how fragile the ethnic fault-line remains.

Crossing the fifteenth-century Turkish Kamen Most (translation: 'stone bridge' though 'concrete bridge' would now be more apt) provides entry into Skopje's old city. No multi-tiered shopping centres here. No designer clothes outlets. No junk food chains. Instead, a vibrant fruit and veg market stands alongside the last remaining Turkish bazaar in Europe. The green market is peopled by peasant farmers, old men and women with alligator skin selling obscenely tasty tomatoes, buckets of glowing blackberries, peaches and peppers, black olives and white cheeses, every imaginable kind of egg laid. Plums. Honey. Beans. Nuts. Pears. Carrots. Apples.

Onions. Potatoes. Wickedly pregnant aubergines. Dense vats of spices. Take a deep breath and inhale.

Enticing this organic wonderland may be but the old city's largely static: here time looks to have stopped around 1912, people appear to be waiting for the Sultan to issue edicts. The bazaar may be car-free but its days as a conduit for Ali Baba fantasies are long gone. Forlorn shops sell gold jewellery, sheepskins, pirate CDs, Rajasthan textiles, air and bus tickets, foreign currency, shoes and clothing. There's a nostalgia here for the colonial past – it feels like Turkey, it looks like Turkey – similar to that for England which you may find in equally odd outposts of India or New Zealand. A little of Istanbul's bustle surely wouldn't go amiss; the only people moving quickly, indeed, seeming to move at all, are the boys delivering glasses of tea on silver platters.

So Skopje's a city divided, old and tired, new and hectic, rich and poor, relaxed and tense, Macedonian and Albanian, Roma and Turkish. Wandering the city, amidst the heat and dust, I encounter peaceful people yet can sense an undercurrent of unease, unresolved tensions. I wondered if this would be reflected in the music but, no, that theory won't wash. A better one involves Macedonia's brutal history lending a fatalism to the nation, a fatalism that infects the music: subdued sufferings are expressed in deeply sensual, nostalgic songs, songs that ripple through the national consciousness. Macedonian music possesses the scent of the Orient – here one of the most potent fusions of European and Asian music came about and in the Macedonian Orthodox Church's liturgies and the folk music of Macedonian and Turkish, Albanian and Roma, this can still be heard.

Igor lives on the fourth floor of a tower block and displays a tendency towards extreme *Withnail & I* habits. He shares the flat with four cats. Four cats who never leave the apartment – Igor dare not even open a window in case they venture out and drop towards the pavement below – and these felines spend all their time either fighting or leaving a trail of fur balls, hair and pee across every terrain. Then there's the kitchen sink, swollen with dirty plates, cups and cutlery. Igor hates doing dishes so invested in a dishwasher. A dishwasher he rarely remembers to fill. The chaos continues in the bathroom – the shower is swollen with hair and the laundry basket is filled with stale clothing beginning to rot. Igor's unfazed by the domestic meltdown surrounding him; instead, being a true Balkan Buddha, he sits and sings the praises of all his nation's citizens – a critical word against another ethnicity never passes his lips. Milošević and Tudjman and their cronies, he notes, they have a lot to answer for. But to Macedonia's Roma and Albanian populace he offers only warmth and the belief that the nation will pull through its varying degrees of crisis.

Maybe it's the Albanian ganja Igor smokes that keeps him so calm while chaos reigns. But I doubt it: in Skopje ganja appears hard to come by so Igor consumes way more tobacco than hemp. This could be an Albanian method of psychic insurrection – cutting off the city's supply of smoke. But the assumption that the ganja is Albanian raises a basic question: is it? Albanians are Europe's new bogeymen, linked to every form of crime going – including drug running across the Balkans – so any ganja toked is tagged 'Albanian grass'. This leads to occasional bouts of spurious nationalism with smokers breaking out of their comatose state to shout, 'Fuck Albanian grass! It's shit. Like everything from Albania. Serbian grass is much better!' The best ganja I smoked across the Balkans was in Skopje, warm, trippy and with a tasty flavour reflective of the Macedonian character. Whoever grew those buds was a green-fingered natural healer.

Odd there's not more homegrown ganja around considering the Balkans remain an agricultural wonderland. Imagine it, fields of organic hemp blowing in the summer breeze. Considering cannabis is indigenous to India and part of the Hindu Sadhus' religious ritual, I begin to wonder if ganja entered Europe with the Roma. Which would be a nice explanation for the explosive contours of

Gypsy music. Sure, I'm being fanciful but…but Macedonia is the birthplace of opium (the vivid red poppy is prominent on the 500 denar note – exactly what a quarter gram of heroin costs here) and opium is a Macedonian word – OPI = to get drunk; UM = mind. The drunken mind. What sweet poetry. Opium was once cultivated heavily in Macedonia's south-east region, its value parallel with if not greater than gold. People would imprint gold coins to their opium pies then cut out the part with the imprint and the opium coin would be treated as legal tender on a par with a gold coin. You can still find opium pies in rural Macedonia where they are kept as a family treasure, never to be consumed and sold only in emergencies. And while trade in opium is now banned it appears farmers can still legally sell opium to the biggest pharmacy factory in Macedonia, ALKALOID.

Macedonians are righteously proud of opium, claiming it inspired ancient Greece's finest minds and Alexander consumed it copiously, introducing it to Asia on his conquests. It would explain those dreams he had too. For centuries opium was one of the world's most valued and praised products, a magical substance that eased pain, exalted thought and increased intimacy. And always it was the mysterious land known as Macedonia, an organic Atlantis, which was whispered of conspiratorially when aficionados sampled their opium – 'subtle and mighty,' wrote Thomas De Quincey in *Confessions Of An Opium Eater*; 'we had some of the best Yugoslavian opium,' William Burroughs reported in *The Naked Lunch*. In the late 1800s Salonika, Aegean Macedonia's port city (renamed Thessaloniki by the Greeks), was the opium trading hub for the world. Macedonians were to find the growing of their beloved poppy restricted due to US pressure in the 1970s. Since then the beautiful red poppy has been banished from Mama Macedonia, grown only under the beady eye of government inspectors.

Igor's philosophical about the lack of illegal highs and suggests we try the best alternative going: the local cuisine. After Serbia (meat, meat and mo' meat) I'm sceptical but a trip to a Greek taverna finds lamb souvalakis so succulent I'm converted. Another night we check a traditional restaurant in the old town. Here we're plied with divine stuffed peppers and sausages of such delicacy and flavour I begin to wonder whether I should be writing on Macedonian food instead of music. The local wines, rakija and beer are excellent but those sausages, thin tubes of animal flesh and herbs, damn, they were a sensual experience.

One evening Igor's channel-surfing, skipping across everything from Russian meditations on communism to Italian porn featuring leather-clad dwarfs, when he calls my attention to a local channel. I'm already impressed by Macedonian TV, beguiling as it is in its diversity, the three state channels featuring news programmes broadcast in Macedonian, Turkish, Serbo-Croatian, Albanian and Romani. Even the Vlach get a look-in with documentaries in their language. A Saturday evening pop show is hosted by a linguistic magician who fields calls in at least five languages as viewers vote for their favourite local videos. And the videos are equally multiethnic – an Albanian pop princess with prominent nipples belly dances around Skopje's bazaar; a Turkish interpretation of Panjabi MC's 'Mundian To Bach Ke' is pure Balkan bhangra; a turbo-folk singer, her video all slow mo' breast and crotch shots, croons lasciviously. Igor translates the song's title as 'I Want to See You Kiss Her (To Remember What You Were Like in Bed)'.

'What's her name?'

'SSS.'

'What?'

'Stupid Serbian Singer.'

On the studio's minimal set a long-haired local rocker named Beni performs. Beni's a Catholic Albanian who sings in Romani and sounds like a Balkan Bon Jovi. Then there's the star of the show – Esma! I'm excited, not just at seeing her but knowing she's in town. Esma still performs close to three hundred dates a year so she's not too often in Skopje. Seated with the host, dressed in a flowing gown with her hair covered, Esma exclaims, 'We are very lucky in Macedonia to have a multicultural show like this.' An Albanian girl rings in and says to Esma, 'I love your music because even though you are very old you are always happy.' Esma grimaces but keeps smiling. 'Can you sing something for me?' asks the unabashed caller. Esma, still seated, breaks into song, her voice rising through the octaves, tearing and hiccupping notes, overloading the studio's microphones, perfect a capella wailing. She finishes (pause), spontaneous cheering. 'She's fabulous,' says Igor. Absolutely. Then it's back to the phone requests in many tongues. 'Imagine this on the BBC,' says Igor. 'The guy fielding calls in Punjabi, Hindi, Yoruba, patois and English.' Imagine? Impossible. The British music media curl up in terror at non-English-language content.

Enough TV, says Igor, we are going out to drink with his fellow Macedonians. Crossing the city, I note a variety of cars and landrovers with UN or NATO tags. Igor explains that when the Kosovo conflict threatened to engulf Macedonia in 2000 the UN were invited in. 'They're OK. But NATO, they've set up bases in Kosovo as part of the US colonisation of the Balkans and their soldiers head to Skopje to party. It's fucked up – the US is setting up in destabilised areas, preying on ethnic conflict the same way Germany did sixty years ago.'

Our destination is Laika, a hole-in-the-wall bar with a soundtrack of Johnny Cash and Lee Perry. Nice. NATO troops are absent, this not being where the local whores work. The owner, a blonde woman who has been busy sampling her bar's wares, keeps coming up to me and saying 'nice to meeeeeeet you' with added hiss to help me realise that she's attempting to be, ya know, ironic. Women apparently outnumber men 60/40 in Macedonia – no one has an explanation why – so I imagine she got a little excited at a new guy being in town. Beyond strange mating rituals the company's friendly though I'm disappointed none of Igor's friends has any

Džansever

Photo: Christian Scholze ©Network Records

interest in Macedonian music. 'Does anyone ever DJ Macedonian music here?' I ask. 'Never. People want what they've seen on MTV or read is fashionable in Western Europe.' Igor admires Esma but admits he owns none of her music. And he's never even heard of Džansever. OK, Igor, you proud Macedonian, time for a history class.

Born in a tent near the Macedonian industrial town of Veles with her father as midwife, Džansever – pronounced Jan-se-ver – had it rough from her first breath. Her family were nomadic Roma and her birth was described as 'difficult'. Raised as a boy – the few photos of her I've found suggest she kept a tomboy image into adulthood – she lost an eye in childhood due to a carelessly thrown dart. It appears she suffered from a spinal defect that led to her being quite hunched in appearance. There's also the suggestion she has a problem with her bones. Her voice is a deep, almost masculine instrument and Macedonia's Roma populace have loved her since she was first recorded in the early 1990s. Popular Turkish singer İbrahim Tatlises heard a Džansever cassette and invited her to perform on his TV show. This won her a Turkish audience and she's since concentrated on singing in Turkish.

Beyond the four tracks she cut for German label Network's compilation *Gypsy Queens* she's never recorded for a Western label. In Skopje's bazaar I purchased a pirate of her latest Turkish CD. The cover finds her now bearing a resemblance to Maori opera diva Kiri Te Kanawa while the music is the Arabesque pop popular in Turkey, OK but no match for her fabulous Roma recordings. Boris Pavlović, a Serb music journalist, recalled seeing Džansever sing in Belgrade.

'The audience was between five and ten thousand people, mostly Gypsy. Ferus Mustafov showed up and began to play and the whole venue stood up and started dancing and then this small young woman shows up, she's got one leg shorter than the other, a hunchback like Quasimodo, eyes going in different directions. She started to address the audience in Serbian, struggled, obviously didn't know Serbian well. I'll never forget what she said. "Fuck Serbian, I'm continuing in Rom!" and everyone laughed. Then she started to sing and her voice is one of the most beautiful I've ever heard, it swept up the whole audience. She's like Frida Kahlo, she's suffered a lot yet she can hypnotise an audience. Recently a wealthy supporter paid for her to go to the US for an operation on her back and apparently she's now in much better health.'

That's all I know. Igor enquires as to whether she now lives in Macedonia or Turkey. No idea. He cracks his knuckles, says, 'Amazing, what an incredible character,' asks amongst his friends yet not one admits to having heard of her. Instead, they want to talk about new albums by Goldfrapp and Blur. Igor doesn't give up, instead getting a theme running: 'She sounds like a figure from a Greek tragedy, someone who the gods conspire against and then reward once she has shown she can overcome these huge obstacles they place in her path.' Nice analogy. Still, I'm beginning to wonder if Džansever is a mythic creature, existing only in my imagination.

As the night draws on the DJ changes and the music becomes MTV rock schlock so we take our leave. Wandering back, Igor explains to me that Macedonia's census results have been delayed for a year. Apparently this is because the Ohrid Accords, which appear to have stemmed KLF-fuelled insurgency, say Albanians are 20 per cent of the population. Fine. But if the census shows they are less than 20 per cent then the Albanians stand to lose the guarantees they were given and thus the Accords are unworkable. Yet if they are more than 20 per cent – say 25 per cent – then the fear of what happened in Kosovo (Albanians' high birth rate swamping the other ethnicities) looms large. Either way, most Macedonians see only darkness in the result. Another pessimistic thought: where Serb youth have embraced Balkan brass, Macedonian youth now allow NATO music to colonise their subconscious. Not the kind of thought to encourage sweet dreams. If only Igor had access to an opium pie…

Esma Redžepova:
We Are Guests on This Earth

*I don't come down on you really with blood and fire,
earthquake and lightning, but you must know, seh, that
within me all that exists too...*

Bob Marley

'Elvis Presley was a Gypsy. Da. I know these things. He never
admitted it but he was a Rom.'

So says Esma Redžepova Teodosievska as we talk all things
Gypsy over scalding Turkish coffee. It's an entertaining suggestion
and, undoubtedly, carries a certain logic; the Memphis Flash's tan
beauty, gentle nature and ability to blend and reshape any music
he inhaled is symbolic of Balkan Roma. Any truth to it? Where
Esma's concerned, simply print the legend. More importantly, I
imagine Esma's making a connection of sorts; she being the Queen
of the Gypsies, Elvis the King of Rock'n'Roll. Think about it: arising
from 1950s urban poverty, Elvis galvanising poor black and white
Southern US music, Esma reinventing Roma and Slav music(s) of
the southern Balkans, two adolescent sirens who sang and danced
with a bewitching freedom. Before Elvis and Esma white trash and
Roma women had no cultural presence, existing only as caricature.
E & E proudly marked their peoples on the world map.

'Many famous singers in Serbia and Greece and Turkey are Rom
but don't acknowledge it,' continues Esma. 'I appeared in concert
with Predrag Gojković-Cune from Serbia once and asked him why

Esma

Photo: Jasna Susha

he didn't acknowledge that he was Rom and he denied it. I said, "Whatever you wish!" I don't have a problem with it.'

What others deny Esma takes pride in, taking the Gypsy soul experience across the globe, impressing all who encounter her. A force of nature? Indeed. Esma's tiny, a plump bundle of energy whose unlined features are a testimony to a life free of cigarettes and alcohol. Today, as ever, she's charming and immaculately turned out. I'm shaved, sober, on my best behaviour. Even though we don't speak the same language – she's fluent in Romani, Macedonian, Serbian, Turkish; I speak English and minimal Spanish – we get on well, communicating easily, her nature being funny, wise, affectionate. And I…well, I have a tendency to get effusive in her presence. Esma listens, oriental eyes sparkling, mischievous smile playing on her lips.

'You're a honey,' she says. Then winks at me. Oh, Esma!

Esma was born on August 8, 1943, to Ibrahim and Čanija

Redžepovi, the second youngest of six children. Ibrahim was born in Tirana, his grandmother an Iraqi Jew, his grandfather a Catholic Roma, the family shifting to Priština then Skopje. Čanija's family were Muslim. Esma's bloodlines reflect a very Balkan miscegenation. Ibrahim worked as a porter, singer, drummer, circus strongman and shoeshine. The Nazi's 1941 aerial bombardment of Skopje cost Ibrahim a leg. That he survived the next three years – dodging fascists intent on the genocide of Macedonia's Jews and Roma while managing to feed his family – suggests the strength of character Esma inherited.

'My father was going to work on his crutches and I was carrying his shoeshine box and a well-off woman who lived in the same street as us came up to him and offered him money. He said, "Lady, thank you for your offer of money but I can't accept it. But you see my little girl behind me. Today she will come around to your house and collect all the shoes in your house and I will clean them and then I will take your money." '

Esma recalls home consisting of a room, anteroom and yard in Skopje's old town. They were poor but not as poor as most of their neighbours, many of whom still lived in mud huts. Education was emphasised by Canija with all six children finishing primary school. Aged nine, Esma was introduced by her brother Fari to Skopje Romaines Pralipe (a local Roma music organisation). 'I was quick to pick up even the most complicated rhythms,' says Esma.

Čanija encouraged Esma's musical gifts and Fari helped her join an amateur folklore group in the Tito Metal Works. In the summer of 1957, while attending a contest in Saraj (a town outside Skopje), she was invited to sing at a talent contest Radio Skopje were sponsoring. Esma entered. Esma won. Forty-six years on she's given over eight thousand concerts, written and recorded hundreds of songs, released dozens of albums, shifted countless units.

'My father was told by other shoeshine men that they had heard his daughter on the radio singing and he said, "No, not my Esma.

She was at home sleeping." He wasn't aware I was in the competition! Stevo Teodosievski was at the concert and when he heard me sing he heard something special in my voice. Perhaps it was my love for singing, my longing to assert myself, my feeling for the music of the east. He approached me to be my tutor. And then he approached my father and persuaded him that he would help me become a good and famous singer and that he would look after me. The following Saturday I set out on my first real professional tour.'

In the 1950s Balkans Roma girls were often married at twelve or thirteen. How, I wondered, had Esma escaped this fate?

'I was dedicated to being an artist and singer, not a wife,' says Esma with evident pride. 'At the age of nine years I realised I was different, I had something special. I was a wonder child and maybe that's why I matured so much faster than the others. At the age of ten I stated to compose. "Tuzbalica", that's my first. At the age of twelve I had composed "Chaje Shukarije" [Beautiful Girl], the most popular song amongst my peers. By the age of thirteen/fourteen I had already composed thirty songs, Roma and Macedonian songs.'

Stevo Teodosievski, born in the East Macedonian city of Kočani, was a noted accordionist, composer and bandleader. A gentle man absolutely dedicated to music, the 'something special' Stevo heard in Esma persuaded him to approach Ibrahim. Stevo guaranteed Esma would be trained as a singer, paid well and treated with the utmost respect. For his part, Ibrahim had to promise not to arrange a marriage for Esma before she turned eighteen. Initially uncertain, Ibrahim realised there was no restraining his tiny songbird. Contract signed, Esma was installed as Ensemble Teodosievski's vocalist. They scored their first hit in 1959 with 'Chaje Shukarije'. Esma brought Ibrahim a kiosk in Macedonia Plaza with her earnings. And not any old kiosk, only the most modern kiosk in all of Yugoslavia was deemed suitable by Esma. In 1961 Esma and the Ensemble swept Yugoslavia with 'Romano Horo', a hi-energy dance tune and effective regional riposte to the Twist.

'Romano Horo's success was the excuse for Esma and Ensemble Teodosievski to shift to Belgrade, 'where the media and music industry was based'. Although only in her teens, Esma's powerful voice – wailing with wild abandon on the hard, Asian flavoured dance track 'Esma Čoček' while equally capable of singing smoothly on 'Kalesh Angjo' – ensures her early recordings possess remarkable energy and spirit; the Ensemble's fervour across fast, complex rhythms matches the infectious excitement of Esma's voice. The music's vitality, Esma's engaging smile, the funky Balkan blend of sounds…no wonder Yugoslavia embraced the tiny Gypsy diva. Esma soon became an emblem for a people giddy with optimism as the 1960s opened up, war and the Soviets behind them, socialism and non-alignment ahead. Nation time, baby! President Tito, recognising in Esma something of the hummingbird's beauty and energy, began employing the Ensemble for state and international occasions.

'In 1960 Tito asked me to perform in Belgrade for the Presidents of the non-aligned world when they met for a political forum. I was the only artist performing – and I was a kid! I was seventeen years old and I sang in front of eighty-six statesmen. Tito introduced me to President Nehru and he made me an honorary citizen of India. Tito was also a hunter and I would go and sing for him at his residencies in Montenegro and Slovenia. I was much loved by Tito and Jovanka [his second wife] and my art was much respected. They showed me to many people and I remember on one occasion Colonel Gaddafi was there and, as they were strict Muslims, I had to sing in separate quarters for the men and the women. This was interesting for me.

'Once Tito was giving my LPs as gifts and he asked me, "Are you going to kiss some of them? I won't give them if you won't kiss them!" He was always making jokes! Tito was one of those people who can only be born once in a hundred years. He was the person who managed to keep peace for fifty years. After his death, as you can see, people were selfish. Tito didn't take anything with him

– he didn't steal, he never put his children into power or did other bad things. We had a very good passport valid for the whole world. We were an open country. Because of the selfishness it's made little countries. I think his concept, his idea, is now what Europe has done, opening itself. Let the earth be kind to him.'

Those less enamoured by Josip Broz might suggest Tito was a vain autocrat, one whose refusal to develop democracy and penchant for voodoo economics laid the foundations for Yugoslavia's bloody collapse. Yet Esma, like many Roma, believes in the Yugoslav ideal he promoted: one people, all equal, sharing resources. 1961 was the year Esma and Ensemble Teodosievski first appeared on Yugoslav TV and began touring beyond Balkan borders. Berlin, Vienna, Paris at the Olympia, the USA – before 'world music' existed there was Esma, a 'folk' singer from an obscure corner of Europe who won a wide following as the planet trembled before the Chelsea boots of Bob Dylan and The Beatles. Not that the West's taste for cosmic pop ever meant anything to Esma – her favourite singers being Kaliopi (a Macedonian female singer); Googoosh (Iran's no. 1 diva); Yulduz (ditto Uzbekistan) and the big fella, Pavarotti.

'Classic Romani music' is how Esma describes her sound. 'It's all traditional. I try to keep the style pure so I don't mix cultural influences while singing with Ensemble Teodosievski. It is a very demanding style, vocally, with many ornaments.'

In July 1963 an earthquake flattened Skopje, killing over a thousand and leaving many injured and homeless. Esma immediately set about playing concerts to raise funds for the quake's victims. She appeared in *Skopje '63*, a film made to demonstrate the resilience of the city's people, singing 'Hajri Ma Te Dike', a song she wrote to commemorate the tragedy. Here the Ensemble brew harsh, overlapping notes to suggest the earth trembling and the sky falling. Esma's vocal, why, it is the sound of grief itself.

Esma and Stevo returned from Belgrade to Skopje in 1989, the rise of Milošević hurrying them home. Today Esma lives in a large house situated directly beneath Skopje's Museum of Contemporary Art; an appropriate setting as Esma is Macedonia's greatest living artist. Her home appears pitched perfectly between the Millennium Cross on Mt Vodno and an ancient mosque whose imposing, stone dome wears a zig-zag crack like an over-boiled egg. Skopje's Old Town is beneath her. Topaana, the city's ancient Roma community, begins just over the hill. A suitable base, then, for this conductor of Balkan energies.

'I've been a rebel since I was very young. I remember when my mother offended me, she called me a bad word, so I climbed on the roof and threatened to jump from the roof if she didn't apologise. An older cousin climbed behind me and he grabbed me. I was protesting, "I want to jump!" And that was all because of one word. I was always being myself and today I'm still my own self. Although I was married to Stevo and obeyed him I was still independent. When I was the first Roma girl to be dancing and singing in Romani in front of the world I was a little rebel and, these days, I remain a rebel. When I saw Yugoslavia disintegrating, the borders being set, dividing into smaller countries, I was the greatest rebel against it. I was saying Europe was opening and we were closing – why? The Balkans should be open. I'm saying the same thing today. The Balkans should be open, we should help one another. No one will help us if we don't love one another. This is why I'm fighting for peace, not to have borders, so people can love one another and the cultures can mix with one another.'

From the outside Esma's house resembles a typical Balkan red brick construction, all unfinished surfaces and concrete driveway. A small amphitheatre alongside it gathers weeds. When completed the house will stand as a museum to Esma and Stevo's achievements while the amphitheatre will host concerts. The Macedonian government has no funds to help and Esma currently channels excess income towards the needy – Kosovar Roma refugees and a mental health institute both recently benefited from her largesse. Inside the house everything is immaculate: large, sunlit rooms, comfortable leather sofas, all mod cons (the TV's on but silent), pale walls decorated with framed posters of concerts and painted portraits of Esma that maintain a consistent level of loving kitsch. Good to see she has a comfortable residence – when Esma and Stevo left Belgrade in '89 the Yugoslav banking crisis swallowed the best part of their fortune, so forcing them to live in a small cabin.

The 90s were Esma's years of pain: Stevo succumbed to pancreatic cancer and his suffering, alongside the destruction of Yugoslavia, left its mark on Esma. Where the young singer was fast and given to great yelps of joy – when she stretched for a vowel you felt the rush, the excitement of an absolutely engaged vocalist – today she conveys Roma eloquence and suffering like no other. Now, when she lays back and wails, you feel those weary blues, mourning her father, mother, husband, nation, people. I rate Esma amongst the twentieth century's most potent singers, the raw, eerie beauty of her voice commensurate with the gospel cry and the imam's call to prayer. Indeed, whenever I hear Esma's voice the suffering, dignity and mystery of the Balkans are immediately tangible. Yet in person Esma never dwells on hard times, preferring to talk of happy days. She recalls how, upon turning twenty-three, she decided it was time to get married. Problem being, she was living in the Teodosievski family home yet Stevo had not made his intentions clear. Esma announced she was leaving the house. Devastated, Stevo asked his mother for advice. 'Marry her,' came the matriarch's reply.

'My wedding was seven days in Skopje and seven days in Belgrade and a big crowd gathered. We held my wedding in Dračevo, an eastern settlement of Skopje, and provided free buses to take people there. That was in 1968 and it was a big event because a Roma girl married a Macedonian guy, especially as I was a popular Roma girl. Then to Belgrade for another seven days and the greatest artists of that time came. The duration of wedding is Roma tradition. A day for wedding, a day for putting henna [in the hair], a day when we present the bride with her presents, a day when we present the groom with presents, a day for bachelor and bride parties. The customs are very interesting and beautiful and the bride wears many dresses during the wedding. It's not like other nations where the bride is wearing a white dress all the time. That's why we don't have many cases of divorce. It's so beautiful – it remains in your memory and you are tied to it. How can a young couple forget that? It's a seven-day ritual of love, laughter, fun.'

Long before Esma and Stevo were married they began adopting Roma boys, often discovering gifted children at weddings or in mahalas. Forty-seven children in total, all given a musical training. I'll qualify the number by noting only five became legal wards of Esma and Stevo. Ensemble Teodosievski, the five musicians currently backing Esma, are graduates of the Esma and Stevo school: Ensemble leader Simeon Atanasov joined them aged six.

'It might sound difficult to raise forty-seven kids, well, it's not easy to educate and teach manners, especially when they come with weird habits because they were from a very poor environment. But when adopted the children see the beauty of life – you are teaching them, creating them – then they grow up and later on you are happy you have done something and I think I'm the happiest person on earth when they gather around me. I love these children, I live for them. We were always together, five or six of them always travel with us.'

Beyond music and family there's Esma the activist: she's helped set up Democratic Alternative (Macedonia's first multi-ethnic political party), is honorary president of the Macedonian Red Cross, campaigns to get women MPs in Macedonia's parliament and finances the Romany Organisation of Women which now goes by her name (ESMA). While Esma's loath to criticise the Macedonian government or her people she is known to have loudly stomped her feet when politicians were slow to help Kosovar Roma refugees

Stevo (far left), Esma and boys, early 1960s

Photo: Esma Redžepova collection

and the ESMA organisation deals with Roma women trapped by poverty, domestic violence, alcoholism…the stations of the cross for sufferers international.

'We share the same beliefs in education for the Roma people, financing schools, taking care of women who have no husband or family to help them, providing medicine for the poor,' says Esma of ESMA.

Her humanitarian efforts have led to Esma receiving many awards. Amongst them are the American Biographical Institute's Medal Of Honour, Roma Woman of the Millennium, the 2002 Mother Teresa Award and two – two! – Nobel Peace Prize nominations.

'This time I've made it to the final ten but I'm there with George Bush, Chirac, the Pope,' says Esma of her 2003 nomination, aware of the absurdity. Let's say she won – what would Esma's message be?

'My message would be that the Roma people never fought anyone, never engaged in wars or occupied any other nation. The Roma have no country of their own and everyone should look up to them because they are cosmopolitan people.'

Esma's greatest personal triumph occurred in Chandigarh, India. Here, in 1976, twenty-three Roma artists gathered for the First World Festival of Romany Songs and Music and Esma was crowned Queen of the Gypsies by Indira Gandhi. The festival marked the high-water point in relations between India and Yugoslavia, Tito and Gandhi admiring one another's flashy socialism and semi-divine right to rule.

'I remember our Aunt Duda telling us that all Gypsies had come from a far-away land of sunshine, a land where there was so much sunshine that it had burned our ancestors a deep brown and so all Gypsies should be dark-skinned! I first went to India in 1968; we stopped there on the way back from touring Australia, and the Yugoslav Embassy in Bombay notified us that Tito wished for us to stay and represent Yugoslavia. I fell in love with India, its rhythms were our rhythms, its language similar to Romani, and the Hindu women use surma [kohl] for their eyes, dye their hair and nails with henna and use herbs, lotions and creams for their skin just as we do. The East is in our blood!'

China, Africa, Turkey, Syria, Egypt, Mexico, Japan: Esma continues to crisscross the globe, constantly touring (285 concerts in 2002), her Roma heritage and the healing power of music keeping Esma moving.

'I worked hard even as a child. I was earning pocket money cleaning a four-storey building, delivering milk to richer people, so I could attend puppet shows, movies and concerts. I wouldn't be happy if I didn't work. People are wondering how I can manage but at one time I held 400 concerts in a year. It was like a movie show – four or five concerts a day on Saturday and Sunday. So it's not hard for me today. OK, the travel itself is hard and it's the worst thing about getting old, I admit this. But I love the music so much. I share the happiness with the people there and it's worth all the hardships.'

I've seen a photo showing Esma mingling with Richard Burton and Liz Taylor at the height of their early 1970s celebrity. Que pasa, Esma?

'Richard Burton was starring in the film about Tito. I sang in Niš and Brioni for him. Elizabeth Taylor was there also and they were unpretentious people. Elizabeth Taylor, when you see her so close, she is very beautiful and Richard Burton was very handsome – honestly! – and also a good actor.'

We break for more coffee. Esma's served fried bread, that staple of poor people the world over. Slot a Goran Bregović CD I've brought along into her stereo. The album is one Bregović cut with Polish pop singer Kaya and track eight is 'Chaje Shukarije', Esma's first hit. Bregović adds a silly, childish rap and some lumpen percussion. Kaya's thin voice copies Esma's vocal. The publishing credit is 'Gypsy folklore/arrangement Bregović'. Esma listens and, for the first time, looks pained, tired.

'That's my song. You know I composed it.'

Why don't you sue?

'Goran Bregović is, I must tell the truth, a man who materialised the music, who took something from everybody and put it in his music. He took 30 per cent of my music and then some of Šaban Bajramović and other Roma musicians. So he made music for business. There's no quality in it.'

Esma lapses into silence, Bregović having ruined her afternoon. Upon arrival I'd noticed she and her guests had been reading coffee grains. So, time for a silly question: Gadje often expect Gypsy women to be fortune-tellers. Is there some truth in this? Do the Roma have greater contact with the spirit world?

'Certainly they have greater contact with the spiritual world,' says Esma brightly. 'Many women are clairvoyant, have the ability of foresight, know lots of things. The same thing goes with the Indian people. They have this instinct – I have the instinct as well – I had it about me becoming a great singer and I became one. Everything has its own reason. So there are people that know the future, the things that will come.'

So...have you ever had your fortune told?

'My future was told once when I was on tour in Montenegro by a Roma woman on a mountain while we stopped to rest. The Roma were making large pots and a woman approached us enquiring as to whether we wished to know about our future. A singer was on tour with us and approached them and the Roma woman said, "No, I won't do it because you are an evil woman." She said it right to her face. As for me, she did not know I was Roma because I was very well dressed. She said, "Come, girl, let me tell your fortune. You are going to travel the whole world. You will achieve great things and have good luck." So you see she foretold me. And that was the time I was a young girl.'

OK, Esma's smiling again. Good. Her faith in fortune-tellers reminding me of 'Magija' (Magic), a recent hit by Macedonia's biggest pop star Tošе Proseki on which Esma sang the chorus (in Romani). 'Magija's video shows Esma dancing around a fire surrounded by crystal-ball readers, fire-eaters and, uh, goats. Subtle? No chance. But Esma insists she likes the video and obviously enjoyed the pop spotlight. Speaking of foresight, did she have any pertaining to Yugoslavia's self-destruction?

'You know, we expected something like that [war]. The feeling became uneasy after Tito passed and the crazy politicians like Milošević took power. It was terrible and I hope it will never happen again. It is not OK for Macedonia to be without Yugoslavia. Yugoslavia was a big family and we all share the same languages, food, culture. I performed in Slovenia recently to 2,000 people, in Sarajevo, in Croatia, everywhere they still love me.'

The US-led invasion of Iraq forced Esma to cancel her 2003 tour of the States. A protest against US imperialism?

'It wasn't a protest. We had arranged to play humanitarian concerts and the war meant it was a very bad moment for humanity. Also, as the boys in the Ensemble are dark-skinned and have Muslim names I could foresee problems. Sometimes there are more important things than concerts.'

Time is tight so I throw in my Džansever questions: do you know her? Do you know where she is?

'She's a good singer but I've never worked with her and have no idea where she lives. Maybe Turkey.'

Turkey? As suspected. Esma, have you ever considered living beyond Yugoslavia's borders?

'If I lived anywhere other than Macedonia it would be Germany. I like its punctuality, cleanliness and public transport.'

Well, fine. When did you first hear 'Djelem, Djelem'?

'It's the first song I ever learned. I've been singing it all my life.'

Why are the Roma people so musically gifted?

'I disagree. It's hard work not any exceptional gifts that make for musical success.'

Every other Gypsy musician I've encountered says talent's a blood thing, natural as breathing. And here's Esma, the hardest working individual I'll ever encounter, stating talent's all about perspiration. Krisi, my translator, will later tell me that Esma speaks Macedonian as if telling fairy stories. Appropriate really as Esma spins tall tales – how Alexander the Great first encountered Roma during his conquests and so sealed the Macedonian link; how Hitler, having been to India aged nine, wanted to steal the energy surrounding Hindu symbols which is why he set out to kill Romas; how Nehru told Tito he wanted to take all the Roma people back to India but Tito told him 'no' because 'he loved us so much!' – and her achievements tend towards the mythic: Esma, the fabulous Queen of the Gypsies.

'Music is the only and cheapest entertainment of poor people,' offers Esma as parting philosophy. 'You can turn on the radio and forget hunger. I have travelled to the four corners of the world and could say it seems to me people forget we are only guests on this earth, that we come on to it naked and depart with empty hands. So why wars? Why evil? It is time to open up to each other, to mix cultures, and to begin to respect each other.

ELVIS HUNA:
I Had to Steal Her

Oh how I'd like to hold her near
And kiss and forever whisper in her ear.
                    The Impressions, 'Gypsy Woman'

Temperature's rising: today Skopje's blistering, one big urban oven. I hover inside, dreading leaving the apartment and its ever-spinning fan, certain I'll melt outside. Even the cats are crazier than usual, the heat making them frazzled, jumpy. Finally on to the street where, I swear, the blacktop is bubbling. Quickly scooped up and hidden from the late afternoon sun yet even the taxi provides little relief, the air that blows in hot as that powered by a hairdryer.

We're heading to a wedding and the address is in the western suburbs. Krisi studies the address and looks bemused. 'It's not a Gypsy part of town,' she says. 'It's actually a nice part of town.' I'm gutted, having imagined I would be attending a traditional Gypsy wedding full of music and dancing. And now it appears I'm going to sit under an awning in someone's backyard. Well, boo hoo. The taxi navigates pleasant, suburban streets and I realise why many Macedonians have migrated to Australia – mad heat and modest, quiet suburbs. Admittedly, there's a lack of swimming pools and gum trees but *Home and Away* could still be filmed here. Suddenly a sonic telex: the sound of a clarinet.

Celebration time: Esma, Elvis and Simeon

There's something about the Balkan Gypsy clarinet, a high, keen sound, snaking through the air, resonant and seductive, the tone suggesting a fabulously Oriental ambience. The clarinet, derived from traditional oboes played across Asia, is one of the oldest instruments the Roma have continually played. Whenever I hear its turbulent tone, fat low notes rising to a piercing flurry, I think of how this music has travelled, what meaning's carried within those notes. *Let's call the children home.* And right now I know – *I know* – that the clarinet is a siren, directing us to the wedding.

The taxi turns and stops: one hundred metres away a large PA is stacked on the pavement. Beneath a boiling Balkan sun a band are playing on the street. The clarinet player who's been sending sonic directions – calling the children home – looks up, mouth agog, and lets go a squall of notes, almost atonal yet beautiful. A shiver runs down my spine, icing sweat on chest. *Carry home, I have arrived.* Around them dance women dressed in all kinds of finery, heads ablaze with henna. Men stand further back, dressed in slacks, ties and short-sleeved shirts. Children are everywhere.

The groom is Elvis Huna, keyboardist in Ensemble
Teodosievski. We met backstage after Esma's May 2003 London
concert and the first thing I asked him was: how did you come
to be named Elvis? 'My mother was a fan of Elvis and I was
born not long after he died.' Well, cool. In *Time Of The Gypsies*
a character's two sons are 'Elvis and Rambo'. Cue audience
laughter. Yet Elvis, I noted during my wanderings in Macedonia,
is a popular male Roma name. Either the King had a big Roma
fan base or a lot of people subscribe to Esma's theory. In London,
when I told Elvis I'd be in Skopje after Guča, he invited me to
his wedding. How could I refuse? And there he is, head shaven,
nattily attired, watching proceedings from the balcony. Spotting
me, he descends. 'Pleased you could make it,' says Elvis. 'Pleased
I could be here.' Believe: the band are good. Let me say that again:
the band are good, damn, they're cooking! Elvis agrees. 'They're
called Južni Kovači and are the best wedding band in all of Skopje.'
How, I ask, has the big day been so far. 'Great,' says Elvis. 'Just a
few complications.'

Južni Kovači play music so potent it burns into the senses, hangs
heavy in the thick evening air. A violinist and vocalist join. Both are,
appropriately, extraordinary. Gazmend, the violinist, is amongst
the most highly rated in the Balkans, lending his distinctive tone
to many Macedonian turbo-folk recordings and playing all the big
Gypsy weddings. The singer, Shadan, is a small man with a big
voice, one of Esma's sons and the only singer she has ever trained.
The drummer smacks toms and cuts the snare with funky breaks
Clyde Stubbefield would admire. The band are dressed smartly in
black slacks and grey, short-sleeved shirts. None of them can be
older than thirty.

Many of the songs are instrumental ora numbers – here only
women dance; the bride and her female guests join hands to
form circles and dance in great swaying circles across and along
the street. Women surround the musicians, dancing ora, weaving

amongst the clarinet and violin, pasting money on the musicians' foreheads and collars. Shadan croons an epic love song and gets fly-papered with denars.

A golden Ford appears and parks diagonally. Out steps the Queen herself. Esma, hair styled, wearing a multi-coloured, pleated cotton dress, heels, and carrying a fan, walks towards us. Her fingers, always heavy with rings, today have nails that are incredible creations, painted liquid green and gold. Esma joins an ora. For a small, chunky woman she's surprisingly nimble.

Elvis's father, Ramiz, introduces himself, says, 'You like a drink?' and pops the cap on a bottle of beer. Thank you, sir. Beer, a cigarette and a chance to watch these incredible women. Such an array of costumes, from smart casual to great silk and satin creations, elaborately teased hair, henna highlights, baroque lipstick and lots of gold jewellery. Fabulous! It's Bollywood meets Hollywood, Gypsy flash, way beyond the trivial tack Versace and Co. offer. Elvis's bride wears a white and gold dress that flows like melted ice cream. Esma leaves the ora and takes a seat, fanning herself furiously. A roasted sheep is delivered on a tray and those of us not dancing tuck in. Finger food. Yum!

7.30pm: still mad heat, not that this slows the revellers, who continue to spin in circles, the sun slowly vanishing behind the Šar mountains, a fierce granite buffer between Macedonia and Kosovo. Then darkness descends and, suddenly, the band stop playing, the PA's stripped, plastic chairs gathered and taxis called. Time to head to a restaurant for the reception.

Arriving at a large banqueting hall several kilometres west of the city centre, I note the bridesmaids have changed dresses and now wear everything from cream-coloured gowns to a sumptuous purple sari. The wearer of the latter is a young Roma woman of elfin Indian beauty. She catches me observing her. I blush. She looks away. Oh, princess! Esma enters in a flowing lime gown and invites me to join her table. Cheese and salami are placed in front of us. There's little sign of alcohol, soft drinks and mineral water being the preferred tipple.

Južni Kovači, now dressed in tan suits, start playing, their sound more relaxed to suit the shift from street to restaurant. A curling clarinet solo introduces a classic ora: the anthem for bride and groom. Elvis and Perihan enter and lights are dimmed. Both are dressed in luminous white, he in classic zoot-suit-style tuxedo, she in flowing wedding dress. They cross under an arch of white balloons, untie a white ribbon, are handed a pin each and set about furiously popping the balloons. Everyone cheers and champagne is served to the couple, Elvis's parents and sister and Esma. Južni Kovači play a waltz, the dance floor fills and the ora begins again. Bal and kan, blood and honey, those two Turkish words that may or may not spell the origins of this region's name, persist in the sound, the atmosphere, the black pupils and beige skin. Južni Kovači up the tempo. The dancing takes on greater intensity. Women shimmering in silk lend the ora's dainty steps a sensual presence.

More meat is served – pork fillet stuffed with cheese and cuts of beef – and a solitary salad is gingerly placed in the centre of the table. Wave a waitress down, 'Pivo!' Finally, beer. A table's moved on to the dance floor and a toddler, surely no older than three, placed on it. Južni Kovači are cooking up Gypsy gumbo – hard, snaking melodies, snapping breakbeats – and this tiny girl throws her arms in the air, shakes her hips, and begins to belly dance. People shout encouragement, decorate her with denars. Tune finished and the tot's father lifts her off the table. Much applause. Opening notes of 'Djelem, Djelem'. All rise and sing to the seated wedding couple.

Južni Kovači's clarinet, violin and vocalist leave the stage, wandering amongst tables, singing praise songs to guests. Denars are stuffed in collars, pasted on sweaty faces. They play with good cheer, celebrating a table of Esma's musical sons, then move on to Esma. Shadan offers a vocal blessing, 'May you live for one hundred years', and she smiles that great, broad Esma smile and blesses him back. He tries to get her to sing. She chuckles, refuses. Simeon of Ensemble Teodosievski rises, takes the mic' and sings a praise song to Esma. Esma rises to toast Elvis and Perihan. They rise and toast her. The musicians return to the stage where they begin an up-tempo dance number.

Esma takes to the dance floor, swaying in front of the betrothed couple. She's passed the mic' and starts singing. The first two numbers are Roma wedding ballads, the ora continues, an elegant, serpentine movement. A table is brought into the middle of the dance floor. Elvis and Perihan step up. Južni Kovači kick into a taut 9/8 čoček rhythm. Esma's leaning back…wailing. Elvis and Perihan belly dance, all white finery, arms spread as if in flight, Gypsy angels, a blur of backbone-slipping, hip-swinging fluid motion. And Esma…Esma's rocking. She's singing 'Esma Čoček', her voice building and rising…throaty Arabic flavours and harsh, guttural cries, dense and wild…Južni Kovači hold the rhythm down, every instrument biting and chafing on a two-note riff – and Esma… Esma stretches back, way way way back, until her shoulders and head are parallel with the floor…Esma lets go a scream…the most intense scream I've ever heard emitted by a living creature.

Then Esma's smiling and handing the microphone over and the band are chugging away on a less potent groove and the magic passes, Elvis and Perihan hop off the table, return to seats, guests queue up to present them with gifts, a huge multi-layered wedding cake lit by sparklers arrives, they carve the cake, people queue for slices, plates of melon appear on tables, the evening returns to one of eating–drinking–camaraderie–celebration. But for a few minutes we were out there, led by Esma into somewhere irrational and ancient, a spirit land, a force connecting her (and briefly us) to what she calls 'the old cultures'. I feel exhilarated and drained. Without a doubt, the best wedding I've ever attended.

◆

Two nights later on and I'm back on Elvis's balcony but this time there's no band playing, no glamorous Gypsy procession dancing ora on the street. The temperature's dropped and all is calm.

'Normally the morning after the wedding I would go to to my wife's family house and eat eggs,' explains Elvis. 'It is a Gypsy tradition. Eggs signify birth and so I eat eggs to signal that we have good births. But as they are not happy with me I went to my aunt's house in Shutka and did it there. And then we kept on celebrating.'

The discontent – 'the complications' Elvis mentioned – arose due to Perihan having slept with Elvis before the wedding. Her family see her as 'begalka', literally eloping. Blessings refused.

'I had to steal her,' says Elvis. 'My family went to ask for her. Her family don't call us. Then my wife tells me that her family think it is better next year for the wedding so I take her to my home and you know it's important that the Gypsy girl is virgin and so we come here and I take her virginity. So we do it and we show the... blanket? The sheet! The sheet. Now her mother cannot go and take her home. For me, everyone is the same but tradition is Gypsy and this wedding tradition stretches back through my ancestors.'

Absolutely: the virgin bride, the bloody sheet – this is deep-rooted in Balkan Roma lore. Yet speak to Macedonian Roma about tradition as still found amongst many Romanian Roma – the kris court, the bulibasha clan leader, the separation of men and women's clothes for washing, marrying daughters at twelve (Perihan is twenty-three) – and they dismiss it as uncivilised. But the bride's virginity remains a core ideal of male/female Roma relations. Most Roma women in former Yugoslavia have, if not exactly equality, the freedom to dress as they wish, are encouraged to get an education and, if fortunate, find a job. But sexual freedom? Don't even ask. Tradition also dictates men and women operate quite separately. Elvis lives with his mother, father, sister, grandmother and Perihan. But only Elvis, Ramiz and I are on the balcony; the women stay in the living room, Perihan popping out to deliver coffee and steal cuddles. Ramiz is a hospitable, wiry man who currently drums in a folklore band. His great passion? Rock music. His all-time hero? Jimi Hendrix.

'After Jimi died I didn't shave for a week. Grief, total grief.'

Is he aware of the *Band Of Gypsies* album that Hendrix cut after he split the Experience?

'No. Were they Gypsies?'

No, black Americans. But he obviously liked Gypsies. Or the concept of the roving Gypsy musician. Ramiz nods and explains that he named one of his bands after a Hendrix tune – Gypsy Eyes. Right, I'd forgotten that one. Electric Ladyland, ay? Da! He's animated, hand weaving through the humid night air, leading with his cigarette, listing his favourite musicians. Santana, he says. It pays to be polite so I do the open palms gesture for 'not so keen' and he begins listing a pantheon of rock monsters: Jethro Tull, Deep Purple, Cream and the long-forgotten Grand Funk Railroad. While GFR may be best remembered in the West as Homer Simpson's favourite band ('the bong-rattling bass of Mel Schacher,' eulogised Homer), their impact in poorer nations should not be underestimated: Cuban maestro Juan de Marcos Gonzalez told me GFR and Steely Dan were his favourite American bands in the 1970s. While Mohammed Sačirbey, Bosnian Ambassador to the UN, loved the Funk so much he inspired them to briefly reform in 1997 and play benefit concerts for a Bosnian children's charity.

'I am folk music and he is rocker,' says Elvis. 'I was playing folk and he was saying, "Come here and listen to this rock music!" But I like folk music.'

'I love to play rock,' says Ramiz, 'but for raising two children, for building this house, I must play folk music for the restaurants and wedding music for the weddings. One week maybe I play four or five weddings for two days. I start at 10am, finish at 5pm. Change at the restaurant at 6pm and finish at 1am. Same on Sunday. In 1977

I played in Alexandria and Cairo on a cruise ship but other than that I've always played music in Yugoslavia. I work so hard and every year I take a one-month holiday in Turkey.'

Ramiz bought the land and built the apartment while his children were small. Elvis explains it is difficult for Roma to get the money to build houses, banks being unenthusiastic about lending large sums to Roma. So the Roma save and save. And then build. Elvis's family are solidly middle class by Balkan standards. Most reports on the Roma focus on either their subjects' extreme poverty (which certainly exists) or opulent wealth (occasionally found). Yet the Hunas are salt of the earth, no different from hard-working families anywhere. They occupy a large upstairs apartment with several bedrooms, an open-plan kitchen/living room and a balcony. Elvis has never experienced racism in Macedonia although, sure, he's aware the Roma suffer internationally. Take the Ensemble's Spanish driver who, once they became solid friends, whispered to him, 'Soy Gitano. Shhhhh!'

'His wife, his children, his employers didn't know. He was so scared that if anyone found out he'd lose everything. But he still knew traditional Roma medicine and used it to help me.'

Ramiz loves London. He visited nine times, purchasing equipment for bands. A Ludwig drum kit, Marshall amplifiers, speaker cabinets and, of course, crates full of records. His reference was *Melody Maker*, the now extinct, weekly prog-rock Bible. London's full of mystery and romance for Ramiz – as the Balkans are for me – he had his first slice of pizza in London, his first pint, recalls cheap hotels in Earls Court, can name stations on the Northern Line. This was Tito time when a Yugoslav passport guaranteed international entry. Today Serb, Macedonian and Bosnian passports are looked at with contempt: Elvis notes that in 2003 he was held and questioned by UK immigration officials for three hours at Heathrow Airport even though his work permit, stating he was backing Esma at a London venue, was in order.

Elvis started playing accordion as a child, soon joining the school orchestra, then getting wedding work in his early teens. He met Simeon, fresh from Belgrade, who told him of Stevo's musical classes. Elvis enrolled and recalls Stevo as an inspiring pedagogue. He started playing keyboards aged fifteen, 'to play in the restaurants', and then went to work for Esma.

'Back then they had a large Chrysler to tour in and my first job was to drive the car. The first time I was on tour with Esma we went to Belgium, Ghent. We drove 2,500 kilometres and I didn't feel tired. I was so excited to be going to Europe. And in 1997 I started to play in the main band after Stevo died. After the first concert I was shaking like a leaf!'

Elvis's male relatives are all musicians – an uncle was a master violinist, a cousin's recently been placed second in a pan-European violin competition – which, he believes, is as it should be.

'Gypsies are the best musicians because they play from the soul. Gypsy music, it's the feelings that make it so special. Let me tell you something about the Roma – we are happy or sad and there is no in-between. And I think that's why the people in Europe, in America, in Japan like our music.'

Esma, he notes, is, 'Incredible. Like a mother to all of us on tour. Always generous. Never tired. Never complaining.' When not touring with Esma Elvis plays restaurants and weddings. 'It's good practice and it is our tradition.' He also runs a fast food outlet with his father, 'Because it's wise to invest your money.' And as to Esma's theory on the original Elvis being a Gypsy?

'It's a nice idea,' says Elvis as he mulls it over. 'But I don't think it's true.'

FERUS MUSTAFOV:
Little Big Man

I blew and I blew, and when I finally finished I was shaking all over; my heart was pounding; I was soaked in sweat, and the people were screaming; the people were clapping, and I looked at Sonny, but I just kind of nodded, and he went, 'All right.' And that was it. That's what it's all about.

Art Pepper, *Straight Life*

My head is an eggshell. Fragile, very fragile. Jesus, what kind of poison do they put in that drink? Bought a half litre of rakija in a plastic soft drink bottle yesterday at the local green market. Home-made stuff. Has to be good. Natural. Well, that was the brief. Demolished it with beer chasers while Igor eulogised Philip K. Dick and his relevance to the slow-then-fast collapse of Yugoslavia. I'm sure it made sense back then, today some infernal residue of the rakija is scrambling my brain. And so we kept talking, kept drinking, fighting off paranoid cats who hiss at me then pee on my maps, all was bright and every concept made sense. But today…today I am not well. On the street Krisi moans about how I've kept her waiting twenty minutes. 'You're insane, running late for an interview with Ferus Mustafov.' My fragile skull agrees with her. 'In-sane in the membrane'…that was a tune. Though I think I'll personalise it as 'inflamed in the membrane'. Krisi, who's not amused, continues to verbally beat me up. Ouch. Ouch. Ouch!

Portrait of the
artist…

Photo: Garth Cartwright

Motel Ferus King occupies a large white shell of a building in
Skopje's north-eastern suburbs. As far as the palaces of musical
legends go this one's surprisingly unassuming, no competition for
the mansion Fats Domino built in the New Orleans projects or
Webb Pierce's Nashville residency with its guitar-shaped swimming
pool. As our taxi pulls up I notice the proprietor standing outside.
And, I admit, I'm surprised. Not because he's expecting us, that's
prearranged, but because Ferus isn't the Ferus I imagined. Music
and the images accompanying it are so potent we often expect
musicians to be larger than life; Ferus's majestic saxophone sound
long ago convinced me he was a Gypsy giant, a man swollen by the
remarkable sounds he conjures. Instead, Ferus is tiny, a shrunk-in-
the-wash urchin with thinning hair, ragged beard, swarthy features.
At first I think it's the rakija, affecting my vision. But no, there he
hovers, three feet high and rising. Thick lips and black eyes lend an
almost Polynesian cast to Ferus's face.

Checking all signs of astonishment, I introduce myself and within minutes of meeting Ferus all South Pacific comparisons are gone. What Ferus really looks like – mischievous and leering – is a Balkan leprechaun. Someone call David Bowie, we've found his laughing gnome…Ferus's fame does not rest on perfect features, MTV stardom or animal magnetism. What he possesses is a wild musical grace, serpentine melodies, his sound so warm and liquid, a sonic narcotic. For more than twenty years Ferus's clarinet and saxophone playing have ruled across the Balkans, establishing him as the dark prince of oros, a man so able to make people move they named a dance after him. It's called the Ferus.

Motel Ferus King incorporates rooms, restaurant, recording studio and offices. The studio is, apparently, noted for knocking out local turbo-folk hits while Ferus's admirers from Turkey and Scandinavia have dropped in to try and capture a little of his magic. The restaurant's spacious and – *perfect* – a monument to King Mus': framed posters of him are everywhere, a large, prominently placed TV has Ferus on constant rotation while a several-metre-long panel painting hogs one wall. I can't resist going up and studying it. Smiling is difficult with a hangover but there, in flat acrylic, is Ferus and his father Ilmi on the left-hand panels while portraits of his son Ilmi and grandson Ferus Jr are framed on the right. The youths are set against a seascape while Ferus and his dad blow in front of a spacey backdrop. All clutch their saxophones and Ferus is wearing a crown.

Obviously, investing weddings with his majestic musical presence has made Ferus a wealthy man. Not that he acts so. Ferus slouches, not making eye contact, chain-smoking. Krisi asks and he answers. But doesn't try very hard. Names, dates, events…much of this has slipped his mind. Sample question: how many albums have you released in your career? 'How many? How should I know? [pause] More than twenty, that's for sure.' Errrrr, great. Strong coffee and some coaxing help and Ferus begins to recall the journey of the man who would be King.

'I was born in Štip in 1950 and a multi-instrumentalist by the age of thirteen. My parents realised I was so good that I should go to the local music school. I stayed at the elementary music school until I was seventeen and then I quit school and went on tour with the band of Tome Črčev. I never went back to school as I knew how to play and why else go to school? I formed an orkestar called Čalgii with violin, tambura, trumpet, accordion and we started playing weddings.'

Štip's a moderate-sized industrial town ninety minutes east of Skopje. What was, Krisi asks, life like in Štip? Ferus looks at her first, then me, with a sort of blank bemusement. It's a long time since he left Štip, a long time since he's even thought about Štip.

Yet Štip shaped Ferus. His father, Ilmi Jašarov, was a master clarinet player and, some claim, the first person to introduce saxophone to the southern Balkans. His mother, Zumrut, is also a gifted sax player. Ferus lacks his father's surname due to the Balkan tradition according to which a child's surname was that of the oldest living male member of the family. The communists, finding it hard to keep track of people when they all had different surnames, enforced the father's surname as the one everyone had to use. Thus Ferus's son is Ilmi Mustafov. Just trying to link these facts has me feeling I'm picking glass out of my brain.

'My father was playing with a brass orkestar and often played with Kočo Petrovski. I was always learning from my father. He was phenomenal. My mother, Zumrut, she plays saxophone too. Ilmi taught her. It's funny, he taught her but she never became a professional musician. She plays well but they didn't play together at weddings or circumcisions or things like that. They'd play at home together with the notes [sheet music] but she never worked as a professional even though she knew a lot about music. She knew what was good and not good when I played but she didn't have a big influence on my playing style. That's more my father and the orkestar musicians I listened to.'

Constant rounds of Turkish coffee, while doing little to calm raging alcohol poisoning, do lend a twisted energy to proceedings. Jana, Ferus's daughter, introduces herself. She does not resemble him in the least, being taller and light skinned – what does Mrs Mustafov look like? Jana, her mother and Zumrut are not featured in the wall painting.

'To get out of Štip I started working the Yugoslav restaurant circuit and ended up in Budva on the Adriatic Sea in 1980. Before that I was trying to get Macedonian TV to record me. They were lying to me, not accepting me. To put it simply, they wanted a bribe and I wasn't about to pay those shits anything! After Budva I met one orkestar from Sarajevo called Mića Radovanović Orkestar. They heard me play and asked me to go to Sarajevo to play at the TV station there. This was 1981 and I was booked to play on a New Year programme. My attitude was "maybe it will work" and then I got a telegram to come to Sarajevo. I got on a plane and was welcomed at the airport and taken right away to record a show. This was my first time to be in the TV environment and recording with other music stars. Because I have a brilliant ear I was opening them [his ears] as much as possible to learn from everyone because some musicians had written down notes for arrangements and others didn't so I had to learn the arrangements by ear very quickly. After we played the first set the directors of the TV station invited me to stay at the station. I stayed there for five years, five good years. What a city Sarajevo was! A pity those idiots had to destroy it. Good music…good people…good-looking women. It had everything.

'We realised things were getting bad before the war. Not that any of us were politicians but we picked up on things. Initially after Tito died all was fine but then those idiots who want to rule us started fighting amongst themselves and the next thing you know bombs are falling on ordinary people. Anyway, before the war some of the musicians I was playing with went to America. They wanted me to come but I don't know...America...I can't speak English and it's very far from home. Sure, it's a rich country and being a great musician I would have succeeded but I thought, "Fuck it" and I came back to Skopje. Skopje or New York – what would you choose? Ha ha ha! I formed a band for a Roma TV show on Skopje TV. Neždet Mustafa was the director of the show. He was an OK guy to work with. He's a politician now. I guess he always was a politician. At least he doesn't drop bombs on anyone.'

Ferus's reputation as Wedding King finds him flown to the US, Canada, Switzerland, Australia, wherever there are wealthy Macedonian exiles wanting a roaring reception. Thus he can ignore the relatively paltry sums offered by the world music circuit. His Slovenian manager once set up a major European tour only to have Ferus cancel at the last minute. Weddings, you see, had come up and Ferus hoped he would understand. Said manager suffered a heart attack. Typically, Ferus is contrary here, stating he'd love to come to London; was I capable of booking him some concerts?

'Most of my work comes from playing Roma weddings. Now I have a nine-member band and I play jazz festivals, festivals of Balkan and Gypsy music. I prefer playing the festivals now to the weddings. It's not the hours – I only ever play for four or five hours at a wedding now – I just like the atmosphere and the respect you get at festivals. The people come because they like the music and nothing else and that's good.'

Ferus digs out a contract he's signed to play a concert in Paris in November. It's as part of a Balkan festival and his fee appears modest (500 euros), considerably less than he would receive at a Balkan wedding.

'People everywhere understand music. What's most interesting for the West is we use our irregular rhythms – 11ths and 25ths – it's difficult for them so they are interested in that. The ora is a 4/4 rhythm while the cocek is a 9/8 rhythm. I also play Arabic music, it has 4/4 rhythms. We've got the best accordion player in Macedonia

A Balkan icon:
Ferus

Photo: Garth Cartwright

with Milan Zavkov. The ensemble is closer to a rock band. We smoke on stage and watch how the audience behave and when we get their feeling for being crazy we are more raucous and then we take off like a rock band!'

Ferus emphasises he can play both jazz and Oriental music. It depends what's demanded. OK, what kind of jazz does he like? A waitress is ordered to grab a CD. It's *Jazz Station* Vol. 2, a cheap compilation featuring everyone from Charlie Parker to Kenny G. Ferus studies the CD and points to track 9 – Stan Getz. All right, I say, Stan and Astrud Gilberto. Bossa nova. Ferus looks at me blankly. Change subject. Ferus regularly works out of Belgrade: any thoughts on the collapse of Yugoslavia?

'I play all over Yugoslavia and the only thing I find strange is when they ask me for my passport on the border. Music I have an interest in. I have nothing to do with politics. I don't understand who is guilty. Women are my hobby. But not politics.'

He chuckles and leers at Krisi, who's keeping an ashtray close at hand in case she needs a weapon. Speaking of women, what does Ferus know of Džansever?

'I discovered her. And produced her first cassette and put her on TV for the first time. She was singing in Shutka at the restaurants. She has a voice and also a presence.'

Any idea how I can contact her?

'No. It's a long time since I've seen her.'

Ferus was employed to provide music for the 1997 Macedonian film *Gipsy Magic*. Every Roma I speak to hates *Gipsy Magic*.

'*Gipsy Magic* is a disaster, a travesty. We're not so retarded as he showed us. There are beautiful houses in Shutka. He made it look like we all live in poverty. I was a producer of that movie's music and they've got me playing on the soundtrack but I wish I hadn't had anything to do with it.'

Ferus then offers us a guided tour of Motel Ferus King. Upstairs consists of five bedrooms. The walls are decorated with photos of Ferus and various turbo-folk babes. He generally stands around the height of their very prominent breasts and grins like he's in pig heaven.

'I played with Ceca and Lepa Brena. They want me for sessions when I'm in Belgrade. I like everything that is beautiful and Ceca is very beautiful! Turbo-folk has been popular but now people are going back to traditional music and so the folk music is going ahead. Every generation comes up with something new and the folk music of the Balkans is very strong now.'

Ferus also travels to Athens, where he records with Greek pop stars. He mentions Vasilas Salias as the best Greek clarinet player. I recall Elvis Huna saying Salias was his favourite musician. Is he Roma? Da. We head to the basement and Ferus unlocks a musty smelling studio. Chairs and equipment are stacked in piles and the scrappy paint and plaster suggest the studio's unfinished. Ferus pulls the covers off the mixing desk, hits Play and, yup, this is a functioning studio. The décor simply fits with the reigning attitude

Seven years old and blowing: Ferus Junior

Photo: Garth Cartwright

that things can be finished later on, a Balkan version of Spain's 'mañana' or Jamaica's 'soon come'.

Ferus begins playing back his latest recordings. 'It's not finished,' he emphasises, yet it certainly sounds ready for release. I'm unsure if Ferus fans will find his new music of interest: bright, pumping jazz with none of the arcane beauty that surrounds his oriental recordings. Like his Bulgarian comrade Ivo Papazov, Ferus appears to equate 'jazz' with Western sophistication. Legend has Ferus and Ivo, back in the 1970s, setting up the phone lines so they could jam, blasting Gypsy jazz to all who listened in. I'd like to ask Ferus about this but he's stretched out in a chair, eyes closed, hands behind head, wordlessly singing along with his solo, lost in space.

The next tune hangs on a repeated saxophone motif. A Hammond organ floods the speakers and the band lock down a walking bass rhythm of the kind Jimmy McGriff once loved. Ferus is nodding, fingers twitching. Another track finds cocek rhythms bolted to a brassy jazz chorus. The final tune is Balkan ambient music, Ferus's clarinet swamped in big drums and synthesiser. Enough. Krisi awakes Ferus from the musical universe he's dozing in and we say our goodbyes. He insists one of his employees drive us back to central Skopje. Krisi breathes a huge sigh of relief. 'He kept on saying to me, "You have my phone number. Use it." Can you imagine?'

Can't help but laugh, Ferus the lecherous leprechaun. Laughter proves painful, my head still suffering a rakija concussion. Kick back, relax, let the brain cells settle. Our driver slots a CD on: Ferus in concert. He and his band are cranked up, loud, playing with the intensity and drive expected of, say, Motorhead. And, as he boasted, they smoke.

Suddenly it's all too much for me, I'm overwhelmed, gasping for air, imagining orkestars as wild and terrifying as Ferus's accompanying Ottoman armies into battle, bringing noise, breaking minds. The sound fills the jeep, intoxicating and, uh-um, a little unsettling, such is the music's fluid, mercurial force. Forget Albert Ayler and late Coltrane and all that other leaden free jazz junk; here, encapsulated in the mad ruckus, this beautiful, silvery, dissonant rush, is a sound both elemental and majestic, truly transcendent music.

The jeep stops at lights. I'm crouched close to the floor, locked into listening, too hard, too deep, head near boiling, Ferus's saxophone and rakija's chemical residue blending madly in my skull. Krisi asks if I'm OK. OK? Instinctively open the door and step out. Dead air... feel like I've been breathing dead air. Surely just heat and alcohol but I'm having a bad reaction, a paranoid flash, the music shaking me into some alternate consciousness. What was it Robert Johnson sang? 'Stuff is gonna bust ya brains out, baby/break you in two.' Find a bar. Order a beer. I'll be sober by evening.

NAAT VELIOV:
Have Trumpet, Will Travel

Speaking of swell people, I might mention Buddy Bolden, the most powerful trumpet player I've ever heard or that was know and the absolute favourite of all the hangarounders in the Garden District.

Jelly Roll Morton, *Mister Jelly Roll*

Skopje's bus station sits beneath the city's historic fort, a location that may initially mislead the new arrival. Clambering down from your coach you see atop the fort a massive Macedonian flag rippling in the wind, red and yellow patterns against the bluest sky. A striking example of emblematic patriotism yet a somewhat futile gesture, old forts and big flags both unlikely to counter internal unrest. Today the bus station is a more accurate symbol of the contemporary Macedonian zeitgeist: wooden benches so worn they could pass as historic artefacts, tiny kiosks offering soft drinks, bottled water, sweets, peanuts and *Anal* magazine, air thick with diesel fumes, platforms crowded with Roma youth trying to sell combs and watches. They're not aggressive but the effort of 'ne ne ne' to their constantly proffered trays is, finally, dispiriting.

Time to kill until the coach for Kočani departs so I return to the bazaar. At the bazaar's heart an impressive oak tree spreads its branches across a spurting and dribbling fountain. If Skopje's citizens feel a tangible sense of dread about the future at least the bazaar remains an oasis of calm, the pace almost somnolent.

Get in the van: Naat and Naat Jnr

Three cafés share the shade offered by the oak's leafy branches and these places of long lunch and slow digestion, all heavy savoury pastries and grilled lamb, keep a flavour of Ottoman times alive. The Turkish taste for all things sweet remains too – I watch a waiter empty the best part of a container of sugar into his coffee. Till the spoon stands up, indeed. Albanian youths stalk the cafés with bottles of bootleg perfume and cartons of Marlboro. Like I really need more fags or a bottle of something masquerading as designer scent. As the dark god of caffeine powers through my veins I ponder turbulence; what whirlwinds have surrounded this tree from acorn to monument? Empires, invasions and earthquakes all failed to topple this mighty oak and amongst its squat trunk, gracious branches and angular leaves there is something of the totemic, the Macedonian spirit rising, emanating from Skopje's historic centre.

Macedonians are a gracious, friendly people, yet strolling back to the bus station I note a social malaise wearing hard on many: women serving life sentences in kiosks, their beauty fading to hatchet faces and cigarette jowls beneath a peroxide thatch. Men shout 'Taxi! Taxi!' but how many fares do they get each day? And, for the record, some of the drivers are cowboys whose numbskull hustle would find them perfectly fitted for a London minicab licence. Then there are the shoeshines, these descendants of Esma's father Ibrahim, ageing Roma men who sit and stare at feet covered in trainers. 'My body feels so weary cos I got the mis-meal cramps,' sang some long dead blues man. 'Right now I could eat more than a whole carload of tramps.' Feels it, knows it. On Kamen Most Bridge younger Roma men and women set out wares on upturned cardboard boxes: lighters, knickers, batteries, alarm clocks, socks, umbrellas, nuts, thermal underwear, electronic gizmos, stockings, pens. Spirited, cocky – they could hold their own in London's street markets – and smiling, these people are not losers. *Patjival o manus an' la vi anda gav xaljardo*. Righteous. Profit. Poor town. Yes.

The coach leaves on time. Navigating through the wrecked estates of the city's Albanian barrios a different kind of tension passes amongst the passengers, no one wanting to be stranded here. Hitting open road the territory is scorched, loose metal and scrub, and the coach, powered by a turbo-folk soundtrack, travels at great speeds, daring the gorges and valleys to swallow it up. Within twenty minutes of leaving Skopje's city limits we're on the side of the road, waylaid with engine troubles. I'm no mechanic but when the driver starts stripping branches from a tree I wonder if I'll ever see Peckham again. Eventually we're under way, the passengers showing no sign of distress – *Vaya con dios* – while I'm somewhere between nonchalance and hysteria. Coach drivers in Northern Pakistan's Himalayan Kush employ a similar belief in extreme speed and divine will sorting things out. Survived that and – as we burn rubber around a mountain road – figure I'll survive this.

Once across the hills surrounding Skopje the land flattens, evolving into broad, mustard-coloured plains. Little appears to grow here, so dry I wonder how it supports even the small flocks of sheep grazing. These flat lands with their mountains in the distance tend towards the monumental – no wonder in the 1960s and 70s Yugoslavia was a favoured location for film productions. Both war films and Westerns were shot across the republics and the land we're currently moving through possesses the dry, opaque qualities that would suit either a lone rider or platoons of men. As we stop for petrol I'm again reminded how Western Europe's safety laws fade into Balkan oblivion as people puff diligently on cigarettes while strolling across the forecourt and refuelling vehicles.

Kočani doesn't mean much to most, a provincial Macedonian city on the way to Bulgaria. But amongst Roma brass musicians Kočani is regarded in the way that, say, New Orleans is by jazz and blues aficionados. Serbia may have the numbers but Boban and Marko nod reverentially when Kočani is mentioned in conversation. Even members of Fanfare Ciocărlia, a brass ensemble isolated in north-east Romania, utter 'Kočani' when asked what musicians they respect. And Kočani today revolves around the stout figure of Naat Veliov.

Naat's a trumpet player and orkestar leader and a hard man to track down as he's always on the move. If not touring northern Europe by van he's playing weddings across eastern Macedonia or rocking clubs in Turkey. Slip Naat's *L'Orient est Rouge* album on the CD Walkman and soak up fat sour notes and brass eruptions. Dust devils dance across desolate prairies while Kočani Orkestar's wild, wonky music swirls around my head. Blow, guys, blow.

Naat's presence is unmistakable at Kočani's bus station. Unshaven, crop-headed, bulging gut, scar face: looks like he'd have Mike Tyson for breakfast. His hooded eyes and cagey manner initially get me thinking an interview with him may be a little, uh, difficult. Not at all; Naat's disposition is laconic and, once talking, he rarely stops. Especially concerning his former Belgian managers.

'The Belgians came to see me two or three times and then went to the French Cultural Centre and got the orkestar visas for France. We went with them to France and played some concerts and they were satisfactory so we decided to make the CD.'

The Belgians are Stephane Karo and Michele Winter, impresarios behind Romanian Gypsy music legends Taraf de Haïdouks. Having established the Taraf internationally they signed Naat to a management and recording deal (with Crammed Discs – home to Taraf). Karo and his co-producer Vincent Kenis recorded the magical *L'Orient est Rouge* album in Skopje in 1997. Tours were booked, the album received great reviews.

'At the beginning everything was OK. They treated me as a brother. Stephane stayed in my house for a month. Michele came to my daughter's wedding. We had a close relationship. But after that the money gets less and less, payments later and later.'

The reality of the Brussels–Kočani divorce is many-sided. According to Michele Winter, 'Naat was always demanding money and offered us cheap recordings for the next album which we had to refuse.' Naat claims he's still owed considerable sums from previous tours. When Naat sold the recordings refused by Karo–Winter to a Turkish label the Belgians severed the connection. Yet three of Naat's then ten-member orkestar chose to stick with Karo–Winter; Naat, it appears, never having been particularly equitable with wages. A new Kočani Orkestar was formed around the defectors and Naat was informed he couldn't trade as Kočani Orkestar, Karo–Winter having registered as owners of the name for Benelux territories. Naat now goes out as King Naat Veliov and The Original Kočani Orkestar. This reminds me of The Drifters, whose manager fired the original group one night and immediately replaced them with Ben E. King and Co. There's now several Drifters working the Oldies circuit; perhaps if the Balkan brass market keeps growing we can expect a plethora of Kočani Orkestars…

Photo: archive Naat Veliov

Naat Veliov and Kočani Orkestar

'I'm really angry because the Kočani Orkestar lived for more than fifty years – my grandfather founded it, then my father led it and then I became the leader of it. Now I can't use my family name because someone from Belgium stole the name. I still don't know the reason why they took the name Kočani Orkestar.'

The messy split leaves Naat lacking the promotional and production muscle Karo–Winter and Crammed Discs offer. He's since released three albums – *Cigan̆ce*, *Gypsy Mambo*, *Gypsy Follies* – through small German label Plane. And he has, in Vera Giese, a dedicated manager. But none of these albums can touch *L'Orient est Rouge* in terms of colour, detail, mood and pure funky swing. What Karo and Kenis did was coax the best performances out of Naat and his orkestar and arrange them so they took on a tactile quality suitable for home listening; a difficult one for any Balkan brass band, so gonzo is the nature of their musical performance. Naat's self-produced albums are decent replications of the orkestar's live performance and have their moments of eccentric inspiration – Balkan mambo! Drum machines! – but rarely demand repeated play. As for Karo–Winter's current Kočani Orkestar, they remain a good live act yet their 2002 album *Alone At My Wedding* proved unmemorable. Hey, that's the music biz!

'I'm talking with all of them [ex-members] except one, the saxophone player. He's the one responsible for the break with the Belgians, he's two-faced. He was telling me to ask for our money, raise the price we charge, and then telling the Belgians that he could be leader of Kočani Orkestar.'

By the time Naat says this he's burned the fever out of his anger, his tone suggesting awareness that he too was stubborn, demanding. Not that Naat's doing badly: his van is a recent model and his phone allows for photo messaging. A work ethic backs this up; tomorrow he's off on another jaunt around Scandinavia, Germany and Austria. Which means Naat wants to get some shopping done.

We wander the streets of Kočani as he selects shirts, collects tailored trousers and looks over an assortment of boots. Naat then buys bags of food – white cheese, olives, candy, cakes, pastries, tinned fish, olive oil, bread. I imagine he's eaten motorway food and wisely sworn never again. Everyone greets him warmly – Naat's obviously a good customer – and kids go crazy when they see him coming; this is due to his TV appearances and habit of giving hundred-denar notes to them. 'What was your Kočani childhood like, Naat?'

'When I was a child I had a strong desire to play the trumpet. I didn't want to go to school and as soon as I was back from school I'd drop my bag and play trumpet straight away. My parents were afraid I'd get sick from playing trumpet all the time. Even in my sleep my fingers were playing trumpet. From the age of thirteen or fourteen I was playing trumpet professionally. Because I was playing professionally I couldn't finish the 8th grade in primary school. Because I was put a few times in the same grade I have a lot of schoolmates and now when I speak with them they're managers, businessmen, and they tell me they don't get to travel all over

Europe like me. So I think I made the right decision of skipping school and concentrating on music.'

Naat's grandfather Ahmed was born into a nomadic family who roamed the Balkans, settling in Kočani in 1913. Of all the Balkan Roma musicians I've interviewed Naat's the only one who can recall his family's nomadic roots. Not that he holds much stock by them.

'My grandfather didn't tell me about the old ways when they lived in tents because he was very young when they chose to settle. His parents died while he was still a child so there was no one to tell him of the travelling.'

Kočani's noted for being a stronghold of Turkish Roma: some local Roma speak only Turkish, preferring to identify themselves as Turks, and Naat regularly plays in Istanbul.

'For four years in a row we have played New Year's Eve in a club in Istanbul. They like everything about my orkestar and are very surprised that I play the Turkish music with good technique. We have lots of our folklore from Turkey, that's for sure. We use a lot of Turkish words in our slang. We speak Turkish Gypsy language as we are Muslims. In the eastern part of Macedonia people are speaking more Turkish than Romani. Remember, we had five hundred years of Turkish government here.'

Shopping for shoes, we encounter Naat's adult daughter. Smartly dressed, with long, bleached hair that contrasts with her olive complexion, she's starting to take on the shape of her father. He lets her select a pair of high-lacing boots before we retire to a local café, where Naat's soon surrounded by friends. Drinks flow and cigarettes are lit yet Naat sticks to lemonade and never smokes. Liquor loosens my tongue: time to ask Naat about the scar decorating his right cheek. Is it true your grandfather grew jealous of your virtuosity (thus ability to generate more 'baksheesh') so attacked you with an axe?

Naat roars with laughter.

'It's not true. Maybe it's inspired by someone hearing the story of what really happened and embellishing it.'

Go on: what did happen?

'My uncle and my father were arguing violently and I went and stood between them to persuade them to stop fighting but my uncle was so angry he grabbed an axe and hit me and it left this scar.'

That's a pretty extreme reaction?

Naat ponders this and shrugs. 'We're still talking. I didn't press charges as I didn't want him to go to jail. Which is where they would have put him if I had.'

No axes are in sight this evening and the atmosphere's convivial. The crowd are both Roma and Macedonian, some musicians, most not. Naat, what makes for a good Gypsy musician?

'To be human and to respect and be respected, to keep your promises and not to lie. For example, in one wedding they are offering me 1,000 euros. It is not so much but I agree to play the wedding because I know this family are honest people, not wealthy people. A couple of days later I am offered 2,000 euros to play another wedding on the same day. Now, if I accept the second offer I would lose my honour.'

Those assembled agree, slap Naat on the back. I rise and offer a toast to his righteousness. Naat shrugs this off and suggests we retire to his house. Kočani's mahala (or 'maalo' as they say here) is built on an extremely steep hill, the houses packed tightly together. We park and start down a narrow, concreted passageway, winding amongst vines and fruit trees, the last remnants from when this was a village built above Kočani. Naat's house is spacious and well furnished. Mrs Naat obviously has a thing for crystal as the cabinets are full of it. Pride of place goes to a widescreen TV with huge, separate speakers.

Mrs Naat directs me to a large sofa and offers cheese, sausage and fizzy water. Waiting for Naat is Redžaim, a local drummer who speaks some English. He earns his living playing in restaurants, 'especially in Germany'. When Mrs Naat shows an interest in my left hand Redžaim explains she wishes to know if I am married. No, not married. This gets Mrs Naat excited and she starts exclaiming in Romani. Redžaim translates. 'She wants you to know that she has an unmarried daughter and are you interested in marrying her?' Now, that's a proposition. What to say? I know, ask what the dowry is. I mean, an unmarried Roma girl in her twenties should come with a veritable treasure chest attached. Then again, Naat has told me that the old Roma traditions have been discarded. So I'm not going to have much luck in the material enrichment stakes. Dammit!

Mrs Naat busies herself in the kitchen, Redžaim lights another cigarette and I ponder on Balkan bride trading. I prefer cuddly to bony women. No problem there then. And friends are always joking I'll return with a Gypsy Princess. Naat likes to describe himself as 'King' so I guess this is as close as I'm going to get to bagging my Princess. But the problems of language, location and the fact that, beyond a mutual admiration for her dad, we probably have very little in common means let's not push this boat out right now…Naat settles into his armchair, flicks through the TV channels and starts noodling on his trumpet. He points to a very well-stocked cabinet. What else can I choose but rakija? He pours Redžaim and me a drink then serves himself a generous measure. 'Cheers,' he says. 'Živeli,' I reply. The Balkan expression 'I'm a Muslim until 6pm' obviously being one Naat lives by. Rakija flash: Naat appears in *Time Of The Gypsies*. What did he make of Kusturica and Bregović?

'The movie presents the real life of the Gypsies. What's in the movie is true. The music in that film is remixing Gypsy music. Bregović, he's a turbo-folker, taking the old wedding songs in a modern way. He's not a very good musician but he's a nice man with a big name and people believe him when he says it's his music.

But it's not. I congratulate him for knowing how to use the music to make a lot of money.'

Naat's recorded instrumental interpretations of 'Djelem, Djelem' and 'Ederlezi': what are the origins of these songs?

'"Djelem, Djelem" has roots when we were nomads, living in caravans, travelling from one place to another. "Ederlezi" is for the Gypsy's holy day. I learned "Djelem, Djelem" and "Ederlezi" when I was very young.'

And Džansever: does he know of her movements?

'She's not very well accepted in Macedonia so has found her opportunity in Turkey. She's a good person and singer.'

Suddenly Naat's attacked by a tiny creature who near knocks his drink out of his hand. Enter Naat Jr. Naat and Jr display a great bond of affection and the seven-year-old grabs granddad's trumpet and treats it as a toy. Orhan, Naat's son and father of Naat Jr, enters and introduces himself in faltering English. He's a gentle young man whose quiet demeanour throughout the evening suggests the word of his father is absolute. His ten-year-old daughter also arrives, squealing with glee at the chance of bouncing on granddad. Friends and musicians enter as the night draws on, some to wish Naat well for his tour, others to check what the orders are for tomorrow. Zahir Ramadanov, trumpet player in Esma's Ensemble, arrives. I'm surprised to see him, thinking he would be in Skopje as Esma has a Sarajevo concert booked. 'No,' he explains, 'we leave very early tomorrow morning, 6am.' Has, Zahir asks, Naat informed me they're brothers? No, I reply, he didn't. Zahir looks aghast. 'He didn't?' There's a discussion in Romani and then Zahir corrects himself. 'Not brothers, cousins. Our fathers are brothers. But we grew up together in Kočani. Even now I only live a few minutes away.' 'There's so much to tell this guy,' says Naat, exasperated.

I imagined Zahir would live in Skopje close to Esma and the rest of the Ensemble. 'No,' says Zahir, 'I am from Kočani and when Esma and Stevo return from Belgrade I choose to live in my hometown again.' Turns out Esma and Stevo attended a Kočani wedding a quarter century ago, one featuring the ten-year-old Zahir playing trumpet. 'Stevo wanted me to accompany them to Belgrade and so I went with and joined the Ensemble.' From a childhood knowing only the Kočani mahala to tackling the world's stages necessitates growing up quickly and, at thirty-five, Zahir's looking a little weary. Or maybe it's the Balkan blues that have added grey to his ink-black hair.

'It's difficult times for everyone in Macedonia, especially Roma,' says Zahir. 'We musicians, we live well, we always have work and can get paid in foreign currency but for the ordinary people there's few jobs and those there are don't pay well.'

Mrs Naat keeps coming in with plates of cheese, tomato, sausage. Naat's darbouka player Ali Memedovski arrives. The rakija and mastika (a local ouzo) flow. Naat remains prone in his armchair, flicking through TV channels, playing with his grandchildren, tuning in and out of conversations. He puts on a video of a recent concert the band played in Berlin. The crowd are up and dancing from the start and the orkestar sparkle. The musicians in the room watch themselves with bemused pride. Naat cuts a swaggering figure in concert, decked out in a natty black and white outfit. He twists gnarly notes out of his instrument, keeping a balance between high shrieks and lower register blasts of sound. On occasion he flavours his solos with jazz, laying back Louis Armstrong-style then going for faster be-bop lines. The audience dances furiously to several different rhythms.

'They don't know our dances,' notes Naat, 'so it always interests me when they get up and dance as it is sometimes similar to our dancing. But often, yes, very different.'

Naat leaves the living room, returning with a framed copy of his first record – a 7-inch vinyl EP from 1977. The EP's colour cover shows the musicians dressed in 70s chic: big hair, big flares, bright shirts. Naat's so young and thin as to be unrecognisable. Standing next to Naat in the photo is Ilmi Jašarov, father of Ferus Mustafov. This was recorded, Naat notes, while he was doing his military service in Croatia. Its success ensured that upon returning to Kočani he took over the orkestar from his grandfather.

'I've been playing weddings since I was a child and as I was the best musician it was only natural.'

The session looks to continue all night until Mrs Naat clears the room, obviously insisting a few hours' sleep is required. I'm offered the spare room but barely kip before the house returns to life. These people either have a great hangover cure or simply can take anything in their stride. I wander to the top of the mahala. Just as Kočani's surprisingly tidy the mahala is equally spotless. Later I'm told Kočani's mayor has made Kočani the cleanest city in Macedonia – if not the Balkans. Yet many houses continue to employ a jerry-built style (bricks, mortar, concrete) and look decidedly wobbly. If an earthquake ever hits Kočani then I get the feeling the entire mahala would slide into the centre of town. Guess it would give the mayor something to clean up.

The musicians gather in front of Naat's van. Orhan kisses his wife and children goodbye. Naat's father, Hikmet, nearly seventy and still playing bass tuba, is bent with age yet determined to bop until he drops. Food–instruments–baggage; they load up the van as their ancestors once did caravans. Naat gets behind the wheel, a fierce glint in his eye.

'My heart, my soul,' says Naat as we exchange goodbyes, 'my music.'

Mahala Blues 2:
Good Music, Good Culture, Good People

Oh, city of gypsies! Who could see you and forget? City
of musk and sorrow, with your cinnamon towers.
Federico Garcia Lorca, 'Romancero Gitano'

Šuto Orizari translates as 'the fields'. That's the official name given
to the world's largest Roma community. Yet everyone, from those
who live here to those who never venture near, calls it Shutka. 'Shut'
in Macedonian is 'garbage' and 'ka' is a diminutive suffix. 'Little
garbage'. Some name. Some town.

To get from central Skopje to Shutka you ride the no. 19 bus. No
air conditioning, hard seats, many stops, a slow, bruising journey.
A journey in which you seemingly travel not only across the capital
but from Europe to Asia. The no. 19 begins on the outskirts of the
Old City, crawls past Topaana's surviving enclaves of pre-63 houses,
trawls amongst the tower blocks, rattles around the metropolis's
hazy outskirts before, finally, depositing riders in Shutka's main
street. You can cut the hour-plus journey to a quarter by taking a
taxi for 300 denars. But most of Shutka's residents can't afford such
luxuries. Get on the bus.

Shutka shares Skopje's hot, dusty ambience. Only Shutka's
hotter and dustier. Indeed, descending from the bus there's
so much dust I feel like I've arrived on the verge of a desert.
Immediately surrounded by Gypsy pigmies – no, hold on, they're
kids, sooty and boiling with glee at having a new Gadje to play with

Dancing in the street

– shouting 'Photo!' 'Photo!', I start down the main street, hordes of ankle biters trailing my every move. There goes an inconspicuous entry…After Kočani's tidy mahala I'm secretly pleased to be in Shutka, the eccentric energies here being very engaging. Shutka was assembled in a hurry after Skopje's 1963 earthquake. Ironically, the majority of the Roma community in Skopje's Topaana mahala didn't find themselves homeless after the quake. But acts of God allow town planners to play at God: they rebuilt Skopje in sheets of concrete and shifted the Roma majority to the city's outskirts, these crumbly fields, Šuto Orizari.

Shutka's a marginalised mahala, sure, yet also the world's largest mahala – 45,000 residents, a defiant city of Gypsies – and residents celebrate their existence with an infectious pride and joy. Some of the houses, built by those who have earned deutschmarks or dollars, are fabulous examples of Gypsy baroque, the names of the occupants engraved in marble or glass, wide staircases and big balconies. There are functional bungalows, solid and comfortable. And narrow, cramped houses, abodes barely wider than a railway carriage. But the grotesque poverty found in Bulgarian, Serbian and Romanian mahalas is not readily seen in Shutka.

'Shutka's not a ghetto,' Elvis Huna told me, 'it's a happy place.' He's right, Shutka's glorious, a jerry-built, hand-made, above-board attempt at encapsulating dreams and the limits you can take them to. Colour? Let's have some! Decoration? Crank it up! Hungry…people here are hungry. For possibilities, achievement, dreams. Imagination rules…think Dr Seuss, Gypsy Gaudis…for this is Roma wonderland. Give this community the funds blown by Blair on the Dome and Garcia Lorca's city of musk and cinnamon towers (and much else) would arise to enthral the world. For these people possess no shortage of imagination: houses curve and curl, squat low and sit high, mix brick and concrete and mortar and tile and…what you can afford, what you can dream. Carved swans and lions are popular symbols above entrances – the former cos they mate forever, the latter for courage – and rainbow hues recall Hindu temples.

Having fled into side streets to escape my army of infant admirers I find mid-afternoon Shutka engaged in a siesta of sorts, market closed, few people about. Dogs relax in the sun, geese march around the yard, families sit on their porch, horses are tethered, Yugos rattle past. Popular pastimes include cultivating vines and racing pigeons. Beautiful children smile and say in a lazy, sing-song manner 'photo' before sullen fathers whisk daughters inside. This is a land of slow dreams and easy, sensual affection. No wonder the best footage Kusturica has ever shot was in Shutka. I grew up in a post-war suburb, grid living, fields of box houses on tidy quarter-acre sections running towards rugby grounds and golf courses and, inevitably, towards more and more houses. Many Yugoslav immigrants shared my West Auckland 'burb, relieved at escaping a nation that had known so much grief during the first half of the twentieth century. Yet they surely missed things – cafés, markets, farm smells, local humour, weary blues, old buildings, the ruins of history, messy everyday stuff that knits a community's soul. And the Gypsies. I bet, tucked up in their suburban comfort, hearing the sound of lawnmowers and sprinklers, radios and TVs, they missed the chatter and music and nuisance of the Gypsies. Subconsciously, damn, I know I did.

Tick-tock: it hits 5pm and the streets erupt with people and music. Lorries unload equipment on to the main street and the reliable grind of a generator kicks off. The first wedding band of the evening play driving, clarinet-led music similar to Južni Kovači, classic Gypsy grooves; an ora forms and swings across the street. Cars turn down side streets, familiar with musical roadblock, even the buses appear un-fazed, adaptable. Summer's here and it's time for dancing in the street. Only members of the wedding party dance yet all are welcome to observe. And they do: the street's heaving with people. Kids like the buzz. Teenagers check one another, and the wedding party's fashions, out. Adults smile wearily, reflecting on their own day of betrothal and all that's passed since.

The singer wails in the hard, Arabic style favoured by Algerian rai stars. The drummer works his kit, building bubbling tabla rhythms on rot-o-toms. Local entrepreneurs arrive, selling popcorn, balloons, lollipops and toy guns. Young men with café latte complexions wear long shorts, football tops, goatees, blond highlights, tattoos on shoulders and chests. Crazy beautiful. Those attending the wedding favour white suits and greased back hair. And the girls, the girls are dressed in Bollywood finery, a blaze of polyester and sequins, bright beautiful creatures, smiling and dancing and dancing and smiling, relaxed and engaged.

Less than twenty metres further down the road another wedding band are starting up, smaller PA, but they get the cocek, the dance of the Roma, moving. The music's good yet there is no applause. I clap after a beautifully ragged clarinet solo and all around glance at me as if I'm, well, retarded. Stupid Gadje! The band's Turkish Arabesque flavour is quite removed from the classic Gypsy phrasing that underpins Esma's music. Yet all Gypsy music shares an emotional intensity that convinces the listener something important is up. And, of course, it is: a wedding!

What's this? A small, awestruck boy dressed in an oversized suit stuffed with denars is standing on the back seat of a blood-red VW bug that's had the roof removed. He's wearing a crown and carrying a sceptre. And the car is covered in streamers, glitter, flags. I assure you, this is a more magical scenario than anything in *Harry Potter*. The car rolls slowly forward, horn a-honking, brass band follows pumping hot Balkan funk. The boy's too young to get married so it must be a circumcision ceremony. Ouch! Circumcision being one of the Islamic rituals Macedonian Roma still employ while having dropped much of the religious baggage. Elvis Huna recalled his circumcision ceremony as 'very colourful and very painful'. The MC was Šaban Bajramović, a friend of his father. 'I remember his big face full of gold teeth singing to me!'

Another brass band approach, can hear the tuba, observe a merry crowd surrounding them. This lot walk fast, bouncing on heels as they come down a sloping street, not turning into the main street, instead heading straight towards a cluster of houses. Obviously an engagement celebration so they're in more of a hurry than a wedding party.

Shutka's packed tight, there's no empty space, thus the market offers solitary open ground. Divided between a covered area offering fruit, vegetables, meat, toys, clothing (Turkish copies of designer brands), shoes, pirate CDs (Gypsy turbo-folk singers, Mariah Carey, Snoop, Jay-Z) and an open area where anyone can sell anything: old shoes, broken electronic gear, children's colouring books that are coloured in, used clothing and underwear…in Shutka if you are desperate enough to try selling junk you may find someone so tortured they buy it.

As is customary across the Indian subcontinent rubbish is thrown on to the street, plastic bags creating raggedy blue and pink wastelands. Hens peck at the trash in the street and men walk their animals untethered – surly goats ransack food scraps before being ordered on. A shack boasting Internet Café turns out to have one computer. 'Connection not so good,' says the youth behind the desk. There's several shops selling food and drinks, a few bakeries and grilled meat stands but that mainstay of Balkan life, the bar/café, appears absent. A variety of Christian churches and a large, unfinished mosque are scattered across the town.

Kemal introduces himself, states that he's been living in Germany, is back in Shutka to see his mum. Please, he emphasises, don't call me Roma. 'Everyone in the world knows Gypsy – look at The Gipsy Kings, very famous band! But Roma, it doesn't mean anything beyond Macedonia. Call me a Gypsy, thank you!' A passing hairdresser announces, 'The women in Shutka are no good! Don't trust them!' Though how he knows this when he's obviously never touched anything but their hair I've no idea. 'I've been to Paris,' he moans. 'Cut hair in Paris!' And somehow he ended up back in Shutka where horse and carts still roar down the main street, dust cakes your hair and trash discolours your trainers.

Shutka's had occasional brushes with international fame: in 1981 Boney M's Bobby Farrell married Jasmina, a Roma model from Shutka who he'd met in Vienna. The wedding was held in the open area normally occupied by the market and, across Yugoslavia, it was A Major Event. *Time Of The Gypsies* established the city as prime cinematic landscape. While the February/March 2001 issue of Benetton's *Colors* magazine devoted the entire issue to Shutka, chronicling many characters and facts yet choosing to concentrate on what I call poverty chic. Y'know, poor people staring at the camera with quotes to reinforce their estrangement. Shutka has many problems, agreed, yet it sparkles with energy, creativity, love.

Sudahan Rušid, the clarinet-playing leader of Južni Kovači (the band who so impressed me at Elvis's wedding), calls Shutka home. He lives in Che Guevara Street, an appropriate address for a musical revolutionary. Close by are Lorca St and Washington St. Say what you will about Shutka but it's not dull. Noticing a gaggle of geese in a

pen I enquire if he employs them for fighting and gives them names
like NATO and Tyson. No, says Sudahan, surprised I'm aware of
Shutka's tradition of fighting geese. I mention *Colors* focused on it.

'That's so strange. Only a few of the old men do the geese
fighting and I don't know where or when they do it.'

Sudahan's twenty-five years old. He has a light aura, the bearing
of a true gentleman, and the dark features of a Roma matinée idol.
Every second winter he heads to Düsseldorf where he plays in a
Roma restaurant/club which hosts 'Miss Roma beauty competitions
every Friday'. He's hoping to give this up. He was invited to play
in Japan in early 2003, but the SARS virus found band members
refusing to fly.

'I knew the virus wasn't in Japan but they could not be reasoned
with. It was very disappointing.'

Sudahan doesn't speak English yet turns out to be fluent in
Swedish. When Macedonia looked to be following Kosovo into
ethnic conflict he took his family to Sweden and stayed a year. A
pleasant place, he says of Sweden, but Shutka is home. How would
he describe Shutka to outsiders?

'Unusual place, unusual people. Not ordinary. And not ordinary
music. I don't want to talk about the life here. People here only
survive through music. If you walk around the neighbourhood all
you may see is suffering. But in spring and summer we have maybe
twenty weddings a day. People love weddings because they enjoy
the music and live for it. That's what keeps me here.'

I ask about Kusturica filming *Time Of The Gypsies* in Shutka
but Sudahan's seemingly unaware of the film. Instead, he talks
about *Gipsy Magic*, a 1997 comedy involving a Shutka resident's
daft attempts to raise funds to get to India.

'The movie was shot here and the actors were the ordinary
people; because the Roma people are very talented they could act
as well as professionals. In the end they weren't paid but people
were happy to be part of the movie. What was depicted in the

Sudahan

Photo: Garth Cartwright

movie wasn't real life. Things don't happen like this. The Roma were shown as rude and cruel and it means the Americans and Europeans, when they see this film, will think we will steal from them. I can't guarantee for every Roma but the Roma in Shutka and Skopje are not like those in the movie. We have good music, good culture, good people. This can be seen in the weddings.'

Sudahan recalls being introduced to Charlie Chaplin's son at a Gypsy film festival: Chaplin's mother Hannah is believed to have been an English Roma and Charlie apparently enjoyed the company of Roma. Sudahan's father was a professional musician but 'he became a Jehovah's Witness and they do not encourage music and drinking so he stopped playing'.

'My grandfather played zurla [a large, deep-toned oboe] in the Tanec Ensemble [the most celebrated folk ensemble in post-war

Macedonia]. My father played saxophone in the ancient style. He was in a brass band and taught me the basics when I was very young. I was thirteen years old when I had a big miracle and fell in love with the clarinet and turned professional and my life was changed. The clarinet offers me a lot and I consider it a part of myself. I practised a lot, a lot, a lot. Ten hours per day for the first three or four years. I'd sleep with it and be practising in my sleep [mimes hands moving while asleep]. Next year I was burdened with my playing – all my friends had girlfriends and my father was saying "Sudahan's clarinet is his girl" and I ended up with a hernia. The specialist asked me what my work was and I said "clarinet" and he warned me that I was practising too much, practising to the point where it was becoming a burden to my being. So I cut back.'

I mention to Sudahan how Memphis bluesman Furry Lewis had a tune called 'When I Lay My Burden Down' – Furry called his guitar his burden. He smiles knowingly. I add his clarinet playing reminds me of Jimi Hendrix, harsh but beautiful, intense yet lyrical. Sudahan nods but looks uncertain. OK, he's unaware of Hendrix.

'The clarinet can imitate the gaida [the traditional Balkan bagpipe] and the kaval [a slender long flute], the duduk [the Armenian oboe] and the šupelka [a small Macedonian flute]. Because of the big opportunity clarinet offered, that's why I chose it. In Greece when you hear the clarinet sometimes you can't tell if it's clarinet, it sounds like all these different instruments.'

Sudahan put together his current band aged fourteen, shaping them into Skopje's no. 1 wedding band. The wedding season (June to September) always leaves him in a state of exhaustion. Making music, night after night, day after day, it's hard work. The physical and mental effort, the emotional turbulence, that goes into creating such magical sounds is something I rarely consider. And your popularity? How did you become no. 1 with no recording contract? No videos?

'Each ten or twenty years there is a style that is modern in one place, and starting this last three or four years the other musicians are imitating my style. It's so new, even for me, very joyful, good for dancing, offers a lot of excitement for listeners.'

We're drinking water, chatting, all is easy. Then I wonder: has Shutka adapted to the large number of Kosovar Roma refugees arriving here? Sudahan thinks for a moment, stands and directs me to his van. We get in and start driving. Through narrow streets, past wedding parties on their way to the main street, past the big houses and the little houses, past gaggles of geese and surly goats, on to the outskirts of Shutka, an area I'm unfamiliar with. We stop by a grassy field. Surely one of the last remaining fields from when Šuto Orizari was originally gifted to Skopje Roma. Correction, we stop by what was once a field and is now a shanty town. Across the field sprout dwellings constructed out of scrap plywood. Polythene is used for the door entrances. Graffiti cover the exteriors. I've seen more sophisticated tree huts.

'Here,' says Sudahan, gesturing at what lies in front of us, 'are the Kosovar Roma. It's a very tragic situation because we have thousands of Kosovar Roma living in Shutka and they live in huts not suitable for human occupation. Some of the lighter-skinned Roma went back to Kosovo and were murdered by the Albanians.'

Well, what can I say? Start thinking of the Edwin Star song 'War'. Not that we're unaware of the answer to Edwin's question. Sudahan asks if I've heard about a boat stuffed with refugees sinking in the Adriatic. Sure. If I'm remembering correctly it was in late 1999 and contained three dozen Roma fleeing Kosovo for Italy. Sudahan looks up as if trying to count the stars appearing in the sky.

'A friend of mine's brother was on that boat.' He ponders the tragedy. 'Why are the Albanians so hard towards us?'

I'm rarely lost for words but upon ethnic hatred I can only offer silence. We stand there, like men at a funeral. The muezzin from the local mosque starts wailing, calling the faithful to prayer.

Snap out of it. What was the line in *Hellraiser*? 'No tears. It's such a waste of good suffering.' Hey, I say, what do you think of the music of Lumi and Çita? They're Kosovar Roma singers whose raw, minimalist style has found them a cult following in Belgrade and Berlin.

'They're super,' says Sudahan, brightening. 'Really modern music. It's in now, typical Roma. I want to record with them. I've practised the tallava style. I'm surprised you know it.'

Tallava (literally 'under the arm') is the music of the Ashkali Roma, those forced to flee Kosovo only to be ignored by an indifferent world, dispossessed amongst the dispossessed. The Ashkali mix shrieking clarinets, elemental electro beats and a vocal style as harsh as that used by the leader of a camel train. How did this music, so un-European in flavour, evolve? Tallava's twenty-first-century blues, a sound created by a people so marginalised their music appears the only code they have to let the world know they survive.

I want to talk about tallava to Sudahan but staring at the shanty town kills conversation. Less than sixty years ago these people were hiding from Nazis. Now the wretched combination of Milošević, NATO and the Kosovo Liberation Army has made them again flee for their lives. Several months earlier eight hundred Kosovar Roma refugees, fed up with the abysmal conditions they were forced to endure in Shutka, set off for Greece. Greece, a nation actively intolerant of its Roma populace, showed no sympathy and refused to let them cross the border. The Roma refused to return to Shutka so set up camp. Esma provided blankets, food and medicine. Their spokesman noted, 'NATO nations caused our problem and they should solve it.' NATO nations, predictably, did their usual see-hear-speak-no-evil. Sudahan, what do you know of the Roma people's sufferings during World War II?

'My grandmother is eighty and so she tells me about this.'

A friend of Sudahan's, Seljo Kraguevac, has joined us. Quietly he adds, 'When the war began the Romas were peaceful people but then the Germans began killing us so many joined the Partisans. This led the fascists to killing even more Roma. My father was a Partisan. Tito liked us Roma because he saw us fight so hard against the Germans.'

Seljo tells me how Shutka has an equivalent to the RSA, a club where old Partisans gather to drink rakija and talk of the days when they were young and fought German, Bulgarian and Albanian fascists, heroes of mighty Yugoslavia. We return to Sudahan's house, a tidy bungalow he shares with his parents, grandmother, sister, wife and two small children. While central Shutka is grungy, Che Guevara street is spotless, a testimony to the residents' aspirations. Inside I'm seated and given an orange soft drink and coffee while Sudahan's sister Perihan buzzes around, eavesdropping as Krisi filters questions. 'How good's your English?' I finally ask. 'Oh, so so,' replies Perihan. 'Better than so so,' I say and she giggles.

Perihan's honey-coloured skin, luminous dark eyes, teased black hair and physical grace suggest she was born to wear a sari. I compliment her on this and she remarks, 'Yes, I like everything from India. The fashion, the movies, the music.' Perihan then mentions she recently got engaged to a boy from Vienna. How did you meet him? 'Oh, he came to visit Shutka in the summer. He is also a Witness.' Is he Roma? 'Yes, Macedonian Roma.' Well, good luck and I hope you enjoy life in Vienna. 'I will,' she says with supreme confidence. Do you play a musical instrument? 'No, but I can sing.' Why don't you sing with your brother's band? I'm sure they would appreciate a female singer to complement Shadan. 'No,' she says firmly, still smiling. Sudahan interjects, 'People don't like singers. Look at Džansever, she is not married. And Esma also, she had to marry a musician she worked with.'

Understood: Esma and Stevo trained dozens of young boys as musicians but, as far as I'm aware, not a single girl. Perhaps 'nečisti sili', the unclean powers, even extend to the Roma community and their perception of music making. Which also raises the unspoken

– at least to me – issue that Esma and Džansever have never given birth. Admittedly, Esma gathered a vast number of 'sons' but within Roma communities childrearing has always been the main focus of female energy. Perihan smiles and says nothing, Roma lore needing no explanation for Gadje.

Shutel TV is on and the engagement of a young couple is celebrated. This consists of photos of the couple and their respective families overlaying various videos of popular Macedonian singers. Sudahan glances at the TV and announces, 'They're from Shutka. They're getting married next summer. I've been booked to play at the wedding.' Shutel TV is one of Skopje's two Roma TV channels. Shutel is owned by Neždet Mustafa, a philosophy graduate who was Mayor of Shutka in the late 1990s and is now an MP and President of United Roma. What does Sudahan make of Neždet?

'I don't talk about politics.'

You mentioned Džansever. Do you know her?

'She is one of our best vocalists. I practise the same styles as she does. She can do Greek and Turkish styles, all Balkan styles, she's got a great range and capability. She's appreciated by the Turks and gets very well paid to sing at their weddings and restaurants. She'd like to do a Romani album but her contract specifies she must only sing in Turkish.'

Hold on. Let me assimilate this information: you are friends with Džansever?

'Of course. We play together many times. My manager and her manager work together. She was here six weeks ago, on TV. If you are not on TV you don't exist. She suffers from lumbago. When she tells me stories of her childhood I want to cry. But now, thanks to her gift of singing, she has everything.'

All right. I'm about to leave Macedonia and finally I've met someone who is friends with Džansever. Where can I find her?

'She lives in Germany now. I will see her when I go to Germany to play a wedding.'

Germany. Hmmmmmm. Home to large Turkish and Yugoslav communities. The great Serb Gypsy singer Ljiljana Petrović (née Butler) also now lives in Germany. But out of bounds for my Balkan trek. So I find something out about Džansever without finding Džansever. Which is, I guess, appropriate, leaving her mythic status intact, an unattainable creature. Sudahan, I say, please send Džansever my regards.

'I will, we spend a lot of time together. We get on very well and support one another a lot. She says of Turkish musicians, "They're very good but academic".' Sudahan pauses, a righteous man in a poor town. 'She says, "They don't have your soul".'

O PORRAJMOS
(The Great Devouring)

They've never filmed it. They never will. But you can imagine cinematic sentimentalists like Spielberg or Benigni being attracted to the initial concept. Date: 1944, site: an industrial town in southern Poland known as Auschwitz, home to the Nazi death camp of Auschwitz-Birkenau. The camp potentate is a man we now view as the absolute embodiment of human evil, Dr Joseph Mengele. Mengele's nicknamed 'the Angel of Death' though why 'the Angel' when he's as pure a demon as any man ever to have walked this planet I don't know. Anyway, Mengele has a mascot. He's a four-year-old Roma boy called Schulka Weinrich and surviving photos suggest a real beauty. All children are beautiful, sure, but Schulka, with his huge brown eyes and head of black curls, is one seriously cute kid. Mengele finds himself very attached to Schulka, dressing the child up, spoiling him with titbits, encouraging him to dance and sing in front of people. Schulka's a Zigeuner (Gypsy) and according to Nazi ideology these talents are indigenous. Along with criminality and inferior intelligence.

Mengele trawls around his various torture and murder depots with Schulka who, like other children in Auschwitz, calls the insane Doctor, 'Uncle Pepi! Uncle Pepi!' Does this read like an Academy Award harvesting screenplay or what? Uncle Pepi is a busy man: whispered reports from all fronts suggest the Third Reich is beginning to crumble so he has to up the extermination rate; Nazism being such that even losing ensures maximum possible damage waged against those most vulnerable. Thus on 4 August, 1944, Mengele ordered employees at Auschwitz's extermination nexus to work

Shake, rattle and roll

Photo: Lars Bartel

extra intensively as he set about murdering all in the camp's Gypsy village. Mengele was nothing if not efficient – 29,000 Roma gassed and cremated in one night. The Roma who care to remember this atrocity call it 'Zigeunernacht' (Gypsy Night). Mengele oversaw the entire operation. At one point, as the doors to the gas chambers were closing, he picked up Schulka, his little mascot, and threw him into the chamber. Even Roman Polanski couldn't–wouldn't–shouldn't film that scene.

I know, I know, you expect to read tales of wild Gypsy musicians. Not another bleak recitation of Holocaust statistics. But the story of the Roma can't be told without reference to this most abominable of crimes. During 1939 to 1945, those cheerless years when Europe went insane, somewhere between 200,000 and 1,500,000 Roma were murdered. Such extreme variation in statistics reflects the lack of methodology when it comes to dealing with the Roma. The former's an extremely conservative one; the latter is promoted by Roma activist-academic Ian Hancock through research and supposition.

Hancock's focused on fighting discrimination/belittlement of the Roma so it suits his crusade to suggest higher casualties. Finally, numbers are inconsequential; the crime and ensuing silence must concern us all.

The first book touching upon the Roma Holocaust was Jan Yoor's 1967 The Gypsies. Yoor's fascinating account chronicled him leaving his Flanders home aged twelve (in 1934) to join a travelling Kalderash Roma tribe with whom he lived for the next decade. Yoor followed with 1970's Crossing, a vivid and lyrical account of Roma Resistance activities in the face of genocide during WWII. 1972's Destiny Of Europe's Gypsies by Donald Kenrick and Grattan Puxon set out a thorough, academic account of the Roma Holocaust. Twenty-five years of silence and fudging broken on 'O Porrajmos' – a Romani term that once may have been used to suggest horrific rapes/abuse and now is recognised as signifying 'the great devouring'.

Yet even today Roma suffering largely attracts silence and, when it does get recognition, denial. Not from Holocaust revisionists who care naught for the Roma. Instead, it's often from Jewish academics intent on keeping the Holocaust (and its related industry) a singularly Semitic affair. Most recently there was Guenther Lewy's The Nazi Persecution Of The Gypsies (Oxford University Press, 2000), an academic's attempt at marginalising Roma suffering for the sake of advancing one ethnicity over another. Lewy's the latest in a line reaching back to when Kenrick/Puxon's book first brought the Roma Holocaust to attention. Gypsies and Jews, the only ethnic groups marked out for extermination by the Nazis, were often united before WWII by their outsider status and musical skills. Today they can be found working together on human rights and musical projects. Dragan Ristic of Belgrade's Kal says of the bond, 'We are brothers in suffering.'

The Holocaust is believed to have destroyed over half the Roma population in Europe, initially getting under way in 1933 when the Nazis took control of Germany – they first banned inter-marriage

between German and Zigeuner. Soon the Roma were being referred
to as 'a plague', 'vermin', 'sub-human'. In January 1940, 250 Roma
children were used as guinea pigs for Zyklon B, the cyanide gas
crystals used in the death camp gas chambers. On December 16, 1941,
Himmler issued orders to have all Zigeuner throughout Western
Europe deported to Auschwitz-Birkenau for extermination.

Why? I mean it: why? The Roma posed no challenge to the Nazi
state. They were efficient agricultural workers and only .05 per cent
of Germany's 1933 population. Simple answer: it was what they
represented. Their colour and wit, freedom and anarchic treatment
of authority, disturbed the repressive Teutonic sense of order.

What effect did the Holocaust have on the Romas' art? The music
that for centuries had endured, night after night invented afresh?
Klezmer, the music of Eastern Europe's Yiddish-speaking Jews, fell
silent as the death camps devoured the Jews. Roma inmates did not
leave diaries or write memoirs or get called upon to give testimony
at war crimes trials. Jewish inmates who survived Auschwitz
recall the camp's Roma singing, music as elemental and essential
as breathing, fascism unable to crush their humanity and artistry.
Other camps reportedly had Gypsy orchestras and Joy Divisions
– sex slaves – to entertain the butchers.

Gypsy music is older, so much older, than Hitler's wretched
tenure. Did much Gypsy music disappear with the klezmorim?
Many musicians were amongst the murdered. But the Roma are
nothing if not resourceful and those who survived (or dodged)
the camps ensured the sound lives, continues to resonate. As
Šaban Bajramović says when he sees Germans dancing today to
Gypsy song, 'Hitler must be spinning in his grave!' Music here
is a refusal to be vanquished, silenced, exterminated. Then
one wonders, did music play any part in relieving the inmates'
suffering? Starved and brutalised but still singing...might the
Roma music we hear today possess a deeper Balkan blues, a
darker, more sombre tone, due to O Porrajmos? 'Blues started

from slavery,' muttered Memphis Slim to Alan Lomax, and Afro-American music possesses a bleaker, more pessimistic hue than that of Africa's traditional music(s). Is there a European or Asian music that conveys the deep blues, the almost unbearable anguish, found in Gypsy song? Think about it.

'Djelem, Djelem' is one of the very few recorded Gypsy songs to touch on the Holocaust. The other I'm aware of can be witnessed in Tony Gatlif's Latcho Drom where an old Slovak woman, Marichka, sings unaccompanied (Jan Yoor noted most Roma song was performed accompanied only by hand claps when he travelled with them) a haunted lament simply called 'Auschwitz'. Marichka's hoarse, blue voice details the man-made hell whose gates boasted in large iron lettering 'Arbeit macht frei' ('work liberates'). Never suggest Germans lack an evil sense of irony.

American academic Carol Silverman noted, 'Many songs were written to express the Rom experience in Nazi concentration camps, such as Ficowski's translation (1991:109):

> I shall never get out of here now,
> I shall never see my brothers or sisters!
> They brought us through the gateway
> And let us out through the chimneys...

In general, Rom songs tend not to depict historic periods but rather speak of eternal themes such as love and poverty, omitting concrete events. Holocaust songs, on the other hand, often include the names of concentration camps. They are modelled on songs of prison life and other laments. In recent years, they are sung less and less, performed only by the older generation.'

That such a cataclysmic event should, largely, have vanished from the repertoire of Gypsy musicians, people whose songs so often deal in pain and strife, is understandable if you comprehend the Roma existence: centuries of oppression having quashed the concept of looking back, of reflection on injustice. 'Of course Gypsies do not know their own history,' noted Roma author Menyhert Lakatos. 'It was not in anyone's interest to enlighten them.'

Records show Allied awareness of Roma trauma yet at the Nuremberg trials not one person was prosecuted for crimes against the Roma and no Roma was called to testify. The US Holocaust Memorial Council was founded in 1979 but not until 1987 (and after much intensive lobbying) was a Roma given a place on its board. The Council's founder, Elie Wiesel, in his speech accepting the Nobel Peace Prize in 1986, said, 'I confess that I feel somewhat guilty towards our Romani friends. We have not done enough to listen to your voice of anguish. We have not done enough to make other people listen to your voice of sadness. I can promise you we shall do whatever we can from now on to listen better.' Talk is cheap: in 2002 President Bush removed the Roma representative from the board.

Romanian Kalderash leader Ion Cioabă has campaigned for compensation for the families of Romanian Roma murdered in the camps – a lack of documentation making this extremely difficult to achieve. I asked each musician I met about Porrajmos. All were aware. None suggested they saw it as anything other than a major tremor in the Europeans' ongoing persecution of their people.

'The Jews have Jewish lawyers and politicians to fight for them,' Esma Redžepova told me. 'We don't but we survive. No matter how hard they try, we survive. We, the Roma people.'

ROMANIA

Choo-choo-choo…dig the rhythm…that slow, loping roll of a mid-twentieth-century locomotive…*Chug-chug-chug*…Romania's trains remain iron horses, noble industrial-age beasts which move with the elemental shake, rattle and roll so required of rail travel… first light lifts the mist across the Hungarian plain…opaque flints of blonde advancing across December's dark and long shadows… *Will the clouds break? Will the sun welcome us into the plains of Crisana?*…atmospheric forces play across this flat, lonesome land… a battle of wills between light and dark…one chiaroscuro morning coming up…*choo-choo-choo…chug-chug-chug*.

Romania by train; you move in almost slow motion, panoramic views of a golden, troubled land unfolding in a series of great, sensual movements…can taste this region with a tangible excitement that's close to erotic…*O. V. Wright's gravelly tonsils on a loop in my skull singing 'Ride…let mah baby ri-ah-i-iiid' across a pumping Memphis backbeat*…Returning to Romania, damn, it's the strangest sensation, akin to a long absent lover discarding her robes and welcoming me back. Admittedly, I'm short of sleep and very, very cold so such metaphors come from a strange part of my skull. I mean, if Romania's caressing me it's with the touch of an Ice Queen – I'm frozen, shrunken into fleece and boots, testicles truly retracted.

Guess nimrods who choose to travel in winter get what they deserve; the carriage I occupy being correspondent to sitting in a freezer with a view. Not that CFR, the state rail network, are known to lack a sense of humour; once, on an overnight winter train from Belgrade, the heating suddenly came on. And on. And on. Soon everyone in the train was removing several layers – even Romanian men of a certain age, long noted for stepping out dressed in leather jackets you might mistake for body armour, shed kilos of dead cow as they stripped down to vests. And then the heating was switched off. This sauna/freezer conditioning continued all night. As the locals like to say, Welcome To Ro-*Mania*.

Border crossings are another highlight of the Romanian rail journey. These include customs officers zealously tearing up already broken seats as they search for contraband and the omnipresent border guard who, upon seizing my New Zealand passport, declares, 'The first time I have ever seen one of these.' He leafs through it, puzzling over the visa from Iran – that gets 'em everywhere – stamps and hands passport back. 'Why Romania?' he asks, puzzled anyone would come not once but several times to a nation so many of its inhabitants desperately wish to leave. 'I like it here,' I say. And mean it, I've a great affection for Romania. The northern regions of Maramureş, Transylvania and Moldavia all offer rivers, mountains, farms, forests, valleys, monasteries, fortified medieval towns and humble villages like nowhere else in Europe. The people can be open,

welcoming. Again, Europe has too few like them. And the music…
Romania oozes music and more legendary Gypsy musicians have
arisen from this fractured country than any other.

Natural magic and much mystery still exist in Romania. Yet
this large nation, one which within its own borders lies across a
geographical, historical and cultural barrier separating central
Europe from the Balkans, is largely viewed by outsiders as a matrix
of clichés – Vampires! Orphans! Dictators! And few can be more
contemptuous of their nation than the Romanians as they dream
of Paris, Rome and Manchester (football's taken very seriously).
The food's often inedible. The coffee worse. They drink sweet wines.
There's ridiculous prejudice against the Roma. And vicious hounds,
not vampires, are everywhere.

Arriving in pretty, provincial Oradea an ice axe is damn near
needed to separate me from the seat. A café offers café nes or
café natural – the latter Romanians boast of being 'black as hell,
strong as death, sweet as love'. Begin swallowing cup after cup
seal style – if love's this vile I'm staying single – until hot caffeine's
unlocked limbs. Now I can think. Now I can speak. *I want to go
to Transylvania.* The woman behind the ticket counter shakes her
head. No train? I don't believe it! There will be a train, perhaps in
five hours or so. We can't sell you a ticket. Come back in four hours'
time. Deep breath. Think Zen. Think calm. Think the tangible
excit— *shut it*. But, hey, I'm in Romania and it all comes rushing
back to me now: I must practise patience. The station possesses
an atmosphere of imminent despair, everyone nervously eyeing
– who's the chicken thief? Who's the informer? – everyone else.

Time to explore Oradea. Dump backpack and leap on to a tram.
Immediately collared by a plainclothes ticket inspector. She speaks
no English and my pleas of 'Tourist! No understand!' fail. Instead
she drags me off to meet a shaven-headed giant who surely once
worked for the Securitate. He says, 'Where are you from? New
Zealand? Auckland, huh? Good sailing, right? Pay this girl two

hundred thousand lei or she's calling the police.' Barter it down to one hundred thousand – two quid – and shuffle off shamefaced. Stupid tourist!

ATMs reject my bank card, the pastries are sour…I'm not up to Oradea's frosty boulevards so skulk back to the station. Most of the station is taken up by huge, dusty waiting rooms where people gather in silence, as if expecting the end of the world. Trying to buy a ticket, I've noted, can be difficult. Trying to recover left luggage near impossible – even though the office boasts twenty-four-hour service I end up searching the station for someone with a key to the room. About the only thing forever functioning are the toilets where, even at 4am, a female attendant wearing a yellow uniform and haggard stare will take your 5,000 lei and palm you loo roll the texture of sandpaper. Best pray the toilets are squat as the seated loos get trashed and rendered filthy beyond belief.

Waiting for my train allows a constant stream of Roma to approach me with goods for sale – a well-tailored jacket, trainers, brooms, babies, kidneys…hey, just kidding on the last two. My endless chorus of 'nu-nu-nu' fails to dent their enthusiasm and I enjoy the spectacle, the women's vitality being as bright as their floral skirts and scarves. Today's been a market day and a couple of dozen Roma women bustle about, puffing on cheap tobacco, infants hanging in cloth wraps around mama's chest, boarding their train in knockabout comedy manner. They provide vivid spectacle, rolling Gypsy chaos in motion, an energy flash amongst the station's torpor. Catch myself smiling, getting back in the Romanian groove.

Finally off, the train to Târgu Mureş winding through a landscape basted with the first winter snows. Transylvania: 'beyond the forest' is the literal translation of those five beautiful syllables yet the power they exert on the Western imagination is so immense the region should be relabelled 'beyond comprehension'. And as the sun sets, all bewitching crimson wash across farmland

and mountains, I reflect on Jonathan Harker's fictional journey into Transylvania and wonder if Bram Stoker, who never visited, imagined quite how cold a train journey through this land of ragged Alps and deep valleys gets.

Arriving in Târgu Mureş I'm met by Mihai, an old friend who, encountering my very youthful self in 1992, proceeded to guide me up the Făgăraş Mountains and into the Alps where all is silence and beauty and the vodka never loses its chill. Back then Mihai was living in Bucharest but that blackhearted city lent grey to his hair and lines to his face so he shifted to Târgu Mureş, closer to those beloved mountains. Mihai is a surveyor and for his efforts he is paid the princely sum of US $100 a month. 'It's like the 1960s,' he says of his existence, 'living for love and peace and not giving a damn about money.'

Mihai is humble, generous, kind, to be in his company is to enjoy time with a gentle soul. I bring him tapes of old English rock monsters – Traffic, Deep Purple, Cream – which he embraces with an enthusiasm comparable to mine for Romania's Gypsy music. Mihai can't understand why I like Gypsy music. He plays me Romanian prog' rock bands and tells me, 'This is the good Romanian music'. I defer. His wife, Doina, fondly recalls seeing the abysmal Uriah Heep in concert – when communism collapsed fag-end metal bands found they had audiences across East Europe. I recall only one Heep song, predictably called 'Gypsy'. It's a one-chord stomp about Gypsy girls whose fathers take a whip to Gadje boyfriends. I hadn't heard 'Gypsy' since childhood until a Bulgarian in London played me it. She, too, expressed enthusiasm at seeing the Heep in concert in Sofia.

As we wander from café to kiosk Stoker's 'children of the night' are nowhere in sight. In Bucharest there are children of the night, runaways, abandoned children, refugees from Satanic orphanages, both Roma and Romanian, who emerge from sewers, barefoot, hungry and ripped on glue fumes, lost boys and girls. But Târgu

Mureş, with its wide, clean streets and Habsburg architecture, offers no evidence of such suffering. Târgu Mureş was once Hungarian in culture and population but Ceauşescu made it a closed city so allowing only ethnic Romanians to settle here. Violent clashes between the city's Hungarians and Romanians in March 1990, ended bizarrely with dozens of Roma men being charged with public order offences. It got worse: during the early 1990s vicious, fiery pogroms were inflicted upon several Romanian Roma communities.

Why do many Romanians loathe the Roma? I can't explain it. Mihai, who hates no one, can't explain it. A glance at Romanian history suggests four centuries of slavery have left an ingrained prejudice, the Roma still being viewed with a contempt fit for slaves. Romanians are descendants of Thracian tribes who mixed with the conquering Romans; strong Tartar, German Saxon, Magyar and Turkish communities made their presence felt across the lands now known as Romania. All arrived, to some degree, as conquerors and various degrees of intermarriage have continued, so creating a strong featured people whose complexion ranges from blond to Arabic. Only Jews and Roma arrived as peaceful settlers. In turn, both would suffer great brutality.

Prince Vlad Dracul (Vlad the Devil) inspired Bram Stoker's fictional Dracula and Stoker casts Gypsies as the Count's nefarious Transylvanian henchmen. Skip the myth: Vlad Dracul is the medieval Balkan equivalent of Hitler. In 1445 he returned from Bulgaria with twelve thousand Roma captives and, in doing so, set in place a system of slavery still intact four hundred years later. The Roma were kept as slaves by the monasteries and the Boyars (landowners), both to work the lands and as artisans, in the Romanian regions of Wallachia and Moldavia. Slavery was slowly dismantled, finally being outlawed in 1864. This launched the greatest Roma migration since they first left India; thousands fled for Bulgaria, Hungary, Germany, France, Belgium, the UK, Latin America and the USA. Silence still surrounds this historical injustice; Romanians tending to grind teeth, start making low, growling noises, when the subject is broached. In *From Russia With Love* James Bond visits a Gypsy camp that comes under attack from 'Boyars – their vicious enemies.' James and the Gypsies kick Boyar ass in fine style. Ian Fleming, what tales he told!

The Romanian government's census result suggests 450,000 Roma currently live in Romania. The Budapest-based organisation European Roma Rights Centre claim the figure is closer to 2.5 million. Academic estimates push the figure to just beneath two million. Whatever, this involves a massive discrepancy surrounding the largest Roma community in any one nation. Government fiddling of figures, local mayors declaring 'no Gypsies live here' and even the fear of many Roma of being recognised as such, so inventing a different ethnicity (in some Transylvanian regions it is reported that as many as 70 per cent of the Roma registered as Hungarians in 1992), all keep the statistics down. The latter option is understandable in a nation where the 2000 Presidential election was almost won by Corneliu Vadim Tudor, formerly a 'patriotic poet' in Ceauşescu's court, who calls for all Romania's Gypsies and Jews to be put in paper boats then set adrift upon the Black Sea. I caught Tudor debating on TV with two journalists while in Romania. He's small, plump, absurdly aggressive and very camp. Viewers could ring in to say 'Da' or 'Nu' as to whether the vile Tudor would be Romania's next President. When I switched channels votes were running 77 per cent in his favour.

The Roma in Romania – a nation speaking a Latin language that uses the word 'Țiganii' (pronounced Tsee-gan-ee), one seemingly derived from the Greek 'Atzinganoi' (which referred to a heretical sect) – possess the numbers to effect political change but not the organisational skills. Self-proclaimed Gypsy King Florin Cioabă lives in Sibiu, Transylvania, but his political and economic (the Cioabăs are wealthy traders of gold and scrap metal) power is focused on his family and the Kalderash caste he presides over.

'Tzigane' and 'Gypsy', not 'Roma', were the terms everyone I met employed. What's the difference, I asked Şulo of Fanfare Ciocărlia, between a Romanian calling you 'Tzigane' and you describing yourself as 'Tzigane'? He thought about this then said, 'it depends on how they say it'.

Romanians may say 'Tzigane' softly or with a snarl but one thing's for sure: Romanians don't want the word 'Roma' to come into popular use. Already they insist that those who employ it must spell it 'Rroma' and any correspondences made between Romas and Romanians – great musicians/great footballers – are looked upon with horror. But the worlds of the Roma and the Romanians are not so separate as many wish to believe.

As we wander around Târgu Mureş I note the local Roma men wear distinctive bushy moustaches and black trilby hats. Their appearance suggests a certain affluence. Intriguingly, I realise I've never seen any of this clan making music. Romania remains home to some forty different Roma groups, of whom several thousand are nomadic (corturari), somehow prevailing against the communist desire to create a sedentary population. Corturari settle for winter then spend summer travelling, many in the region around the Romanian/Bulgarian border. The nomadic Roma tend to keep themselves more separate from Gadje society than their settled (vâtraşi) brethren and they may employ such traditional laws as the kris (a Roma court) and the bulibasha (local leader) alongside taboos that go back to India's caste and cleanliness laws.

The post-Ceauşescu government's failure to build a strong economy and civil society lends Romania a distressed, anxious identity. And nowhere is this more obvious than Bucharest. Arriving by land, you sense Bucharest before you see it; the psychic dread of the city seeps through the Danube basin, crawls across the flat Wallachian plains, leaving in its wake what I can only describe as a choleric premonition. My breathing gets tighter, the nape of my neck tingles, there's something in the air...It's not just

Romica Puceanu

©Electrecord

Bucharest's closing presence I'm reacting to. The route I'm following is one innumerable armies have taken over the centuries. Tatars and Turks, Goths and Austrians, Nazi and Red. Imagine the blood spilled into this black earth, the fertile terrain surrounding my train hosting, surely, burial grounds stretching across millennia; thousands of anonymous bones rest here bleached by soil and time. The winds that swirled around the Transylvanian Alps now blow softly around my head and appear to whisper, 'History is bunk!'

Indeed, the history of Romania has not been a kind one. And Ceauşescu's legacy was one of reverse alchemy, turning Bucharest from 'the Paris of the East' into the ugliest capital city in Europe. Apparently inspired by North Korea and Versailles, he insisted on a third of Bucharest, its historic Byzantine quarters, being demolished and replaced with a field of palaces so lacking in spirit, imagination, wit, I suffer indigestion whenever I see them.

Admittedly, I have friends in Bucharest and their sunny company makes up for the capital's flaws. Well, almost. Bogdan meets me off the train, dismisses my descriptions of the spectral beauty that

is the walled Transylvanian city of Sighişoara, and boasts the real
Romania is right here in Bucharest. He's correct. I'm just not sure
how much 'real Romania' I need. Back at his apartment we watch
Atomic, the Romanian pop video channel. Romania has long
produced phenomenal musicians from all ethnic groups but the
nation's attempts at pop-rock are dismal, lacking even the trashy
energy that characterises Serb and Bulgarian efforts. In Romania
the power ballad appears to have never died and most of the singers,
no matter how glossy the video, possess spectacularly bad teeth.

We head out to meet Henry Ernst, a Viking-looking German
national who discovered Romanian brass band legends Fanfare
Ciocărlia. His wife is a Roma from one of the Bucharest mahalas
('A German married to a Gypsy? Well I never!' said Doina when
I mentioned this in Târgu Mureş) so Henry spends considerable
amounts of time in a city he holds little affection for. Henry points
me in the direction of Muzică, a CD stall in a functional shopping
mall, where reissues of classic Romanian Gypsy recordings are
available. I purchase CDs by Romica Puceanu, Gabi Luncă, Toni
Iordache, Dona Dumitru-Siminică, four artists whose work can
be measured alongside US jazz/blues icons or Cuba's equally
venerated old masters of mambo. The fact that all four prospered
under communism suggests Ceauşescu's rotten regime employed
apparatchiks who had some feeling for music.

Romica Puceanu, a tiny, chubby woman born into a family of
noted Gypsy musicians in 1928, sang with fabulous grace and good
humour. Fuelled on cognac, wrapped in silk and fur, capable of
virtuoso vocal performances, Puceanu spent a lifetime singing in
taverns and at weddings, infusing songs with a big-hearted joy and
tenderness. Returning from performing at a wedding in 1996 her
car left the road and little Romi left the planet.

Dona Dumitru-Siminică, born in 1926 and dying seemingly
forgotten some time in the 1980s, possessed an ethereal voice,
all murmurs and sobs, a crooner whose weaving of vowels and

consonants suggests the human soul naked, burning. Dona, whose two surviving photos suggest an anxious head waiter rather than one of the great Gypsy soul magicians, sang the salon songs of the eighteenth and nineteenth centuries. In his music there are traces of a land much darker and stranger than anything Bram Stoker conjured up.

Toni Iordache, born in 1942, was master of the cimbalom, an instrument that entered Europe with Roma as the santoor. Initially worn around the neck and picked with tiny hammers, the cimbalom was modified into a larger size and furnished with legs and a pedal by Hungarian instrument-maker Jószef von Schunda. As an adult Toni represented Romania internationally, though a drugs bust in the mid 1970s – a quantity of Turkish heroin was found hidden in his instrument – saw him jailed. Behind bars, using scraps from the workshop, he built his own cimbalom. Romania's stony rulers could not bear the absence of his sublime sound and he was freed after serving eighteen months. He died too soon in 1987.

Gabi Luncă is the only surviving artist from the golden era yet these days she too is silent. Her accordion-playing husband Ion Onoriu died in 1997 and Luncă effectively retired from performing her repertoire of traditional Gypsy songs. Gabi is still known to sing but only in honour of God and her performances are coordinated by a Pentecostal church group who are intent on saving souls in this land of Orthodox heathens. The US-funded organisation obviously consider it quite a coup to have a legendary Gypsy diva amongst the congregation and thus reward Gabi well for leaving songs of Roma lore to sing for the sanctified.

Romanians tend to be very touchy about Gypsy music, generally claiming 'Gypsies copy Romanian music'. Challenge them to match the Gypsies with equally fine Romanian musical performances and their bluff is called. Romania does have a rich folk music tradition, though much of the music is dissonant – drones, squeals and stomps best describing it – so lacking the warmth, the soul of Gypsy music.

If the music of Romania's peasants is as harsh as their lives that didn't stop Ceauşescu using folk music as a nationalist tool during the 1980s: Romanian TV was chock full of beefy peasants singing odes to new tractors and bright socialist mornings. The tiny tyrant tormented his long-suffering citizens by exporting the bulk of agricultural produce (hence severe food rationing), uprooting entire villages (the squalid tower blocks they were forced into being 'modern') and banned every form of contraception (so leading to the nation's infamous, overflowing orphanages). Insane and wildly paranoid, he demanded every phone be tapped while coddling up to the West. Nicknamed 'America's favourite communist', Ceauşescu received the ultimate package holiday: a 1979 invitation to Buckingham Palace, honorary knighthood included. Back home in Romania the TV showed nothing but non-stop footage of The Great Leader's royal triumph.

These days Romanian TV is a diabolic mix of game shows, Latin American soap operas and violent American films. Exiled Romanian novelist Norman Manea wrote immediately after Ceauşescu's fall, 'will television – the daily trivialiser – overwhelm cultural life?' Norm, you couldn't even begin to imagine: everyone has the TV on all day. Bogdan works as a cameraman for a TV channel ($400 a month salary; good for Romania), an average day involving filming politicians and car crashes. Heads of state and headless states making for prime viewing. Roma also feature regularly as news items. The first item I see finds a Kalderash matriarch flanked by her two daughters, both pouting, sloe-eyed beauties. The matriarch is campaigning for compensation for Kalderash gold confiscated by the communists. The camera slowly pans over the fat gold rings and bracelets the three women wear. 'They have no papers documenting their losses,' notes Bogdan. The second item involves the inhabitants of a poor Roma settlement on the outskirts of Bucharest: why aren't the children attending school regularly? A girl, about ten, says she is happy to go to school.

A man, perhaps her father, says he realises an education is a good thing. But there are problems. Upon this he doesn't expound. But, to be sure, there are problems.

The news items were straightforward, non-judgmental. Rich Gypsies with gold. Poor Gypsies lacking education. Two sides of the same cliché? Or a reflection of the huge social division within Romania's Roma? In Bucharest I will ask people this. None offers an easy answer. You must understand, says Henry, both interpretations are true. Welcome To Ro-*Mania*.

FULGERICĂ:

Slave to the Accordion

Lots of these guitar players, they play fast, don't concentrate on no soul. You play fast an' with soul.
Albert King to Stevie Ray Vaughan

Wake up with fever. A psychic reaction to landing in Bucharest? Nice idea but more likely this has followed on from my chilly wanderings through icy Transylvania. I'm crap in cold climates, my South Pacific bloodlines collapsing as soon as the sun sets. Trekking around the outskirts of Sighişoara I passed a garbage dump where a rectangular dwelling had been created out of cartons and sheets of plastic. Recall Jivi's comment of the Roma living 'on, from and upon garbage'. And they manage to do it without freezing to death. Incredible. The three boys who obviously call this home approached smiling, intrigued.

'Romanian?'

'Nu. Englez.'

'Englez? Nu Romanian?'

The conversation continued like this for a few minutes, me increasingly unsure they even had a concept of England. Latin America having taught me that it's pointless saying New Zealand, my nation non-existent to many Third World minds. Go to move on and notice their mother washing her hair outside the plastic shack. She smiles sweetly – this is a great family of smilers – these people who have so little share a smile so easily. The boys, realising

Fulgerică and Angelica

I'm off, offer the open palm salute and I shuffle my coins amongst them. 'Patjival o manus an' la vi anda gav xaljardo.' My stock Romani proverb. They laugh. Good luck, sweet princes, in this distressed land you're sure going to need it.

Danni, Bogdan's wife, serves me sweet tea and I try and gather focus. Do I hear a brass band or are hallucinations accompanying the fever? Look through the window and, yup, marching slowly behind a black van are half a dozen brass musicians. All right, the day has begun. I wander into the Bucharest morning feeling not too great but certainly better than whoever occupies the back of the van. The musicians and mourners are a mix of Roma and Romanian and while there's no tradition of brass music from Wallachia the horns blow a blue, funereal funk.

Ceauşescu didn't get much right but he did leave Bucharest with a fast, functional metro. I ride into Piaţă Unirii, exiting to see, lurking in the near distance, the world's second largest and worst building. When The Great Leader got things wrong he did so on a thermonuclear scale. Once called Palace of the People

– Ceauşescu starved them to build it – the hulking monstrosity is now called the Palace of Parliament, housing as it does Romania's politicians. Why do I visit this monument to absolute power whenever I pass through Bucharest? There's nothing admirable in the wretched edifice. But such extreme hubris provides a glimpse into the psyche of those who run Romania. So there it sits on an artificial hill, looking like an overwrought wedding cake. To think that for the Palace alone Ceauşescu ordered the clearing of twelve churches, two synagogues, three monasteries and 7,000 homes.

Walking down Boulevard Unirii, the street Ceauşescu demanded be longer and wider than the Champs Elysées, reinforces the sense of The Great Leader's levity: he called Boulevard Unirii 'The Victory of Socialism'. Locals renamed the street 'The Victory of Socialism over Romania' and so it seems, the boulevard's parched fountains, dead foliage and grubby marble plateaus reinforcing the city's sense of bereavement. Entering the Palace I pay 150,000 lei and feel fortunate to have skipped breakfast – the entrance hall alone is such violent kitsch my gut's twisting. Look at this place – plaster ceilings done out in gold paint, an extravaganza of dripping crystal chandeliers, elephantine white marble columns, staircases wider than city streets, pink marble walls…an Essex mansion on steroids, a temple of genuinely fetid taste. $3.3 billion was spent on this dump and wandering through it, the silk curtains and handwoven carpets, I realise you'd have to spend a fortune to build such a shithole. Outside again I hurry away – stare too long at the Palace and you'd surely wish you were blind – recalling how, on my last visit, I dragged Mihai along. He'd never been inside before. I asked how it made him feel. 'Hungry'.

Time to get things on a more human scale. Time to head towards the bar where I'm meeting Constantin Fulgerică, the foremost accordion player in Romania. Fulgerică, at thirty-eight, has little experience of the West although he has released a fine album, 2002's *Fulgerică and The Mahala Gypsies*, on the

Dutch World Connection label. Beyond a handful of dates in the Netherlands he's not toured behind it, being one of Romania's most in-demand wedding and restaurant musicians. Arriving at a chilly, empty bar I wonder if this is the right location; the blunt tables and soulless ambience suggest a down at heel restaurant. Which, considering Bucharest's waning economy, it probably was. The waiter, as grey and grumpy as his city, provides a traditional Romanian breakfast, beer–vodka–cigarettes, perfect for scouring my mind of architectural transgressions. The city scenes outside – people walking, people talking – all blur until a sharply dressed couple stride in.

Fulgerică – baby face, sharply dressed, shoes shining – is accompanied by his translator, Angelica Trancă. Angelica is also Roma although it turns out she's not a professional translator; instead she's a managing director of a trading company. She looks it: short-haired and power-suited, every inch the professional. Their connection comes through Fulgerică having married Angelica's sister, 'who he loves very much,' adds Angelica with droll emphasis. She's the first Romanian Roma professional I've met and announces, 'I'm not married but if I took a marriage it wouldn't be to a musician. They're away too much. Anyway, I'm not that keen on Gypsy music. I like disco, house.'

'I'm from a musical family in Braşov,' says Fulgerică. 'My father played violin. My mother's father played clarinet while my father's father played double bass. All my uncles were musicians and then in 1965 I came into the world, determined to play accordion! I've been playing since I was four. At eight I was already good. I played in a folklore festival in Târgu Jiu and won first prize. I grew up learning from the musicians in my family and all we played was Gypsy music and Romanian folklore.

'I went to music school for elementary school but I didn't stay there long as I knew I was going to be a professional musician and by the age of thirteen I was playing in restaurants and at weddings.

I arrived in Bucharest aged seventeen. I knew I was a very good accordion player and had to establish myself amongst the crème de la crème of musicians. And that's always been here.'

Fulgerică's prowess – 'bottled lightning' is how admirers describe his playing – quickly established him on the Bucharest restaurant scene. Romanians may be reluctant to give the Roma much respect but, as Fulgerică observes, 'They love us when we make music'. And for those Romanians who had money, even during the worst of Ceauşescu's privations, there were always restaurants open with Tzigane bands playing. The fee for playing restaurants is small, the baksheesh from those eating and drinking being the reward. So Constantin played and played and played. And his ability, his deft touch and fine discipline, found him alongside the last of the Gypsy soul legends.

'I got to play weddings alongside Gabi Luncă and her late husband Ion Onoriu. And I got to play with Romica Puceanu at Hunedoara Restaurant. I played that restaurant from 1990 to 1999. I loved working with Romica, she was a great lady, very funny, very warm, and always singing so well. I also worked with Neluta Neagu, he's a good Gypsy singer, for several years. Working with the great singers and the master musicians was an honour for a young man like me. They sang all the old traditional Gypsy music. And they were near to the public by the simplicity of their songs.'

Fulgerică orders another vodka. Same for me. What does it take to be a great Gypsy singer?

'The most important criterion is to sing well. It's important to have a warm voice and with every performance to be close to the audience.'

And what makes for a great accordion player?

'Well, I play a very personal style and I employ influences from all around the country.'

Was there, I wondered, any chance I could come along and witness Fulgerică rock a restaurant while in town?

'It's not worth playing them any more. The economy in Romania is so bad there's now no baksheesh.'

But I'm informed you go to Paris and play in restaurants?

'That's true. There's a Romanian restaurant in Paris that booked me for six months. It was good, well paid.'

Weddings are what keeps Fulgerică going. Tomorrow he and his band are flying to Spain for a wedding.

'It's rich Romanians getting married so we will be there for seven days. Weddings are my only source of income. When we play them we start at 5pm and finish at 6am although we may only play for two or three hours as we are the stars. Things are changing with weddings: they're getting rid of cimbaloms and double bass, replacing them with synthesisers and drums. I'm not happy with this but what can I do?'

Not a lot. Gypsy music in Romania is mutating and nothing hints at this more closely than Tony Gatlif's 1997 film *Gadjo Dilo* (Crazy Stranger). The film, set in rural Romania, finds French drifter Stephane living amongst a traditional Roma community and learning lessons in joy and sorrow, the pleasures of vodka and dancing to Fulgerică's hot Gypsy band. Yet it's not Fulgerică's band. Well, not so you can see. Gatlif, obviously tipped to Fulgerică as king of the tavernas, hired him and recorded two numbers that appear in the film. Yet he cast Adrian 'Copilul' Minune – the most popular contemporary Gypsy singer in Romania – as accordionist. Logical? It's a movie. How does Fulgerică feel about *Gadjo Dilo*?

'I've never seen it.'

'I've seen it,' offers Angelica. 'It was on an arts channel. I think the director has mixed things up for the success of the movie. The reality is not for now. Maybe fifty years ago people lived like that. But not now.'

What Angelica's unhappy with is *Gadjo Dilo*'s portrayal of a very traditional (and poor) Roma community. They sing, dance and live in tents, making few concessions to the modern world.

The film ends with a vicious anti-Roma pogrom so making for unsettling viewing, especially for a Roma woman trying to live peacefully in Bucharest.

Gadjo Dilo is more accurate than Angelica admits. Accusations of rape and/or robbery in rural Romanian towns led to the burning of several Roma communities in the early 1990s, communism's fall allowing hatreds full vent. And some Roma communities remain as traditional as that in the film. *Gadjo Dilo* is, for me, the best film yet made about East Europe's Roma. Avoiding the stereotypes Kusturica and co. tend to trade in, *Gadjo Dilo* captures the humanity – flawed, funny and beautiful – of a traditional Roma community; no frame rings false.

Since his 1983 feature debut *Les Princes* (Roma family living on a dilapidated French housing estate), Tony Gatlif's become cinema's Gypsy auteur. The majesty of the music and images in 1993's *Latcho Drom* ensures it remains his most successful, yet 1996's *Mondo* (a young Roma boy wanders France), 2000's *Vengo* (Andalusian flamenco drama) and 2002's *Swing* (Manouche musicians in France) are all remarkable viewing. Anyway, I digress. The music local Gypsy star Adrian 'Copilul' Minune plays is manele. And Fulgerică doesn't approve.

'I'm not a fan but people at weddings are asking for it. The musical situation in Romania is bad: there aren't many good musicians these days, not like in Serbia. Since the revolution there have been many changes but most of them have been bad. Ceaușescu was bad but the music was good then. Now the music is not related any more to the traditional Gypsy music.'

Fulgerică and The Mahala Gypsies is a masterpiece of economy and style. He leads the band through an intense workout, their traditional roots being powered by an urban anxiety. Fulgerică should be at the forefront of a new wave of Romanian Gypsy music. Instead, he's the final doyen of a generation, a prince aware his kingdom is turning from him.

'I don't advise young people to play the accordion because it's hard work,' says Fulgerică, shrugging at the extinction of tradition, 'and in order to be good you become slave to the accordion. Hard work and a lot of troubles. A Titanic amount of work!'

Fulgerică and Angelica are off and I'm back in central Bucharest with an afternoon to kill. Every surface is tagged with graffiti, the sky burdened with rusting cranes, the only bright buildings being fast food outlets. I note a surge in designer cafés, their prices obviously not catering to your average caffeine-craving Romanian. The packs of stray canines that once roamed the streets are less evident. But the stray children, many barefoot, are still obvious. On the metro a boy, perhaps ten, gets on with his little sister who's no more than two. He prostrates himself, bowl in front of his head, and launches into a desperate riff. No one spares a single lei. The following morning he enters my carriage, no longer accompanied by his sister, still begging, still receiving no reward. Bogdan believes the kids work for professional criminals. Maybe. But it's still a wretched sight. At the next station a smaller boy, maybe seven, cuddling a puppy, gets on and begins to beg. He does somewhat better. Romanians love dogs.

Taraf De Haïdouks:
You Don't Learn This Job, You Steal It

Every true work of culture is a work of resurrection,
a work of remembrance that creates the remembered
moment anew and blends it with the present moment
to create the possibilities of the future.

Michael Ventura, *Shadow Dancing in the USA*

Visit Clejani in summer...heat crackles...the buzz of insects fills the air...all movement slowed to rural drift until evening descends and the dirt streets erupt into life...children spill out of shanty houses...people queue at kiosks for bottles of sticky beer...a turkey's slaughtered, gutted, cooked on an open fire...and music...music adds flavour to the soupy atmosphere...gets shoulders rolling and legs stretching...locals aware that for all their discomfort, poverty and frustration they live amongst princes, musical aristocrats received as stars in Hollywood and with honours in all the great cities...a violin slices the still thick air into eighths. Let's just dance...

But in winter, as the season happens to be, Clejani is mud. Roads that were hard and kicked up a golden dust when I last walked on them are quagmire, sucking at my steps, hungry for boots of Spanish leather. Fields once ripe with maize are now dank and forlorn, only the husks of last season's crops remain, left to rot in the rains. Come on, I tell myself, things may not be so picturesque but it's still Clejani, the music still spills out of here like oil across

Photo: Klaus Reimer

Enter the Taraf

Saudi sands – *Splat!* A puddle attempts to engulf me. But it's too big to be a puddle…more a…more a swamp. *Goddamn it!*

Clejani lies some thirty kilometres of bad road south-west of Bucharest. Backtrack to earlier in the day and I'm heading there in a Dacia, Romania's answer to East Germany's Trabant. Our driver is Ioniţa, a Clejani native now living in Bucharest. I'm accompanying Stephane Karo and his wife and daughter. Karo – lanky, chain-smoking, wry, Belgian – is the man who put Clejani on the world's musical map after drifting here in 1989. Appropriate really as, back then, Clejani was off all maps – Ceauşescu, rabid with paranoia, had banned maps of Romania, so Karo wandered through the dog days of communism, a towering, French-speaking drifter who strode into peasant villages and began miming a violinist, desperate for directions to this musical Shangri La.

Clejani should have been easy to find; for generations it was celebrated across the Wallachian plains as home to lautări – the name once given to the trade of fiddler that's evolved to specify the Tzigane caste of professional musicians. These lautări having been called upon to play at weddings, funerals and festivities for as long as human memory recalls. And for decades Romanian ethnomusicologists have written books and made recordings of Clejani's lautări. In 1986 musicologist Speranţa Rădulescu took a Swiss colleague, Laurent Aubert, to Clejani. Aubert recorded a six-man band and arranged for Ocora, an ethnographic label funded by Radio France, to release a CD in 1988. The CD, *Roumanie – Musique Des Tsiganes De Valachie*, is what Karo had chanced upon and as he repeatedly listened to the album, soaking up unknown pleasures, he became determined to seek out these master musicians who were buried way, way behind the Iron Curtain.

By the autumn of 1989, Romanians were sour, hungry, fearful, especially when it came to giving directions to rank strangers. Thus it took Karo two weeks to find Clejani. Arriving, he found the village home to both Romanian and Roma, the latter living where the road stops being sealed and turns to loose metal. And once directed correctly to Tzigania – Gypsy town – he stood in the street and began performing his violin mime. *Look, look, people! What a sight! A giant playing an invisible violin! Yes! Really! Some crazy Gadje who's as tall as a tower! And he wants music!* Lautari began grabbing instruments, throwing open doors, leaping fences, slogging through the mud, oblivious to the snow, rushing to encounter him, sure the stranger was hiring musicians for a wedding. *Me! No, me! Da, da, me!* The giant seemed oblivious to the Gypsies thronging around him. Karo kept miming and mouthing *Neacşu Nicolae. Neacşu Nicolae. Who? What? Never heard of him!*

Anyway, I'm a much better musician. Don't listen to him, you need accordion, not violin! Me! Yes, me!

Karo had not walked many kilometres, endured cold beds, foul food and worse weather to embrace the first lautări fiddling in front of him. So he stood there, letting snow settle on his shoulders and tint his moustache. Eventually the commotion calmed and some of Tzigania's women pointed him in the direction of a ramshackle house. Inside, staring out at the commotion, sat an old man, gummy and toothless, leather-skinned, black eyes hard as opals, violin clutched in hand. Could this, wondered Karo as he strode forward, be the man I have been searching for?

Nicolae Neacşu was having similar thoughts. Could this, he wondered, be my angel who has come to this God-forsaken hole to bring me, Nicolae, back from the dead? Nicolae Neacşu was sixty-five in 1989. Or sixty-six. Or sixty-seven. It depended on memory, how much he had drunk. Not that it mattered. Having survived fascism and communism, war and famine, Neacşu was established as a master lautar. But by 1989 he was earning a meagre living selling contraband cigarettes. Throughout the 1960s and 1970s he played at weddings, funerals, restaurants, the baksheesh earning him more than a factory or farming job. And in 1986 when the Swiss man and Speranţa assembled a taraf it was Nicolae who they had as lead musician. He even got sent to Switzerland to play his music. The Gadje sat and applauded. Nicolae could not quite believe Switzerland. A land so clean and wealthy...so close to paradise...so far from Romania.

When Nicolae returned to Clejani he talked incessantly of this land of milk and honey, cuckoo clocks and pink people, until all had enough and would flee when they saw him. And as the cancer called Ceauşescu chewed on Romania, people lacked money for musicians. So when the Gadje giant sat down, brushed the snow off his shoulders, lit a cigarette and motioned for Nicolae to play he drew the bow across his ancient violin, smiled a toothless smile, and knew the God of the Gypsies was a kind and just one.

From this chilly beginning took flight the extraordinary saga of Taraf de Haïdouks. As soon as Ceaușescu fell Karo returned to Clejani and assembled a thirteen-piece band. He named them: 'Taraf' is an Arabic word believed to have arrived in Romania with the Ottomans. It means celebration players. Haïdouks were romanticised outlaws who, in Balkan Robin Hood style, robbed the rich and gave to the poor. The 'de' suggests the French connection that was sealed when they flew to Belgium.

Whooomp! Hit a pothole that felt like a landmine. Ionița shrugs and steers us back on course. 'That's our signal we're getting close to Clejani,' says Karo.

Clejani's nondescript, inanimate: bleak houses, steel kiosks selling anything going and concrete drinking holes plastered with Coca-Cola, beer and cigarette ads. Ionița explains how, in the sixteenth century, a Serbian prince ruled the area and built a church, school and language institute for diplomats and merchants. These days Clejani's little more than a dusty speck in an arid land yet memories of former glories arose when, during Milošević's wars, a Serbian envoy appeared in Clejani to call on the mayor and claim the prince's bones.

'It was a wealthy Serbian guy named Miša Anastasijević who owned much of Wallachia and he developed Clejani,' says Ionița. 'Miša brought his Gypsy slaves, who were singers and musicians, and gave them houses and they were under his custody. We've been settled here ever since, families of musicians.'

The Romanian part of the village feels desolate, closed for winter. A dirt road signals we're entering Tzigania. We arrive and there's no one about. Everyone is hibernating, avoiding the cold and damp and fog and mud. Through the mist people start to appear, kids oblivious to the cold, a woman wrapped in a shawl, a jolly drunk Romanian hoping for a free drink. Pretty soon we're surrounded. Which is to be expected when you're riding with the King. Having radically changed the fortunes of many Clejani households, Karo commands attention. And his wife is Margareta, daughter of Taraf accordionist Marin. We decamp to Marin's house for coffee and Fanta. Word's quickly out that Stephane's in town and throughout the day a trickle of musicians, friends, admirers, wannabes, hustlers and hangers-on will drop by. Marin's wife attends to the household menagerie of pigs, cattle, geese, cows, chickens, goats, cats and dogs. Marin's ever attentive to guests while tickling his granddaughter.

Initially, there seems to be little in Marin's house to suggest he's part of a major musical outfit who appear in films and sell-out international tours: the toilet remains outdoor and water's drawn from the well. Yet the house, made from concrete, is solidly built, warm, well furnished. Much of Clejani's Roma population live in sub-standard housing, structures barely pledging shelter during winter. Marin's house is professionally wired up for electricity consumption; many residences rely on illegal cables run from the street's few wonky power lines.

Caliu, the band's flamboyant violinist, invites everyone to his house. He's the closest Taraf have to a star, his dark features and speed-demon playing making him the classic Gypsy violinist of lore. Caliu looks like he's just arrived from India, and his house, like his playing, speaks loudly: painted gold and lime; the exterior's decorated with the kind of abstract print patterns found throughout Hindu art. Inside, dense rugs cover the walls alongside religious kitsch and glossy photos of semi-naked women. Puppies appear from everywhere. Thick Turkish coffee is served. A bottle of vodka's opened. Sweet white wine poured. Caliu's teenage daughter speaks remarkably good English – none of the Taraf can utter more than one or two phrases – learned from concentrating on US TV shows and asks for money, 'to go to the disco'. The TV is on, people play music, everyone smokes, sausage and pickled peppers are served. This is the comfy Romanian winter experience.

Marius, one of the Taraf's younger musicians, invites me to visit a family further down the street. The home, essentially a single-room structure made of mud, houses a double bed and simple wood stove. The roof barely contains the structure and part of the front wall has crumbled to let in the elements. A smiling, if drawn, young woman lives here with her two small children. 'Very poor,' says Marius. 'Very difficult. The people here have little. This is the fate of the Gypsy.' I'm not sure if he wants me to hand over a donation or just observe how badly the non-musicians in Clejani live. I look at him. He shrugs. We leave.

For more than a decade a floating pool of musicians have made up the touring/recording Taraf, the core regulars earning a very tasty income. Yet no investment, no development, appears in Clejani. Marius is dressed in designer gear – what his coat cost would cover repairs to the hovel's structure. And as his father is Ion Manole, one of the Taraf's founding violinists, the family's not short of cash. But community spirit, beyond music and family, isn't evident. I reconnect with Ioniţa and suggest that the musicians should develop Clejani. The look he gives me is somewhere between sad and contemptuous.

'The fact is the guys from the Taraf are a special kind of people. One day they have $1,000, the next nothing. They live for today. Some of them live at the same level as they did in 1990. Others support up to twenty people.'

Ioniţa's a trained accountant who's escaped Clejani – purchasing a Bucharest apartment – and values education and a work ethic. If his former neighbours are too stupid and lazy…to hell with them.

'I shifted to Bucharest because these village schools, they're no good, and in Clejani some people get very big heads. I want my children to get a good education – my father emphasised that I had to study and, believe me, sometimes it was very hard. I would play a wedding all weekend and then have to be in school on Monday morning. Back in Ceaușescu's time you were obliged to have a work place, you couldn't just be a musician. No job? Then you go to prison. But not one of the lautări went to work. Instead, I had them all down as working for me because I was the accountant of an agricultural association. The Mayor of Clejani was actually managing them and the president of the agricultural association was a friend and a fan. So whenever we were checked on it was fine.'

By the late 1980s a decline in weddings and Speranța Rădulescu's refusal to have accordion on her recordings left Ionița dispirited.

'Speranta wanted only old guys and no accordion. She considered accordion to be a very modern instrument. She didn't like the big cimbalom either, only the little one. Those ethno-musicologists are crazy, telling us musicians what we can and can't play! Initially I didn't trust Stephane so I passed on the invitation to go to Belgium with the other musicians. I was running a disco-bar in Clejani and it was going well and I didn't want to give up my jobs. Then the others returned and told me about Brussels.'

They told him by leaving Romania you 'taste paradise'. Paradise consisting of plentiful second-hand clothes, TVs and umbrellas – violinist Costică returned with three hats on his head. This excitement at escaping into Europe is understandable: wandering through Clejani's muddy back streets is like slipping through time, catching the scent of a medieval Balkan community. In summer an idyllic rural vibe surrounds the village as horse-drawn carts trot past, groups of women weave in front of their houses and maize dries in small tee-pee formations. But winter brings pneumonia and emphysema to those stranded here and cloaks my visit in melancholy: Nicolae Neacșu passed into the next world on September 3, 2002, and while the band have kept going his crab-like presence is missed both on stage and in the village.

Ion Manole, long retired from the Taraf, followed him six months later saying, 'Nicolae is calling me from the other world.'

They were funny old men, veterans of Tarafs rooted in the nineteenth century that featured violin, Pan pipes, cobză (oud), and small cimbaloms, men whose haunted eyes and fear of the modern world meant they still possessed the shadowy presence of wandering Gypsy troubadours from centuries past. Pan pipes now only exist in formal Romanian folk orchestras while the cobză has disappeared. And with the passing of Ion and Nicolae there goes a connection to a vintage Romania and the lautari who made it dance.

I visited Ion once in Clejani and he tried to sell me his violin. Nothing new in this: the Taraf hustle audiences for baksheesh, busk out front of venues and offer instruments on stage to the highest bidder. But his gesture had a sad edge. It was spring 2000 and Ion, though retired due to hearing problems, was still on wages. Yet he looked mournful, gutted of spirit, and kept on talking about his poverty which made no sense. Most likely family members had swallowed his earnings. And without his role in the Taraf he was fading. Nicolae was made of tougher stuff and played right up to the end. On stage in Yverdon, Switzerland, he announced this was to be his last concert and he would now go home to die. A week later in Clejani – sixth sense or instinct? – Nicolae Neacşu turned to dust.

The funeral of Neacşu was a perfect example of the Taraf symbiosis of celebration and sadness: the musicians set up outside Nicolae's house, playing throughout the night while female relatives stand guard over the coffin, swatting flies and burning candles. Nicolae, dressed in his finest suit, crucifix in hand, trilby placed on coffin's edge, looks only a little more grey than usual. Caliu leads the Taraf; weeping, he serenades Clejani's primeş (master violinist) with eloquent violin flourishes. In the morning the Taraf reassemble and the music continues. As the sun shines it could almost be a festival, smiling children surrounding the musicians. Then an Orthodox priest arrives and all is silence. He says words over the coffin. A loaf of bread with a long, thin, burning candle planted in its centre is held aloft during chants in front of the house. The coffin's then lifted into a horse-drawn cart and literally hundreds of people, all of the inhabitants of Tzigania, friends from surrounding villages and Bucharest, international Taraf associates and a large village band, accompany the cart to Clejani's church. A young man carrying a large wooden cross strides in front of the procession. The coffin is carried into the church and a simple wooden cross with 'Nicolae Neacşu 1924–2002' roughly painted on it is placed at the head of the coffin. Friends, family and Taraf members kiss Nicolae goodbye. Cacurică, ancient master of the small cimbalom and Nicolae's longest serving musical partner, is distraught. On to the cemetery where the band strike up again and Stephane Karo, aghast at losing his mentor, this oracle of Romanian Gypsy musical lore, is bowed and pale. The sun shines brightly and, I note, everyone is in casual wear. Nicolae's wake carries on well into the night, all the lautar in Clejani striking up when the spirit takes them.

Nicolae's primitive genius is best demonstrated on 'Balada Conducătorului' (Ballad of the Dictator), a traditional epic poem – a favoured Balkan ballad form – over which he improvised new words about the fall of Ceauşescu. Recorded only months after the tyrant was toppled, it opens with Marinel Sandu weaving a soft, mesmerising pattern from his small cimbalom. Neacşu strikes his violin up, tearing holes in space, letting notes creek and crack, then slowly tells the tale of the fall of Ceauşescu, his voice both harsh and gummy. He stops singing, bows the violin and begins to tug on a horse hair attached to the instrument's bottom string, creating a sound like, well, the earth opening and closing. Tony Gatlif included the Taraf in his 1993 film *Latcho Drom* (Good Journey). The film follows the Roma migration from Rajasthan's deserts to Andalucia's slums via carefully staged musical performances. The Taraf's performance – one of Neacşu and Sandu, the other an exuberant village gathering – helped propel them into large concert halls across Europe, the US, Latin America and Japan.

While still wearing nylon shirts and slacks the Taraf became widely celebrated, ethnic chic, hired by fashion designers and rich art patrons. Yehudi Menuhin, who knew something about violins, was voluble in his praise. While Johnny Depp exclaimed, 'These guys can play a music which expresses the most intense joy. They are among the most extraordinary people I have ever met.'

Depp got to meet them on the set of British director Sally Potter's 1998 movie *The Man Who Cried*. He plays a Gypsy the way Western actors tend to – pouting, intense, monosyllabic…Joaquin Cortes without the flamenco moves. Taraf are token ethnic colouring. The film's kitsch melodrama, an art-house turkey. But the Depp connection benefited the band. Not that they knew who Johnny was when he requested an audience. 'Who is Johnny Depp? I am Costică!' exclaimed the beefy violinist. When Depp subsequently flew them out to Hollywood to serenade him while he imprinted his palms in Sunset Boulevard cement the Taraf came to rate him considerably higher.

'Am-er-i-ca! So big! So far from Romania!' enthuses Marin. 'Here, there is nothing. In America, everything. Hilton Hotel. Sunset Boulevard. Johnny Depp. Thousands of people arrive. Police everywhere. Very good!'

The band's only discontent with their Stateside popularity is the matter of where to smoke – a real problem for musicians seemingly born with fags between fingers. They were then embraced by Californian pointy-heads Kronos Quartet who recorded and toured with Taraf. This proved a variable spectacle: the Gypsies tried to hold back and play formally but once the spirit caught them they'd take off, leaving Kronos behind and bewildered. KQ had learned the Taraf tunes in the classical manner of writing them out on sheet music. Yet the Taraf can't read music and never play a piece the same way twice. Thus fitting their freeform style to the Quartet's classical formalism proved near impossible.

'That was a joke,' says Ioniţa of the collaboration. 'We were forced to learn our music as it was on the CD but we always play as we feel. The Americans, they didn't understand that and Nicolae, he was a tricky guy, he wasn't about to hand them his secrets.'

And what secrets: on stage Neacşu was the band's anchor; his irreverent approach to form and tone, ability to express infinite sadness and ecstasy, would bring the music home after Caliu got too flashy. Offstage he was humble, good-humoured, especially when talking violin.

'We were very poor,' he recalled for the *Honourable Brigands* album sleeve notes. 'When my father died, I was very young, my mother went to work in the tobacco fields so she could afford to buy me a violin. She's the one who taught me music, in bed in the evenings. She hummed "la-la-la" and I copied. Later, in Tzigania, I started playing for the girls. You don't learn this job, you steal it. A true lautar is one who, when he hears a tune, goes straight home and replays it from memory. The one who plays it certainly won't teach you! Yes, the violin is light in your hand but heavy to learn. Like mathematics.'

You don't learn this job, you steal it: as the Taraf's youngest member once legged it from Brussels with the takings from a European tour Nicolae's statement carries a greater irony than he surely imagined.

Neacşu lived long enough to participate in the Taraf's triumphant Band of Gypsies homecoming concerts in December 2000. Karo, accompanied by engineer Vincent Kenis, had produced three superb studio albums – 1991's *Musique des Tziganes de Roumanie*, 1994's *Honourable Brigands, Magic Horses and Evil Eye*, 1998's *Dumbala Dumba*. The first two albums captured the Taraf's core repertoire, their ability to play hard and fast and soft and slow, to sing sad, to sing saucy, to sing of tyrants falling and haidouks robbing, to make music like no one else on the planet. *Dumbala Dumba* extended this with guest appearances from female singers, lautări from the village of Mirsa and percussionist Napoleon, a Ursari famous for beating out startling rhythms on barrels, chairs, spoons (and for naming his children Billclinton, Schwarzenegger et al.). The title track, sung by Viorica Rudareasa, is one hundred and thirty seconds of Gypsy joy.

> Dumbala Dumba
> Margareta, do not flee
> Come press yourself against me
> So we can have some fun
> Dum de dum de dum
>
> My love is a big boss
> He sells and takes no loss
> He sells it to the pretty ones
> In exchange for chewing gum
>
> I may be small, but I am sweet
> I'll wear shoes with high heels
> And my skin may be too brown
> But I've got talent, I've been around.
>   (translation Tongues Untied)

While each Haïdouk album sold over 20,000 copies – solid for European ethnic music artists – they played for much larger concert audiences. So Karo decided to release a live album. But it wasn't to be any ordinary live album. The Taraf may have won over the West but back in Romania they remained unknown beyond Clejani. So why not celebrate their success with two concerts at the Arcub, an Art Deco hall tucked behind the Intercontinental Hotel? Record the

Music school
Clejani style

Photo: Klaus Reimer

concerts, get Tony Gatlif to film it, fly in international media and treat the whole thing as a huge party. Naturally, I had to attend.

Bucharest in December…it redefines the term 'grim' and the expected chaos is already under way when I arrive: Gatlif's had a heart attack so sent his twenty-two-year-old daughter Elsa along to shoot things, Stephane's face is horribly swollen after a dispute with a taxi driver and he appears to be near meltdown, the Arcub's management are trying to cancel the concerts having realised they are a Gypsy event, citing 'fear of damage to venue', a Japanese journalist has been robbed on arrival in Bucharest, food poisoning and flu rampant…Still, things can be sorted out, a little baksheesh here, a phone call there, lots of vodka…all is under way. Michel Winter, Karo's business partner, announces the Kočani Orkestar (minus Naat Veliov) will be guests, the concerts being an opportunity to cross-promote Balkan acts.

Saturday afternoon finds everyone in minibuses heading for Clejani. On arrival, the Kočani Orkestar are visibly unimpressed, this kind of rural poverty being what they left behind generations ago, and I sense they can't wait to get back to Macedonia. The village's communal hall ('barn' being more accurate) is where Ioniţa used to hold his discos. Various Taraf members and other Clejani lautări play, we're served damp salad and scorched mutton – in Romania no one, not even the Roma, can cook – and the Kočani Orkestar play a brass blast which leaves the locals both impressed and/or confused, this type of Gypsy music being alien to Clejani. Three teenage girls get up and belly dance and several journalists stand and twitch, the whiteboy shuffle. Clejani's kids whoop, obviously finding Gadje dancing hilarious.

I drag Bogdan and Mihai along, both less than enthusiastic about going to see a Gypsy band. They walk away, if not converted, certainly feeling very humble. 'Those guys are really good,' says Bogdan. 'Really, really good.' Which they were. But not great. The concerts were punctuated by sound problems – microphones feeding back, horns distorting – and the band, while playing as brilliantly as ever, were more self-conscious because of the cameras, the media blitz, so lacked the eccentric energy that normally marks their gigs as amongst the very best. Still, it was great to see the Taraf rocking Romania and those connected to the band had a really good time, dancing down the aisle and whooping with wild, Gypsy joy.

This time in Clejani and the climate is as bitter as that seminal weekend. Ioniţa is tiring of Caliu's chatter – internal politics arise – so he, Costică and I drop in on the cosy home of lead cimbalom player Dimitru 'Cacurică' Baciu. Alongside Nicolae and Ion, Cacurică is one of the musicians Aubert and Rădulescu first chanced upon and he's never been out of the Taraf line-up, his magical way with the small cimbalom he wears around his neck being central to their sound. Cacurică's close to seventy, could pass for twenty years older, tiny, bald, pot-bellied, a Gypsy hobbit. The small house he and his wife occupy is bright and cosy, perfect for Balkan Bilbos. Cacurică insists on serving us sour homemade wine. Ioniţa, has life changed much since the fall of Ceauşescu?

'Nothing's changed.'

'Revolution? Phffft!' adds Costică.

Of course, a great deal has changed but everyone I encountered, whatever ethnicity, spoke with deep pessimism about 'democracy'. 'It was a coup, not a revolution,' many say of an uprising whose aftermath found The Great Leader and wife executed while his former henchmen dressed themselves in shiny, Nu-Democrat cloaks and held on to power. Current President Ion Iliescu was a Ceauşescu stooge who ruled Romania with a mix of brutality and incompetence from 1990 to 1996. He took four years off and returned to power in 2000. Revolution? Phffft! This and the bitter taste left by thirteen years of social and economic turbulence mean politicians are held in contempt and money's all people believe in.

As twilight unfolds we return to Caliu's and the atmosphere resembles a Brueghel painting of a village winter celebration. Men sing and get drunk, children chase dogs and dance, teenagers flirt, animosities surface – a musician now excluded from the Taraf stands at Caliu's gate and shouts abuse – cornbread, boiled eggs and more wine forthcoming. Poorer citizens beg cigarettes, families gather their kids and demand 'Photo! Photo!', a woman wrinkled as a walnut and on the wrong side of sixty offers to hump me for a fistful of lei. The musicians think this is hilarious and tell me she's good. She responds with a thrust of her hips. No? Cigarette then? Sure. And a few lei, da? The atmosphere is easy and everyone is having a very, very good time. Finally I realise Stephane is surely waiting for me with his family at Marin's house. Make my excuses. Leave. I know the way. Straight across this puddle.

Mahala Blues 3:
Who is Killing Balkan Music?

The gold eye shone, not with the practicality of sex, so necessary to its survival, but the promise of it that promised other things, another life, deliverance.

James Dickey, *Deliverance*

Sunday morning awakening...hog breath...vinous mind... wrecked on the shores of Bogdan and Dani's sofa. Such is the Bucharest Saturday night experience. Bogdan and Dani live with Dani's mum – a pensioner who has a one million lei (£20) monthly pension to exist on – in Crângași, a characterless working-class district in north-west Bucharest. Determined to face the day, I trail Dani and her mum as they head to the local street market. The meat's indoors, everything else is laid out beneath a porous ash sky. 'Everything else' being root veggies alongside bruised apples and pears. Righteous men/poor town? Bucharest keeps testing that theory. Weary pensioners proffer bowls of potatoes. An old man, wrapped in a threadbare smoking jacket, moustache neatly trimmed, scavenges for discarded produce. Chill wind whips the air. Both shoppers and stallholders wear the tired, watery eyes that accompany constant struggle. A tiny café space is busy serving vodka shots alongside café natural. Men, their faces creased and tight, play blackgammon and share cigarettes, each puff savoured. Grey, grey, grey. Sky and people and food and cityscape, all is grey. The Roma are everywhere, weary pockets of colour: men vend

Photo: Garth Cartwright

Bucharest: Out on the street

vegetables, women shoes and clothes, their daughters stand with trays of parsley. And the sons, the sons sell cassettes.

Cassettes are how music still circulates in the Balkans. Especially in Romania where only a select few can afford CDs. Forget about downloading music: who owns a computer? Cassettes are sold everywhere: in tiny kiosks beside bus and train stations, amongst narrow shops in the main streets and, especially, in markets like this one. Here youths set up tables and racks loaded with cassettes. What's on offer is near 100 per cent manele – a Romani expression for 'good thing' – and the true sound of Romania today. They might have some traditional (Gabi, Romica) Gypsy cassettes and the odd Western act (Spice Girls, Baha Men). But these largely gather dust. It's manele the lei are spent on.

Cassette stands are predatory places and the atmosphere around them is similar to that in Soho specialist music shops: think you know your shit? Are you hard enough to shop here? Seeing I don't speak the language and have little idea of what's hot manele wise this ain't the easiest task. Then I encounter Remus. Remus

Romanian music
megastore

Photo: Garth Cartwright

speaks some English and doesn't proffer the evil eye while I skim cassettes. Huge relief. At least 50 per cent of what he offers are cassettes by Adrian 'Copilul' Minune or Nicolae Guța. The rest are less famous singers and manele compilations whose covers feature semi-naked women so letting you know the music's 'hot'. Hip-hop, R&B and dancehall all employ the same imagery, the international proletariat obviously unable to resist shelling out for anything decorated with big breasts.

Adrian 'Copilul' Minune I recognise from *Gadjo Dilo*. 'Copilul' means 'the child' and, apparently, for several years most people did think he was a fat kid as opposed to a height-restricted adult. Nicolae wears the kind of moustache Freddie Mercury once favoured. Cast my mind back to Camberwell. Taking time out from wiping windscreens, one of the squeegee Gypsies was flogging lame street rag *The Big Issue* outside the supermarket when I strolled past, Fanfare Ciocărlia on the CD Walkman. I bought the *Issue* then tried to strike up a conversation. 'Romania?' 'Da.' 'Tzigane?' 'Da.' Pass the headphones. The initial look on her face was one of confusion. Finally, having worked out they were singing in Romani, she smiled. 'Romania music! Gypsy music!' Yup. Fanfare Ciocărlia. Good, innit? She looked blank then said, 'Gypsy music. Adrian. Guţa. Da!'

The difference between what the West's world music industry sells as Gypsy music and what the Roma listen to back in the Balkans can be huge. Sure, in Serbia Šaban is King and across Macedonia Esma reigns. But this is akin to African Americans acknowledging James Brown and Aretha Franklin. Don't mean they're listening to them. And in Romania the breach seems wider than anywhere else. Fulgerică is respected but he's no pop star while Fanfare Ciocărlia and Taraf de Haïdouks exist only for Western audiences. That they play superior Gypsy music, rooted in tradition, means nothing. The local Roma aren't listening. What they want is Adrian. And Guţa.

'Guta can do traditional and he can do manele,' explains Remus. 'I think he tried the traditional in the West but decided to stay in Romania where he must sing manele. We call Adrian "the King" and Guţa "the Emperor" because we love them both.'

Adrian is the don, his cassettes easily outnumbering Nicolae's. They've cut numerous duet cassettes which feature their heads badly Photoshopped onto the bodies of Formula 1 and Speedway drivers. Got to chuckle – I can't imagine more unlikely-looking pop idol material. Both also appear on the Miss Piranda 2003 compilations. Miss Piranda is Romania's Gypsy beauty queen/celebrity event of the year: top manele stars serenading the babes. With cassettes costing a quid each I pick up a selection: current manele hits, Adrian's greatest, Nicolae in concert. And a couple of anonymous traditional efforts. Then I head over to where Henry's staying.

The mahala Henry stays in is situated in the south-west of the city. There's a dozen or so mahalas around Bucharest and this is one of the smaller ones with forty or so families existing here. First impressions suggest the mahala's ostensibly poorer than Crângaşi – mud streets, craters, epic puddles, horses tethered outside houses, rabid mongrels behind gates – yet the houses vary from simple structures to large, spacious environs. And everyone has some semblance of a garden. The mahala reflects the inhabitants' move from country to city and Bucharest's authorities have left it to take shape as such.

Henry's initial involvement with Romanian Gypsy music came through Moldavia's Fanfare Ciocărlia. Having bagged the world's hottest brass band he shifted south, searching for new talent. Around Bucharest he found dozens of musicians. One of them, the percussionist Nicolae Ioniţa, he managed to smuggle into Fanfare Ciocărlia. 'They were all jamming at a party and when there was a break I said to Fanfare "What do you think of Nicolae?" and they said "He's great!" so I said "Well, we need a percussionist. Let's use him." That's the way you have to be to make deals with Gypsies. No hard line decisions, instead sneak around them.' It helps that Henry got Nicolae a gig as Henry married Tanţica, Ioniţa's daughter, seven years ago. Ioniţa is lautări, originally from Clejani. He owns a spacious, unfussy house with lots of bedrooms to accommodate his extended family.

I arrive to find everyone returning from church. Two months ago Florin, one of Ioniţa's nephews, and Minodora got married: Orthodox ritual dictates the couple return and once again repeat vows. You know, just in case the honeymoon heat has been fading...Cold cuts, bread, sweet white wine, vodka and Coca-Cola are all placed on the table and introductions made. Florin and Aurel were, it turns out, members of Rom Bengale, a contemporary Gypsy band Henry managed a few years back. By all accounts they were good, very good, heirs to Taraf and

Fanfare. But they were young and it went to their heads. And into their veins.

Bucharest is on the heroin trail that starts in Afghanistan and ends in West Europe's morgues, jails and methadone clinics. Bucharest, with its Mafias and desperation, is a perfect place for unloading excess stock and Rom Bengale collectively succumbed to the needle. The band fell apart. Families were torn apart. Members were busted and jailed. Aurel and Florin avoided the worst but still had to cope with addiction, withdrawal and the slow, unforgiving process of piecing their lives back together.

Henry puts on the CD of Mitsoura, a contemporary Hungarian Gypsy band based around the unique vocals of Mitsou. He's impressed. Florin and Aurel aren't. Mitsoura sound more Bjork than Balkan; Aurel whispers 'Woody Woodpecker' then rummages through my cassettes and pulls out Ceca, puts it on and immediately he and Florin are happy. 'It's kitsch,' says Henry, disapproving. 'She sings good. The arrangements are good,' replies Aurel. 'It's pop music, not even good pop music,' says Henry. 'The borders are all broken down now,' offers Florin. Nicolae enters the room and the discussion turns to the collapse of Rom Bengale and Romanian Gypsy music.

'Rom Bengale were a big power and a good idea,' says Nicolae, 'but the world wasn't ready for it. Maybe now. But now is too late.' Aurel now plays in the Mahala Rai Band, a grandiosely named project Taraf entrepreneurs Winter and Karo have launched with *Electric Gypsyland* – a remix CD featuring DJ interpretations of Mahala Rai Band, Taraf de Haïdouks and Kočani Orkestar. Straight-up: I loathe remix albums. Now, I love Jamaican dub – Scratch, Tubby, Fattis & co.: respect – which invented the genre to extend reggae's sonic cosmology. But the European remix album was a bad 90s phenomenon, inept (con)fusions aimed at milking punters swept up in the decade's rave craze, and *Electric Gypsyland*'s no exception. The Balkan grooves have been filtered out until all that's left is the drudgery of the EU dance floor. In Serbia Vanjus, of Modern Quartet (who remixed Kočani Orkestar), informed me 'I fucking hate folk music so I stripped everything but the clarinet' of MQ's effort. His comment provides a succinct review of the CD. Even Aurel expresses no interest in *Electric Gypsyland*. 'For the West,' he says and shrugs. Nicolae disapproves of both the remix album and The Mahala Rai Band. 'It's shits like you that are killing off the traditional Gypsy music,' he tells Aurel. 'If I only make a copy of the old ways, of Taraf, of Fanfare, I wouldn't go anywhere,' replies Aurel. 'I have to take the music forward.'

Manele also raises temperatures. Henry loathes it. Aurel suggests Henry accept it. 'Manele is a phenomenon and it can't be stopped by anybody. In the beginning it was invented by Gypsies as a party music and later adopted by Romanians. It's a universal music that can be performed by all ages, from very young to very old. The old music, the traditional music, is done. So nobody asks for the old music.' Florin simply raises a pierced eyebrow and asks, 'Who is killing Balkan music? MTV or MTV?'

Florin's a singer and accordionist whose current income depends on wedding work. At the moment this means he lives on around 100 euros a month. His wife, Minodora, is articulate, confident and obviously believes in Florin's promise. She's also very beautiful in the classic Indo-Roma manner, all Bambi eyes and ironic intelligence. Initially shy around this Gadje, she's soon firing questions at me, trying to work out what I'm doing here, a neighbourhood where white boys fear to roam. Do I only like Gypsies for their music? Or do I like them as they live? Am I married? How do I survive alone? Can I cook? Minodora's originally from Braşov, an attractive city in Transylvania. My brother, she says, is an entertainer but not a musician. I field a dumb guess: he's a bear-tamer. She laughs, emphasises NO! Turns out he's a professional stripper in an all-male Roma troupe who work out of Tokyo.

'Do your parents object?'

'Of course not, we are a modern family.'

'And you learned to speak English from TV?'

'Yes, I like action movies. Schwarzenegger and Van Damme.'

'But they hardly speak.'

'Hasta la vista, baby.'

We break to eat: roast pork, meatballs, mashed potato, pickled peppers and gherkins. There's much laughter about the church service with the priest getting Minodora to repeat that she will 'obey and serve her husband' when it's obvious she's the decision-maker. Being amongst the Roma I'm reminded how Indian they remain – nods of head, polite gestures, gentle smiles. Nicolae talks of his father, Pascale, a fabulous violinist who was selected for the original Taraf line-up but declined as he was scared of flying. Nicolae lives comfortably yet he's nostalgic for communism.

'During Ceaușescu it was better for Gypsies, especially for musicians. As a musician there was quite a big freedom and musicians had lots of jobs to perform at weddings and people had money to spend. The main part of the Gypsies had a better life than now. Everyone had a job and playing at weddings gave us additional money. Now we're happy if we get one wedding job a month. Back then we were often invited to go by plane to the coast to play for big weddings. We'd stay in nice hotels. Life was easier.'

'Most Gypsies liked communism because it gave them houses, paid them to have children,' adds Henry, who grew up in East Germany. 'They don't see the faults in the communist system as we do. Censorship never affected them as they had no desire to read Western literature or talk of politics. And when the revolution came Gypsies were the first to lose their jobs in the factories. Partly this was discrimination and partly as they were the least punctual workers. Not that your average Romanian is much better. And the Gypsy community here still doesn't put much emphasis on

Big hits…
Manele cassette

NICU va recomanda: Super Manele 2003 vol.2

Nicu Paleru
Vali Vijelie
Cristi Dules
Liviu Pustiu'
Florin Salam
Nicolae Guta
Nelly
Leonard
A-tentat feat. Samir
Claudia
Kamarad
Catalin Arabu'
Play A.J.
Adrian Copilul Minune

Photo: Garth Cartwright

education – musicians do, at least as far as learning musical skills – but the majority, their blood is not towards this system.'

The TV comes on and we watch a documentary on the rolling crisis that is Michael Jackson and his clan. How, I wondered, did this extended musical family feel about MJ's saga? 'Phewhhhh,' says Aurel, 'he's just gone crazy.' The others nod, saddened their original American idol is so tarnished. Soon the music is back on and Crenu, Nicolae's teenage son, is sifting through a suitcase full of manele cassettes. 'We call Adrian "The Wonder Boy",' he says. 'These days he is so famous he doesn't even play for the Gypsies any more, we can't afford him; he only sings at the Gadje weddings.'

Crenu puts on my Guča live cassette. On it the Timişoara-born singer works his way through a selection of manele hits, a couple of traditional folk numbers and a Romani version of 'My Way'. His voice is frantic, revved up over a synthesiser and violin backing. Everything sounds rushed and cheap, very twenty-first-century Romania.

Tales of manele singers who rose to great heights only to lose all in Bucharest's casinos are swapped. One took advances for weddings, blew the money and never appeared to sing. He's now destitute, an untouchable amongst outcasts. And a discussion gets under way about summer. During summer the extended Ioniţa and Uniţa musical families spread out over Western Europe, busking on the streets of Germany, Belgium, Holland, France, Spain, Austria, any nation where euros can be harvested and a tourist visa isn't required, working to entertain the Gadje with music as their ancestors have done for centuries.

'Music's native to Gypsies,' says Aurel, 'something coming from inside. And if Romania offers us nothing then we go elsewhere. We share our gift. Lucky Europe.'

Fanfare Ciocărlia:
Brass On Fire

It is not down in any map; true places never are.
Herman Melville, *Moby Dick*

Relief, baby, relief: we're leaving Bucharest. Florin and Minodora accompanying us, Henry manoeuvring through this battered, unforgiving city whose name translates without irony as 'joy'. Potholes make automobiles zig-zag capriciously, weary children surround us at intersections hoping to sell newspapers or beg a few lei, the sense that everything and everyone is coated in lead...As the metropolis dissolves into weather-beaten houses and the flat alluvial plains of Ialomiţa district extend in front of us I experience a sensation close to euphoria. Somewhere several hundred kilometres to the north-east is Zece Prajini, the invisible village of legend, a place not found on any map. A local musician, when asked once how to find it, cryptically suggested, 'He who searches for it probably sails right past. Unless he senses when to jump...' I like this concept, dropping off the radar screen, but can't quite get my head around the jumping.

Henry, what's this about jumping when sensing Zece Prajini?

'Well, Zece Prajini's built along a train line but the train doesn't stop there. And there's no sign marking it so for those who didn't have a car or motorbike, which is most of the residents, you have

Back in the day: Fanfare Ciocărlia

to wait until the train slows to take a curve and then jump off. Or on, if you are intending to catch the train.'

Zece Prajini is home to Fanfare Ciocărlia, currently the planet's hardest working, highest grossing Gypsy band. Their invisible village of Zece Prajini is in Moldavia, that much cleaved north-western region of Romania. Today a good chunk of Moldavia is incorporated into the Ukraine while a large, amoeba-shaped blob of territory is now the Republic of Moldova, Europe's poorest nation; one whose misery is compounded by an ethnic divide between Russian (placed there by the Soviets after WWII) and Romanian citizens. The latter dream of reunion with mama Romania but President Putin, that dark master of the East, will not hear of such.

Wintry acres of farmland spread in every direction, fallow but for ice and crows. On the horizon ghostly lines of poplars form a spiky spine. The motorway is remarkably smooth after Bucharest's broken roads. 'Of course it's a good road,' says Henry, 'the EU paid Italian engineers to design it and Italian workmen to build it.' No one, it appears, trusts the chaos of Romania. Henry drives with

Photo: Dragos Lumpan

Ioan makes a point

the speed and clean-precision moves of someone very familiar with Germany's autobahns but not for a minute does he let his concentration slip: the TV news is full of 'tragedie' and 'fatalitale', road-kill being a league Romania excels in. Easy to see why – wheezing trucks, ancient Dacias and horse and carts slow the traffic so leading to bouts of kamikaze overtaking. And at night drivers refuse to lower their lights from high beam. I slip *Iag Bari*, FC's third album, into the CD player. As the brass swells and roars Henry reflects on what led him to finding a lost village full of master musicians.

'I started to travel in Romania fifteen years ago and in 1996 a farmer told me of a village of brass musicians. This was new to me, that's why I went there, driving an old Ford, stopping and asking directions, until I crossed a railway line and pulled into the first house of the village to see where I was. It was Ioan Ivancea's house and he, it turned out, was one of the master brass musicians of

Zece Prajini. I told him I was curious to hear brass music and in a couple of minutes the complete village was outside. That's 400 people and 80 musicians. It was so amazing I ended up staying not one day but three months and assembling a brass band. Fanfare is a French word that's passed into Romanian and is used to describe a brass band. Ciocărlia, that's the Romanian for a lark's song. I returned to Germany and sold everything I had to make one tour.

'When I went back to the village to gather the musicians and get their visas the band realised I wasn't joking. It was 1996 and I managed to book ten concerts in forty days. As you can tell I was not very professional! It was a huge success but a financial catastrophe – thousands of marks lost! We paid the promoters and the band but nothing was left but debts for me. Still, it was the best forty days of my life. Two months later a radio station called me up and asked for the band. I told them it was not possible. They insisted they wanted to book the band for their world music festival. I made some calculations for visas, flights, hotels and fees and rang them back with what it would cost. Within two minutes they had agreed. This was the signal to make the band professional and I founded Asphalt Tango with my friend Helmut Neumann that day.'

Fanfare Ciocărlia have since gone on to release three fine albums – *Baro Biao*, *Radio Pascani*, *Iag Bari* – a live DVD, and have circled the globe many times. Arts festival in Adelaide, concert halls in Tokyo, techno clubs in Dresden, Fanfare know no limits to where and what they can play, their hard Balkan funk attracting punks, ravers, headbangers, suits…musical catharsis for all who dare engage with it. Years of playing weddings – Roma weddings lasting for days and Romanian weddings where you might end up receiving a beating if you don't know a popular tune – have lent Ciocărlia the ability to deliver a stunning brass blast.

We cross into Moldavia yet the landscape remains unchanged. Then a sea of power pylons spreads in front of us, giant, crab-like constructions slouching towards some communist Bethlehem. The metal forest recedes and again everything is tilled earth, bare vineyards, concrete viaducts, dead factories. Anslem Kiefer's sculptural paintings, thick with convulsive landscape and political imprint, could be modelled on this muddy Moldavian gloom. Occasionally a new outcrop of apartment buildings, disarmingly painted bright pastel colours, leaps out before we return to the black and brown, green and grey. Florin and Minodora are turning the backseat into a lurve zone, all cuddles, discreet kisses and giggles. Maybe it's something in the air: the poet Pushkin was exiled to northern Moldavia in 1821 only to fall in love with Zemfira, a Gypsy princess. What chance I'll inherit Pushkin's luck?

Romania's motorways are conscious of the twenty-first-century traveller – petrol stations sell soft drinks and sweets, occasional restaurants find the waiting staff dressed in 'authentic' peasant colours – but the villages we drive through are literally dying on the vine. This is a land where peasant farmers are denied access to EU markets and ignored by their own government (Romania didn't have an agricultural policy until 1998) and, once again, I'm recalling Mississippi's ruined delta hamlets. Rural settlements, all thin electric light and puffing chimneys, float in limbo, people shifting out, ghosts shifting in, dust in the wind.

The sense of absolute despair and imminent violence hangs heavier in the American air yet something wild lingers here too. Hard drugs, readily available weaponry, a diet of high-octane TV and low-fibre food, too much of nothing…how many generations of Balkan youth need be left to rot before their intolerance and hopelessness can match that of the US underclass? Florin, hugging Minodora in the backseat, is a reminder of how easy it is to stumble in Romania. He got lucky, found redemption. But other members of Rom Bengale, counting out the years in Romanian prisons, were less fortunate.

Darkness falls as we enter the small city of Roman, and fascist spectres burn my mind. During three foul nights in November 1940, Iron Guards massacred 4,000 Jews here and in Moldavia's capital of Iaşi, butchering many in the cities' abattoirs. Approximately 400,000 Romanian Jews were murdered here or in the death camps on Romania's borders. The Roma were also massacred, 70,000 being deported to death camps in Transdniestr, the chunk of Ukraine Hitler gifted Marshal Antonescu. Yet fascism still bubbles in tainted Moldavian minds: in October 2001, Ion Rotaru, Mayor of Piatra Neamţ, the city immediately west of Roman, announced he was going to force the city's Roma populace to relocate to a converted chicken farm six kilometres outside town where 'the black plague will be surrounded with barbed wire and watched by guards with dogs'. International reaction forced the Romanian government, busy applying for EU membership, to halt Rotaru's construction of what can only be called a concentration camp. As ever, Ro-*mania*.

Today in Roman there remains one synagogue. It is maintained by Roman's sole remaining Jewish citizen, an elderly man who still performs the cleansing and prayer rituals, so ensuring the synagogues are living spiritual temples. The synagogues may live but fascism effectively exterminated one of Europe's richest Jewish cultures. Interested parties, largely from outside Romania, come searching for traces of the klezmorim whose music once resonated across the region. And whom do they turn to so as to find these traces? Gypsy musicians.

Descending from the van, I seem to catch the too familiar scent of blood riding the bitter evening air. Not that we're in this nondescript city to check Holocaust history; Fanfare's Costică 'Cimai' Trifan lives here. Cimai's spacious apartment is furnished with large leather sofas and paintings of Jesus. The latter contrasts with Cimai's stage persona: goatee, blazing black eyes, incendiary trumpet solos, all suggesting a musical Mephistopheles. If Cimai's a tiger on stage he's a pussycat at home, pouring drinks, serving salami and reflecting in halting English on Fanfare's leap from village poverty to urban comfort.

'When we started touring Germany then Europe we were very, very surprised. Surprised at the audience reaction and surprised at the life people live. We are not used to being more than a few kilometres from our village. None of us had passports before Henry arrived. Life was difficult because the factories had closed and people did not have the money to put on weddings. But now we have seen the great cities and our village philosophies have changed.'

Cimai's unaware of klezmer influences in Fanfare's sound, suggesting, 'Local Romanian and Gypsy music are what I know. We steal a lot of musical styles – all Balkan countries, Bulgaria, Macedonia, Serbia – and we are able to transform radio hits.'

As for the Holocaust, Cimai simply shrugs. He's aware Moldavia's Jews and Roma suffered but no one directly from his family. And why talk about such tragedy? No good can come of such. As for everyday racism, he's unaffected but adds, 'There are lots of different Gypsies in Romania so I can't speak for all of them'. The Piatra Neamţ débâcle? Never heard of it. This is understandable: these musicians glean their information from TV news, a medium unlikely to show foreign criticisms of local lunatics. And, maybe, Fanfare, like so many Roma elsewhere, have developed psychic defences, blocking out the loathing Tziganes draw.

Pro-TV has a Romania Day special packed with local celebrities. The one Roma involved is, inevitably, Adrian Minune. Releasing up to twelve cassettes a year and singing at several weddings every weekend has made the Gypsy man-child wealthy and, when the show's host asks him how it feels to be rich, he replies, 'It's very good. I'm building two new houses in Şoseaua Kiseleff [Bucharest's most exclusive boulevard].'

Cimai's wife and Minodora serve dinner then retreat to eat with the children. A sliced tomato is added to complement the fried meats. On TV a rare event, a Romanian film, is showing. It's a comedy called *Carcear* (Cop) and stars the nation's most popular comedian, Mugur Mihaiesca. *Carcear* deals in a form of broad slapstick once beloved by British comedians. Florin and Cimai find it hilarious, Henry chuckles and I figure the language barrier is causing me to miss the punchlines. When I retire to the hotel bar, a solitary waiter maintains the ancient East European custom of expressing obvious discomfort at having to serve anyone. Back in my hotel room, MTV has a headbangers' special full of ugly Americans roaring about how much they suffer. Well, boo-hoo, you big heavy metal cry-babies. I sleep well, dreams full of Zece Prajini, the invisible village now tangible, almost in sight.

Morning: Henry and I are off early, leaving Florin and Minodora to sleep the sleep of newly-weds. Cimai is Minodora's uncle so they surely have much catching up to do without Gadje around. We drive out of Roman and leave the highway for a dirt road, passing through a landscape where little has changed in the last thirteen years. Actually, little here's changed in the last thirteen hundred years. Villagers walk their cows to the fields, a spidery forest covers the rising hills, water is drawn from wells, man and beast plough the land, geese dawdle down the track defiant of our four-wheeled incursion, puffs of smoke arise from cottages that look to have leaped from Brothers Grimm fairy tales, men cycle past wearing long overcoats and cachules (traditional peaked wool hats) on bicycles built in Chairman Mao's factories. The road rises steeply and soon we're sailing through cloud, a rising sun burning the mist away to reveal a rolling, tawny landscape over which hawks glide. While Bucharest was wet, the winter rains leaving swollen puddles across broken streets, northern Moldavia is yet to be scalded by storms. 'By this time of year the roads are often reduced to mud tracks and driving to Zece Prajini is extremely difficult,' says Henry. 'To have conditions like they are today...it's magnificent.'

Soon we're descending into the valley, passing a lake coated in ice, and I get my first sighting of Zece Prajini: squat houses made of mud, brick, concrete and tarpaper, many painted luminous colours, wells out front and a menagerie to the side of the house. Note more cows, goats, chickens and turkeys on the main road than humans. Country living? Deep country. We swing into Ioan Ivancea's house. Ioan's bleary, not long awake, wearing a shapeless Hugo Boss sweater, his big, jowly face cautiously welcoming, checking this new Gadje with pen and camera in hand. Marie, his wife of almost fifty years, offers a glorious gold tooth smile while continuing to husk maize. Marie and Ion look to have been shaped by the Moldavian clay, ingrained in the hills that loom above their valley. Recall Carla Thomas taunting Otis Redding with 'you country, straight from the Georgia woods' and think, yeah, Gypsy soul indeed. Breakfast follows: cold meat, hot soup, bread, coffee, vodka.

'Where would we be without Henry?' says Marie as we settle in. 'Without him this village would be dead.' Don't mistake this for an idle compliment; when Henry arrived in 1996 the village's brass bands had largely fallen into disarray: the economic collapse following the end of communism had cancelled extravagant weddings and few of the children showed any interest in learning an instrument. Now the hills around Zece Prajini are alive with the sound of music.

No one's sure how Zece Prajini became a laboratory for future Balkan funk but by the 1920s the region's German communities were dancing to waltzes and polkas: the Roma in this region of Moldavia found brass instruments more suitable than string instruments for fingers hardened by farming. Ioan suggests the Hungarians in the region liked spicy food and thus spicy music. Good theory but it fails to explain why the Romanian diet is so awful yet their music so tasty.

Ioan's two-room house is Gypsy Classic: green ceiling, yellow-patterned walls, rugs, tea towels, weavings and posters, images of Jesus and flowers, puppies and kittens, covering every surface. Marie cooks on a wood stove. Ioan's built a new house next to his old one but Henry's never seen him inside it. Instead, he and Marie appear ingrained in their original homestead, unable to shift what is a tiny physical distance but, perhaps, psychically a huge journey.

At sixty-four Ioan's Fanfare's patriarch, leader and sage. He broods on questions, aware Zece Prajini's oral history rests in him and his band. 'We are of the Ursari tribe, the bear-tamers' tribe,' says Ioan, 'but it is a very long time since anyone here tamed bears. Zece Prajini's name? Our ancestors were serfs for the local Boyar from Dagița [a neighbouring village] and were living on the steeps of the surrounding mountains. This was such a harsh existence, people struggled to carry water and firewood to the camp, so one day the tribe elder approached the Boyar and asked for a space in the valley. The Boyar was a good man and gifted them ten fields in the valley to live. Zece Prajini's name translates as Ten Fields. Since then all the families have farmed and played music. And always will.'

Ioan then adds, 'Unless the young generation of Gypsies turn to shit. I grew up with the music of Romica [Puceanu], Gabi [Luncă], Dona [Dimitru-Siminică]. This music is the real music of the Gypsies here in Romania. We only had it on records and tapes as we could never invite them to our weddings. The new music, it's bullshit.'

Sufficiently animated – he recalls with contempt how a recent French interviewer assumed Fanfare were still living in tents and caravans – Ioan starts on politics.

'On tour I was watching a programme about the Third World, countries much poorer than Romania, and it gets me thinking why this fucking Bush and – what's that asshole's name?'

'Blair?'

'Da. Blair. Bush and Blair, why are they invading Iraq and creating terror rather than helping the world's poor?'

Ioan may glean his information from TV yet his house is the only one I visit in Romania where television's electronic eye isn't a constant presence, a forcefield of trivial distraction. I'm yet to find a Romanian Gypsy musician who reads a newspaper and I don't see a book, not even a Bible, throughout my time in Zece Prajini. Ioan's never heard of Piatra Neamț's rabid mayor. I explain. He shrugs. Romanian fascism, he says, we've seen that shit before.

'During Antonescu's regime there was a very big hate of the Jewish and Gypsy people and a lot were deported to camps. A few people from this village were deported to camps. My father was forced to join the Romanian army and sent to fight on the Russian front. He served three years in a Gulag. I remember there being two Jewish people in this village in 1946 or '47. Their name was Leibovitch and they ran a bar. We never had much musical connection although in Roman there was a Jewish choir and sometimes we would play with them at funerals. During the Ceaușescu era a lot of Jewish people disappeared. Perhaps he sold them like he sold the Germans.'

And Transylvania's self-proclaimed 'Gypsy King' Florin Cioabă, what are your thoughts on him? Cioaba courts publicity, although generally of the more positive kind than what followed when he arranged the marriage of his twelve-year-old daughter in October 2003.

'He's a politician leading his party. We've never worked with him, we're different clans. As for the marriage of his daughter, our parliament was talking to him, saying, "You call yourself king but you don't put your daughter in school to get an education. What kind of king are you?" It's a stupid tradition to marry a girl so young. Who can respect you if you do things like this?'

The wedding attracted international attention and EU condemnation, so allowing Romanians to beat on the Roma ever harder. Thing is, only a minority of Roma still practise the child bride tradition, one linking them both to India and an older Europe where life was short so all married young. Also, as Cioabă noted, the EU complain loudly about his daughter's marriage yet remain content to let most Roma live a marginal, impoverished existence. And until Romania develops a civil society, one that engages Roma as equals, some Roma will defiantly hold on to such customs.

Ioan's farm grows maize, potatoes, beetroot, wheat. He owns 'a cow, a horse, five sheep, lots of chickens and turkeys'. While on tour he employs men to work the fields. His relationships with Romanians remain cordial but recently he's noticed spite.

'They start to get jealous and say, "Dirty Gypsies, they think they are very rich". If I go to their villages I wear old clothes and if they ask me how much money I earn I say, "As much as God allows me" but I never give a figure. But the younger generation of musicians ignore this. They show their cars and clothes.'

Henry offers a wan smile and suggests we visit Şulo, the tenor horn player. Şulo's from one of the village's poorest families and to make up for this he's proved adept at spending money: his house was Zece Prajini's first to have a bathroom and indoor toilet, something which had the whole village gawping and raised Ioan's ire: who needs a sit-down indoor toilet when you've squatted outside all your life? Drawing up at Şulo's, Henry does a double take – currently under construction is a two-storey house with balcony. Şulo saunters out, a Gypsy Jean-Paul Belmondo.

'What's this?' asks Henry.

'The old house is too small for two growing kids,' says Şulo nonchalantly.

We retire inside for more coffee and vodka and Şulo announces he's going to build a lake and fill it with fish. The TV is on but silent. Panjabi MC blasts out of the stereo. Marinela, Şulo's wife, attempts to serve us more food while her husband reflects on his good fortune.

'No other job in Romania provides this kind of money so it's absolutely possible to build as I do.'

Ralf Marschalleck's feature-length 2001 documentary *Iag Bari* (The Big Longing) filmed Fanfare at home and on tour: Şulo, in

Japan, takes a call from his wife announcing she's given birth to a son. 'Is he white or black?' he asks. 'Well, of course I ask that,' he says, laughing when I mention it. 'I was so happy to have a son and I want to know how much colour he has.' For the record, his toddler is dark-eyed and pale-skinned.

'*Iag Bari*'s OK but he missed the comedy of the village,' says Şulo. 'What Kusturica gets he didn't.'

We walk to Bar Soare, the musicians' local, which has Zece Prajini's only telephone. Beneath the chilly sun cigarettes are smoked, vodka drunk, and gossip swapped as members drop by to catch up with Henry. 'Every year there's discussions as to who's in the band,' says Henry. 'They all have a family member they want to bring in. A trip like this involves me sorting things out, smoothing things over.' Outside a small Orthodox church Şulo proudly announces this is the first 'Gypsy church in Romania', Fanfare having pooled funds to build the concrete block edifice. Does Şulo, I wonder, worry the local Romanians might hate him for his wealth? 'No, as musicians we are treated with respect. But others, they are considered' (he spits) '"Tzigane".'

Horse and carts pass on the way to the mill. Occasional cars and trucks cruise through. Only the local school director, in a bright yellow jeep, roars through, spitting dust and stones. The musicians curse him. 'He takes the children from the next village home as they live five kilometres from the school,' says Şulo. 'The children here live three kilometres from the school but they have to walk there and back. Because they are Gypsy.'

By 3pm the Carpathian Mountains, just to our east, are making their fierce presence known with a chill that cuts through scarf, fleece, thermals, boots. We retire to the house of Monel, Fanfare's bass tuba player. He's a big man given to great displays of affection towards his children and guests. Monel serves coffee, fizzy wine, cold meats, bread and a fermented cheese that's a local delicacy but, to the soft bellies of Henry and me, inedible. 'Sastipa!' he

says, teaching me the Romani expression for 'cheers'. In Zece
Prajini Romani is the first language but at school all lessons are
in Romanian. Henry tried to persuade Fanfare to build a bilingual
school instead of a church. No chance; he may be their manager
but God calls the big shots.

Ethno-musicologist Charles Keil studied the Roma musicians
of Iraklia, Greek Macedonia, noting their attitude to music was
that of craftsmen, not self-conscious artists. I mention this to
Monel. He thinks, then answers, 'I consider I'm an artist. When I
worked in the factory I was a worker. Now, firstly, I like what I do
– you can't say that in a factory – and it's a job that inspires us.'

Monel's not only inspired but seemingly indifferent to the cold,
regularly leaving the door open as he pops out for wood and wine
– Henry and I swap expressions for 'Do you live in a barn or what?'
Finally a large ceramic stove is fired as mist descends across the
valley. Suddenly an Orthodox priest is upon us, entering the room
holding a silver crucifix and waving a spray of basil soaked in holy
water. We all rise. In my time I've done some weird shit but this is
definitely my first experience of kissing a crucifix while a bearded
bloke in black has chanted prayers and slapped me with basil. The
priest pockets baksheesh, leaves; spiritually cleansed, we return to
wine and cigarettes.

Whatever blessings the priest uttered don't appear to be
working: Zece Prajini's electricity fails and the village is thrust
into darkness. We head to the house of Gişniac, the drummer, for
dinner, passing on the way a tiny mud house of eccentric beauty.
'The village's only violinist lives there,' says Henry. 'As you can see,
he doesn't get much work. Instead, he makes and sells brooms.'

Dinner is vegetable soup, bread, fried chicken, vodka and ţuica
– a local equivalent of grappa – eaten by candlelight and, blissfully,
TV-free. Florin appears, he and Minodora having arrived to stay
with her grandparents. We all trek back to their small house where
the conversation's about collecting tokens from packets of coffee: if

very lucky you will win a TV. Or even an apartment. Minodora's grandparents fancy a new TV. Minodora and Florin dream of owning an apartment. Minodora's grandfather is a handsome man, his features recalling Edmund Hillary and Robert Ryan, noble men of yesteryear. Henry asks him about playing the violin, which he once did, and he proceeds to tell his entire life history. The most interesting part concerns how, one night, he and his future bride got off a train and started to walk.

'After ten kilometres we reached my aunt's house. We could stay there. But Gypsy tradition insists that once we have spent a night under the same roof then we are "married". Yet if I am to marry this girl how can I be sure that she is a virgin? Young man, let me tell you how I did this. Listen carefully as one day perhaps you will wish to get married and this advice may be useful.'

Sweet reader, there are elements of Roma lore that can only be passed from mouth to ear. And this information remains such. So, perhaps, one evening we will encounter one another across a crowded bar or at a Balkan crossroads. And then I will whisper such secrets your way. But, till that time, the mysteries of the Gypsies must remain such.

Electricity returns and we can hear a jam session kicking off in Bar Soare. Florin would like to accompany us but, being married, he can no longer attend such events. Henry and I head out to find Fanfare's Daniel on saxophone, a keyboardist playing bass patterns and a drum kit so minimalist it's simply bass, snare, cymbal. They're cooking up an oriental jazz gumbo and the local youth – the unmarried – form circles and start to dance the hora.

Henry enquires after two teenagers he remembers were always playing their instruments along the railway line. Arrested for stealing three chickens from a neighbouring village, they were sentenced to five years' imprisonment. Such is justice and the Gypsies. Temperatures rise when the drummer gets on the mic' and starts singing Adrian's hits. He's loose and fluid, his oriental

Photo: Garth Cartwright

Public transport, Zece Prajini

pop verve sparking through the bar. The youth cheer and dance in couples. Water's thrown on the floor to soak up the dust. One youth, all ravaged features and hip-hop threads, is a fine dancer and girls circle him, the Gypsy Travolta. A mirrorball spins, we gulp vodka, teenagers take turns on the mic', there's more smoke and dust than air, good humour and high energy galvanising all.

Stagger back to Gişniac's house where his wife, praise be, has the ceramic stove blazing. So warm, so nice. Gişniac's built a bathroom but has stuck with his long-drop toilet. The fear of Ioan? Perhaps. I want to stay indoors but desperately need to pee. Hurry outdoors and, avoiding the ominous long-drop, stand in a field and piss streams of steaming urine at the full moon, laughing at the absurdity of it all, me a refugee from Auckland's disembodied suburbs knee-deep in rural Romania, navigating through the time of the Gypsies, living amongst Tziganes, a territory where there's no phone lines and intermittent electricity but dozens of the world's most naturally talented brass musicians.

I laugh and piss, all the soup and vodka and wine and zuica forcing itself out, my mind expanded till I'm almost tripping

on alcohol and cold. This unbearable, unbeatable cold. I swing
round, leap towards the house – wood fire a-burning – completely
forgetting Gişniac's gateway's entrance is designed for folk
smaller than I. It sounded something like you get in cartoons:
THHUUUNNNKKK!!! So. Here. I. Am. On my back amongst the
mud and cow shit and vegetable scraps. Semi-conscious, I stare at
the night sky and wonder if it will snow. Stars are stars and they
shine so bright. Gişniac's savage mongrel circles me. He's probably
scented my blood. Gişniac's pig oinks nearby. He's a huge fucker,
surely carnivorous, must be trying to break out of his pen to
munch on me. The chickens cluck at my idiocy. In the distance
I hear a trumpet wailing through the fog. Brass on fire and Gadje
on ice.

TEHARA BRISIND DELA
(The Rain May Come Tomorrow)

'Da. I go to school. Here in the mahala. It's OK. Better than the school
for the retards. Lots of the poor children go there. The teachers from
the retard school come here every year before term begins to make
their classes full – they go around the mahala and tell people to send
their children there because the school provides the children with
food and clothes. I don't know what they learn but for poor families
it is good. They just have to get a signed note from the local doctor
to go. And the doctors always sign it. I'm twelve and I think I would
like to go to school for maybe two more years but my father says if
the government don't give him anything for me going then he will
take me out of school to work with him in salvage. We collect bottles,
cardboard, tin and when we have a ton of it the Serbs come and buy
it. What would I like to do? Lots of things. Be a policeman or a bus
driver or like Van Damme in videos. But I'm a Gypsy so I guess I will
have to work with salvage.'

As our collective optimism for the new millennium rapidly dims
it's worth wondering what the Roma hope the future holds. They've
had a difficult – to say the least – last thousand years so I imagine
a smoother journey through the next ten centuries is desired. If the
immediate future looks grim the onward rush of humanity means
events and attitudes are changing on a massive scale and, hard as it
may be to believe, this also involves the Balkans.

One hundred years ago the states I travelled through were agrarian
nations, filled with peasants, overshadowed by the disintegrating
Ottoman Empire, illiterate communities whose lives were determined
by rituals of church and work, dominated by absolute rulers. The

Roma were marginalised then and they remain marginalised now. Sure. But today they have the weapon of knowledge – of their origins, their place in the world and their rights. Chafing against this, they have those Eastern European characteristics of ignorance and arrogance, violence and intolerance. For the region to truly prosper an evolution in consciousness is needed.

The Roma future is, hopefully, the same future we all share. Gypsies are supposedly intuitive fortune-tellers but this remains one area no one's going to pick possibilities out of a palm or crystal ball. Black America will remain what Roma struggles for rights and recognition are measured against during the next few decades. A nineteenth-century French observer's description of the Roma as 'Europe's Negroes' still holds; the cruelties of slavery and pogroms are visible reminders of a brutal past whilst overt discrimination and folk devilry remain constants. And, of course, ever-present musical genius. The US has wealth and a liberal tradition; to be Roma in the Balkans is to be coming through slaughter. Yet they keep coming. And coming.

Blatant discrimination can be challenged: across Eastern Europe too many Roma children are either denied access to education or put in 'remedial' classes where they are caged, kept away from white society, treated as if morons. Yet the entrenched racism of these nations treats this slewed schooling as normal – Slovakia's former prime minister, Vladimir Mečiar, described Gypsies as 'mental retards' while the Czech Republic's Pop Idol 2004 TV series found the most talented competitors being Roma (predictably) yet the public ensuring they would not win (predictably).

EU anti-discrimination policies can't teach tolerance yet they do set a progressive template. Spain's a good example of a nation now employing strong anti-racism laws against institutions and individuals who are found practising anti-Gitano measures. That said, any EU enthusiasms may be naïve considering, as the new member states joined in May 2004, Holland's Mr van der Linden (Head of *the EC Delegation to Slovakia) proposed the forced separation of Romani children from their parents in order to resolve the 'Roma problem'. Tehara Brisind Dela: the rain may come tomorrow...a hard, bitter rain.*

Gypsy legend has Kaloome the Gypsy, having overslept, arriving too late when God was giving out everything on earth. God couldn't change the destiny of these people he'd condemned to eternal wandering so he gave them music and dance. Since time immemorial music has been the Roma's gift to the world. Today it remains their CNN, a cultural statement second to none. Across the centuries the Roma have been denied access to legitimate art, so they have made their own. Deprived of formal education, they've created a compelling way of keeping their culture alive – an incredible, instinctual fight to preserve the integrity of language by people who may often be illiterate. Sentenced to death by ruling elites they turn death into beauty, forever challenging convention, musical rules, artistic expression, communicating the soul of a people and their phantom nation.

Music is a sacrament. This has been true for thousands of years of human history, save the last 100 or so. Today it may primarily exist as entertainment, simply another commodity, yet the mechanisms of music, how and why it affects us the way it does, are still mystical. Good music carries an incredible, invisible strength, one that communicates with the human heart and can act to inspire in so many ways, none more so than as an anti-oppression agent, slicing through prejudice and ignorance. And if music can't initiate regime change at least it offers alternative ways of feeling and seeing, expression and consciousness. Gypsy music, with all its alchemic abilities, remains for the Roma a tool of liberation.

Grief, melancholy, frustration, dissatisfaction, alienation, loss of family, economic insecurity, a sense of powerlessness against unjust power, of being a commodity rather than a person, of losing your roots, such is the subject matter of Gypsy song, these deep-rooted

Balkan country music

Balkan blues. And at the beginning of the twenty-first century many of us could claim to share in such emotions, to know also that the world's gone wrong. As Western popular music grows forever more banal and mercantile it is to the Roma and their Gypsy musicians, these soothsayers of song, we increasingly turn.

BULGARIA

A Sargasso Sea of tower blocks...thousands of apartments stacked like crumbly Rubik's cubes...a vision of dystopia worthy of Fritz Lang's *Metropolis...Welcome to Sofia, baby.* That's what I imagine a multitude of silent voices warbling – cement sirens, locked up in these grim towers – as the taxi rips along this monolithic neighbourhood's asphalt spine. Name of said urban ocean? Druzhba ('Friendship'). These buildings may stand as monuments to communism's cheerless vision but capitalism's found a use for them, their exterior walls now appropriated for gigantic advertisement hoardings. If billboards were vertical instead of horizontal (and painted on to apartment blocks) this is how they could look. I observe all from a dilapidated Skoda – suspension shot, doors broken, filthy – costing me more than a London black cab. This must be love, my ceaseless return to Balkan cities, it has to be love. Recall a Velvets song, one about some kinds of love being better than others, and reflect that a love of the Mediterranean or the Caribbean could be – as we sweep through canyons of concrete – better than Balkan love.

The Bulgarian experience involves traversing a nation leaking psychic unease; this is old Europe, an ancient land, yet Bulgaria's twentieth century contained much carnage and paranoia, so marking it as a surly adolescent on the international stage, one few have time for. Most associations with this geographically and ethically varied nation remain stock clichés: Tintin's Iron Curtain escapades, grotesque weightlifters, villainous secret police armed with poisoned umbrellas and plots on the Pope. Oh yeah, cheap skiing and plonk too. Yet wander around Bulgaria and something of a Balkan paradise is revealed; much beauty exists here. Alongside all the elements of a Balkan hell; look out my taxi's window and recall urban abysses I have known, Sofia ranking amongst them.

I mean, these tower blocks…severe concrete Triffids…Bleak House…wonder if the residents in each building refer to home as 'the Coca-Cola building', 'the Shell Oil building', 'the Toyota building'. In a world where people increasingly define themselves by brands this would make a certain wretched sense. As the traffic jams I notice individual inhabitants standing on discoloured balconies, tiny figures trying to enjoy the smidgen of afternoon sunshine falling their way. Force down the window to get a better view. Inhale…inhale an atmosphere of…*entrapment*? Entrapment, yeah. Poor urban communities weighed down by environment, the air thick with exhaust fumes, the constant throb of car engines and roar of planes overhead, the slow drain of spirit, each day like the one before, nights spent guzzling rakija, watching TV, hearing your neighbours flush parts of themselves through the plumbing.

The Skoda farts and slips a gear, driver curses, raspy Shop curses, the Shops being the peasant population, infamous for their impenetrable dialect, who once surrounded Sofia and have filled it over the last century. What a tongue-twister of a language. 'Az ne razbiram' is the only expression I recall: I don't understand. Onwards we rattle, leaving the advertisement-apartments behind, now passing houses, green spaces struggling against omnipresent industrial grey, people on the streets, skipping through lanes of traffic, navigating cracked pavements, manoeuvring children and bags of vegetables. Note a middle-aged man modelling a walrus moustache and walking a large brown bear. Impressive moustache. Mind-blowing bear. Muzzled and on a chain yet...I grew up amongst proud owners of pit bull terriers and Rottweilers but a pet bear...un-be-liev-able. Not that the locals appear to pay much attention; the driver simply shrugs and offers 'Da. Tsigane' to my frantic gesticulations.

I'm filled with wonder – where is he taking the bear? A stroll round the neighbourhood? To earn money from tourists? But it's spring, not exactly tourist season. And Sofia's not exactly a tourist town. Also, he's not carrying a gadulka, the one-string violin normally employed to get bears two-stepping. Maybe owning a bear is comparable to owning a dog and he's simply out for a stroll. Scenario: he's living in one of the apartments we passed and decides 'pleasant afternoon, get some fresh air. Let Todor stretch his legs. "Honey, I'm just going to take the bear for a walk."' And why not? Bulgaria is the last nation in Europe to have the Ursari – the Roma bear-tamers' caste – still earning a living from their ancient livelihood.

Bulgarians remain fond of the dancing bears although this occasionally causes problems: Emil Diamandiev was grabbed in a bear hug and badly mauled in central Sofia. The bear's owner, Radi Ivanov, told local TV: 'I can't understand it, my pet is usually as good as gold. I bet this man was drunk. It's well known that bears cannot abide drunkards.' The West takes a dim view of dancing bears; Brigitte Bardot's helped finance Four Paws, a $250,000 bear park near the village of Belitsa in south-west Bulgaria. The park has a visitor centre and six bears, all purchased for $4,500 per bear from Ursari. Each bear's space is surrounded by two fences and includes a small swimming pool and trees. Their food – bread, honey, fish, fruit and vegetables – costs $150 to $200 per bear, per month. The average monthly salary in rural Bulgaria is often around $100.

Sofia, named after the Greek word for wisdom, has rarely observed enlightened leaders at the city's helm. Founded by the Thracian Slavi tribe several centuries before Christ's era, Sofia's geographical location found Macedonians, Romans, Goths, Huns, Slavs, Magyars, Pechenegs, Mongols, Tartars and Bulgars (a warlike Central Asian tribe who gave the nation its name) all plundering the region while the Roma and other smaller, more peaceful Asian tribes followed in their wake. In the late fourteenth century the Ottoman war machine rolled across Bulgaria, crushing and subjugating. The Ottomans proved wise tyrants: inviting different ethnic groups to settle – aware immigrant communities work hard while divide and rule was then, as now, an effective colonial political policy – Vlach, Armenians, Karakachani and the Roma all arrived in considerable numbers. Sephardic Jews fleeing the Spanish Inquisition were welcomed (Bulgaria's retained a uniquely pro-Semitic philosophy). As were Muslim Circassians fleeing the Russian Empire as it laid waste to their Caucasus homelands (so laying the foundations for today's Chechen conflict).

The brutalised Circassians were not content with refuge, choosing to inflict revenge upon Bulgaria's rural communities. Their pillaging of Orthodox villages helped fuel anti-Ottoman efforts and the subsequent uprisings would lead to the Russian–Turkish War (1877–88): hundreds of thousands died before the

Ottomans withdrew. At the Treaty of San Stefano independent Bulgaria's borders were determined to include Macedonia. Yet the Western powers, fearing Bulgaria would be little more than a satellite state of an increasingly powerful Russia, gave Macedonia back to the Turks. This slight determined Bulgaria's abysmal political manoeuvres during the twentieth century: on the losing side of the 1913 Balkan War, siding with Germany in WWI and WWII (Macedonia being bait), Soviet skivvies till 1989…kingdom rise and kingdom fall.

Safely lodged on the fourteenth floor of a central city apartment – no signs of large paw prints in the dusty entrance – I make contact with Rumiana. Rumi's the secret heroine of my Bulgarian adventures, forever navigating chaos with lipstick style and nervous, witty grace, smoking countless Victory cigarettes, each puff symbolic of her unwillingness to let the forces of Gypsy musician disorder overrun all that is planned.

'Twenty-one years I've worked with musicians,' says Rumi, 'and I thought I knew every trick they could pull. But some of these guys…they're unbelievable.'

Rumi's a singer and linguist. Back in the Comecon days she performed on the Bulgarian cabaret circuit, toured the Soviet Union as part of singing socialist packages and sang on cruise ships sailing Baltic seas. Today her brand of Bulgarian pop's been superseded so Rumi now translates for musicians. And most of the Bulgarian musicians she translates for are Gypsy, as they attract a semblance of demand from the West.

'Before I started translating I had never met a Gypsy,' says Rumi. 'If I had any impressions of them it was that they would be quite rough people. But I find they are very nice people. For me this is a pleasant surprise.'

The Roma make up somewhere between 300,000 (official census result) and 800,000 (NGO estimate) – 10 per cent – of Bulgaria's population. Some claim they first arrived in the land once known as Thrace at the beginning of the ninth century ACE. This is, maybe, a little too early but as the Roma moved through the Byzantine Empire they certainly were here by the twelfth century. More Roma accompanied the Ottomans as soldiers and musicians, metal-workers and animal-tamers. The Ottomans referred to the Roma as cengene or kipts (Copts) and while many Roma converted to Islam they were viewed with reproach – Roma women discarded the veil; their music and dancing rarely in tune with Islamic orthodoxy. Still, their nomadic lifestyle and traditional occupations were allowed and, in general, the Roma received better treatment here than their brethren then in Christian Europe.

The first schools aimed at educating Roma children in the Balkans were opened in Bulgaria in 1910 (Roma literacy then stood at 3 per cent), but as Bulgaria see-sawed through crisis after crisis, war after war, the opportunity to build a civil society was forfeit. Bulgarians remain proud of their nation's refusal to deport Bulgarian Jews to Hitler's murder camps. They're less vocal on how Bulgaria's pathetic pro-Axis government, desperate to meet Nazi quotas, rounded up the entire Jewish community in occupied Macedonia and Thrace (11,000 *in toto*) then shipped them to death camps. And Gypsies? Bulgaria's occupying forces, ripped on fascist rhetoric, acted savagely, say surviving Macedonian and Greek Roma. Yet within Bulgaria's borders the Roma apparently suffered less than brethren in much of occupied Europe.

Socialism should have meant liberation for Bulgaria's Roma. Should have: Bulgaria's Stalinist rulers determined that ethnic minorities would be forced into assimilation programmes; the campaign to create a homogenous nation of Bulgars began in the 1950s by banning nomadism, so forcibly settling many Roma into poor housing, rudimentary education and menial employment – cheap labour for socialist society. At the same time, Bulgarian-speaking Muslim Roma were pressured to Christianise their names. President Todor Zhivkov, the smiling slaphead who ran Bulgaria as a personal fiefdom, lacked Ceauşescu's taste for palaces, instead delighting in increasingly eccentric nationalist policies.

As perestroika opened up the Soviet Union Zhivkov opted to obstruct change, bullying minorities being his preferred tactic to distract from Bulgarian communism's increasing malaise. In 1984 Romani was banned, as was dancing and playing musical instruments considered 'Gypsy'. This involved people playing/ dancing kyuchek (a widespread Roma genre), playing the zurna (keyless oboe), even though it was the most distinctive instrument of the region, even wearing the shalvari (wide pants). All were considered 'Turkish and hence not purely Bulgarian'. In 1987 the publication of Roma newspapers was banned and the only Romani theatre closed. Foreigners interested in the Roma were described as spies or tools of imperialism. Corresponding pressure was put on Bulgaria's million-strong Turkish population to change their names. This sparked small uprisings (violently suppressed) before leading to a mass exodus of Bulgarian Turks to Turkey in 1989; Slobodan Milošević and cronies watched with interest.

Zhivkov's extremist policies are now removed from the statute books yet most Bulgarian Roma, impoverished and largely excluded from civil society, feel the situation today isn't discernibly better. Unlike Romania, where the nation's master Gypsy musicians were recognised and recorded by apparatchiks, the vaults of the state Balkanton label are empty: to Stalinists running the Culture Ministry music existed only as a nationalist tool, thus recording Gypsy music was forbidden.

Gypsy music went unrecorded, sure, but don't ever imagine that a few corrupt Stalinists and their enforcers could silence the Roma: weddings became the focal point for musical creativity and social exchange. The freedom expressed in Gypsy music

The brothers Iliev, 1970s

began appealing to young Bulgarians, many following the major wedding musicians, especially clarinet player Ivo Papazov, whose fluid technique and roaring orkestar attracted several hundred fans whenever he put reed to lips. Concerned by Papazov's rising popularity, the authorities had him arrested, beaten and sentenced to a labour camp in 1982. Papasov somehow avoided the camp, surviving to enjoy tenure in the West as a Thracian jazz-fusionist. Meanwhile, in mahalas across the nation, Gypsy music was fermenting, waiting to rise.

Bulgaria came back to life on November 10 1989 (the day after the Berlin Wall fell), when Bulgaria's Communist Party forced Zhivkov's resignation, arresting the dictator for 'inciting racial hatred'. Shaking off shackles and ditching dogma, Bulgarians embraced their roots; three thousand years ago the aboriginal Thracians were infamous for orgiastic tendencies: getting high on hemp seeds, practising polygamy, allowing young women sexual freedom and, as all true pagans do, tattooing. And chalga, a Gypsy-patented electronic music, is very true to the Thracian spirit.

Chalga and US hip-hop are what twenty-first-century Bulgaria resonates to. These occidental and oriental cousins share hybrid bloodlines – post-modern music(s) promiscuously assembled from the debris of several sonic forms, vivid with ghetto fantasy – and involve high-talent turnover and hints of criminal involvement: Gypsy chalga star Kondio, who hit no. 1 in Bulgaria in 1998 with 'Doko Doko' (the first song sung in Romani to achieve this), was arrested in June 2004 and charged with trafficking Bulgarian Roma girls to Spain and Portugal for the purposes of prostitution. A seventeen-year-old Bulgarian Roma girl accused Kondio of preparing documents for her to go to Spain after she had been bought from another trafficker...Few Bulgarians speak English yet Eminem and 50 Cent are youth icons, their fast mouths and tattooed torsos being the new male absolutes. And in Misho Shamara Bulgaria has a homegrown hip-hop star. Misho's inept rapping mixes mumbled English and Bulgarian while his videos, shot on wobbly camcorders, are stuffed with gyrating bikini babes and thug pose.

Next to Misho chalga appears quite, well, refined. Not that most of my Bulgarian acquaintances professed any time for chalga. Rumi is aghast when I mention wanting to interview chalga singers. Diana, a London Sofia acquaintance, dismisses chalga while relishing metal uglies Guns N' Roses and Man-O-War. Feeling alone in my chalga enthusiasm, I call Nick Nasev, an Australian whose Balkan roots have found him spending considerable amounts of time in Macedonia and Bulgaria. Nick is, to say the least, something of a chalga fan.

We meet in central Sofia, a labyrinth of diesel fumes and designer boutiques; someone has money to burn and they're not your average Bulgarian. I'm feeling grim, the Balkan tendency to never put the cap back on the bottle once again leaving me worse for wear, so Nick suggests we head to a traditional workers' café. Here he orders a bowl of soup and a beer, places both in front of me and insists I consume. This, he emphasises, is the Bulgarian cure for hangovers. The soup is cold and contains tripe…I grovel…my stomach hurts too much to swallow anything, the beer will only increase my current addled state…Nick, his accent located between Sofia and Sydney, is insistent. I slurp soup. Ugh! But a sip of beer does help vanquish the tripe. So I slurp and sip and sip and slurp and by the time I've ordered coffee (the sugar comes in packets decorated with naked women: *très* Thracian…) my brain's stopped fizzing. 'Folk remedy,' says Nick. Agreed. Time to talk chalga.

'The word "chalga" is of Turkish origin and it refers to the urban music of the Ottoman empire of the late nineteenth century and early twentieth century. However, modern chalga is the equivalent to turbo-folk of ex-Yugoslavia, laika of Greece and manele of Romania. Chalga continues the old tradition for humorous songs yet where before folk songs would be about meeting a young boy by the well after riding a donkey it's now moved on to meeting a rich man with a white Mercedes at the Currency Exchange Bureau. As well, the lyrics have used shock value and there are many sexually suggestive songs.

'Chalga really started when the communists were toppled. Musicians would sing the Yugo songs they heard on radio broadcasts and add their own Bulgarian lyrics. This started the mass plagiarism that still affects chalga. The first major band was Kristal, who consisted of Bulgars, Romas and Turks. This set the stage for the multi-ethnic nature of chalga. While detractors dismiss chalga as "Gypsy music" or "truck driver music" its fans revel in a genre that combines all of Bulgaria's ethnic cultures.'

One nation under a chalga groove? Hard to believe, sure, but chalga might just lead Bulgaria's first ever pop culture revolution. Gypsy chalga singers Azis and Sofi Marinova are amongst Bulgaria's biggest stars while Reyhan and Sevdzhan, two seventeen-year-old Muslim Roma girls, crashed the charts in 2003. On video the duo flaunt proud Asian bloodlines and beautiful bodies wrapped in black leather. Just as white America's wholesale racism was crippled when confronted by the talent and beauty of Sam Cooke and Lena Horne, Orthodox Bulgaria can't consider the nation's Turks and Roma ignoble peasants when their songs command the clubs and their videos – undeniably sensual, wonderfully sassy – dominate TV screens.

'The Roma are a pragmatic people,' says Nick. 'They've always been good at adapting music forms to play what's popular while adding their own flavour. You can also see this when it comes to religion. The Roma can be Christian or Muslim while getting on with each other and everyone else. Like other nomadic peoples who adopted Islam (the Kazaks and Turkmen of Central Asia), the Roma were particularly attracted to Sufism, which, with its blend of spiritualism, appreciation of music and relaxed attitude to observance, suited the Roma way of life. It's beyond the realm of your book but Roma involvement with the development of Mevlana music of Turkey is significant.

'Sufism was strong throughout the Balkans although it's not as prominent as it was pre-World War II and when it was announced that the Whirling Dervishes were going to come to Adelaide my father and grandparents dismissed them, saying they were Gypsies! I found out from my grandfather that the Muslim Gypsies in his area [Gotze Delchev in Bulgaria's Pirin Mountains] used to have bizarre trance-like ceremonies with the best music that was at odds with the conservative behaviour of the Turks in town. Studying the dervishes of Tetovo, Macedonia, and Prizren, Kosovo, many were Gypsy.'

Needing to digest both tripe and knowledge I suggest we go walkabout. Sofia's the highest capital city in Europe and this leads to climatic extremes: freezing in winter and now, early May, boiling. Heavy weather, a Balkan speciality. Along Maria Luiza Boulevard Café Vienna and Manhattan Café suggest tangible dreams of West Europe and the USA while large outdoor bars spread from Aleksandar Nevski Church, a massive marble blur of Orthodox baroque. Here Sofia's elite recline, balancing cigarettes and espresso, wearing Ray-Bans and Prada (courtesy of Istanbul's pirates).

Sofia's architecturally banal – ugly oversized buildings, monolithic plinths shadowing boulevards, grey on grey, too much traffic and too little imagination – but I'm content to forget this, observing that the human architecture is much more interesting. Through the centuries miscegenation has gifted Bulgarians with a tough, quixotic beauty, quite unlike anywhere else in the Balkans, cheekbones you could shave upon, smouldering eyes, Asiatic pout. De-licious. The food's fabulous as well – succulent meat dishes, ripe red wines, potent cheese, tomatoes that explode with taste… someone write a hymn to the shopska salad! There's a real sense of pleasure, of carnal knowledge, in both the Bulgarian food and physique.

By the time we reach the Central Railway Station – the least helpful, most debilitated transport hub in Europe – I'm itchy to escape downtown. In the distance Mt Vitosha looms. Nick suggests we take a bus to this natural playground at the city's outskirts. I've another idea: let's visit some Roma friends who live in a south Sofia mahala. It'll be an expensive taxi ride, says Nick. I propose we walk: we've all day ahead of us. And, hey, it'll provide you with time to share your Balkan knowledge.

'Did you know that Bulgaria loves a clairvoyant?' asks Nick.

No. Go on then.

'This is reflected in the fact that one of the patron saints of Bulgaria, Sveta Petka (St Friday), had the powers of clairvoyance. The most famous Bulgarian clairvoyant of the twentieth century was Baba Vanga (Granny Vanga), who, at age six, had a vision of the Virgin Mary. The Virgin offered her either sight or clairvoyance. She chose the latter. She once saw a vision of the Bulgarian city of

Varna being engulfed by water, after which it was discovered that Varna sat upon an aquifer! And she also foretold Hitler's defeat before he invaded Russia. Baba was renowned all throughout the Balkans and a whole cult grew around her. She died poor but a celebrity in 1996 and now her shrine is a site of pilgrimage.'

Clairvoyants or Gypsy fortune-tellers – what do you prefer, Nick?

'Personally, I stick with reading coffee grains.'

I'm sure this fails as a historic question but those bloodthirsty Circassians, is it, uh, true they produced the Balkans' most beautiful girls?

'Let's just say the Sultan was said to prefer them for his harem above all others.'

With that thought in mind we begin our long walk.

Jony Iliev:
The Fate of the Gypsies

Did you ever dream lucky
Wake up cold in hand?

Langston Hughes

Central Sofia, midnight, and amongst a warren of back streets
Rumi and I are searching for the Casbah. Not too much lighting
and not too many people around. Sofia's largely silent at night, a
stricken economy forcing people to stay home in front of the TV,
so the places that are open tend to, well, la vida loca, y'know? Street.
Street. Street. *Where is this goddamn joint?* And then, hey, located.
We approach the Casbah's impressively solid door to be greeted by
an equally solid doorman. Rumi engages in conversation with this
man mountain, turns, says 'the Mafia wish to know if you have
any weapons on you?' 'Trade or exchange?' I reply. Rumi laughs
her deep, wicked laugh and nods, indicating – *what?* – 'Yes, he has
guns'. Yikes! OK, chill, recall that in Bulgaria nodding and shaking
the head signal direct opposites of the West European gesture.
World upside down? Sometimes to this weary voyager that's how
the Balkans appears.

Mt Vitosha looks at me. Comparable to pit bull observing cat
– what else can I tell him? Travelling light I tend to leave the Uzi at
home? If I wish to purchase a weapon I'll look no further? – then
shakes his head having determined I'm a non-combatant and waves
us through. The club's underground milieu (spacious, loud, dark)

Go, Jony, Go

Photo: Garth Cartwright

takes a few minutes for senses to adjust. OK, mmmhhhmmmm. The Casbah is striking. No grotty mirror balls and fake velvet trim, instead the club's interior offers a tasteful approximation of Middle Eastern décor.

Comfortably full for a Tuesday night with more females than males, which gets me wondering but, no, I don't want to think those thoughts and why can't they all just be here cos this is a club where they know their sounds: the DJ mixes Bollywood, bhangra, Turkish, Arabic and chalga – fuel for the Balkan funk machine – then Jony Iliev and band take the stage and cook up Gypsy gumbo so spicy impossibly beautiful women leap on tables and furiously belly dance. Shake it like a Polaroid picture? Hey yah, indeed. Jony's in good voice, wailing over clarinet and dancing bass patterns, a swirling electronic force field of sound crunching around him. Somehow, someway, Gypsy musicians even manage to make a cheap Casio keyboard possess Oriental bite. Order a large rakija, blag a Victory off Rumi and recall the last time I caught Jony performing in Sofia was in a way grungy restaurant where the drunken clientele groped dates and fell into food. The Casbah's definitely a more classy gig. And so the evening proceeds: tune/table/shake-it/outtasite!

Jony Iliev's a gifted singer and songwriter who, for twenty-two of his thirty-four years, has rocked mahalas, restaurants, clubs, weddings and concert halls across Bulgaria's south-west. He has a voice on him, one that can swap between the ornamented vocal style favoured in chalga and much Gypsy music to a softer, more raw and soulful vehicle, a croon almost. Long a legend of wedding music, Jony was a chalga star before setting out to win an international audience. He's a lovely man, always gentle and accommodating. Whenever Jony and I part he puts his closed fist across his heart then opens it outwards. Solidarity? Indeed.

On stage I recognise Jony's much bigger brother, Boril, a master clarinet and saxophone player who shares with Jony a penchant for long, wavy hair. In Spain flamenco's Gitanos favour wedge-like mullets. Jony and Boril don't commit quite the same hair crimes, actually they both possess fabulous ringlet hair, but a hair tie might bring some order to things. There's Camen on guitar. Radev drums. Jony, Boril and Camen grew up in Kyustendil, south-west Bulgaria. The fact that none of them speaks a word of English, Bulgarian baffles me, and the little Romani I know is deemed unintelligible, means smiles–handshakes–gestures are often our tools of communication.

The musicians take a break so letting the belly dancers reconnect pelvis to leg bones. Jony joins us. He's a small, handsome man, devilish goatee, brown eyes sparkling with all the magical possibilities that he, a Gypsy prince, natural Balkan royalty, sees opening in a vivid future. The language barrier is truly a drag, I'd so like to engage him in a conversation on life, universe etc. Instead we shrug and laugh and Rumi translates pleasantries and then Jony indicates time to take the stage again. And when will he play until? Till the club empties out. Maybe 4am tonight. 6am other nights. Getting the girls dancing, performing praise songs at tables that pay for the privilege. This is it, singing till you're hoarse, several nights a week, pumping out chalga for a living, the daily grind of the Balkan Gypsy musician. Rumi, who's spent way too much of her life in music venues, can't be tempted to stay longer.

Wednesday: rise to a drizzly morning so switch on TV Planeta and kick back with coffee. TV Planeta is Bulgaria's leading music video channel and watching it provides a good key to the contemporary Slav psyche. The performers are largely chalga although popular ballad and folklore ('fakelore' says Nick) videos also get a spin, accommodating viewers nostalgic for Zhivkov's Bulgaria. The female singers, whether bottle blondes or those proud of their Oriental colouring, share with Serbian turbo-folk singers a predilection for micro-minis and push-up bras. The male singers appear to be impersonating a constipated George Michael. And then there's Azis, the camp King of chalga, who's quite unlike anyone else. Jony, having left ARA – a chalga label – now never appears on Planeta. The videos are understandably low budget, often highly sexually suggestive – porn rather than mainstream cinema seeming to influence their look and content – and aspire to casinos, gold jewellery, yachts on the Black Sea, Rome, Venice... in a word, Bulgarian bling-bling.

Rumi arrives in her Peugeot 405, the car's crimson colouring matching Rumi's hair, lipstick, sweater, coat. Americans used to refer to citizens of the Eastern Bloc as 'Reds'. Maybe they'd seen an image of Rumi. Rumi shudders at the sight of TV Planeta. I shrug guiltily. Just research, y'know? We leave, heading for Jony's mahala, driving through the city's southern suburbs. Stationary at traffic lights a Roma man on crutches, his left leg absent, hobbles up and knocks on Rumi's window. She lowers it and they chat. The lights change and he steps back, hailing goodbye as we move off, not a lev having been exchanged.

'What was that about?'

'Oh, he's been at that junction for years. I always used to give him something, one lev or fifty stotinki, then I saw him interviewed on TV and he claimed he could earn up to one hundred lev/euro a day! Boy, did I stop giving him money then. It turns out he has a "manager" who drops him at that spot every day in a Mercedes. And, of course, it's the "manager" who keeps most of the money. Last winter when it was really cold I gave him a wool sweater but I never saw him wear it. This junction is his life and he appears quite happy with it.'

'And what were you talking about just then?'

'Oh, he was complaining that today was a bad day. Yesterday was a really good day and he made a lot of money but today he's finding no one's giving.'

Alongside fortune-telling and music, begging is the trade most associated with the Roma. Which gets me wondering: is Rumi's friend another legacy of India where beggars often compete for rupees by advertising mutilations? Or a reflection upon how capitalism's trickle-down economics works in the Balkans? Bulgaria's economy is ranked just above Romania's and the nation's social welfare system evaporated with communism. We continue south, nearing the ring road that circles Sofia. Horse and carts suggest the mahala and soon the streets are alive with children, black-haired and tan-skinned, ragged and sooty and waving at us. This mahala's called 'Fakultet'. I take this to be a jest at the fact so few Roma go on to higher education. Turns out the mahala includes buildings once part of the university complex. Facultet then could be, I guess, an inspiring name. More so than 'Cambodia' and 'Abyssinia', labels other Sofia mahalas are tagged with.

Facultet's a poor part of town – roads are rough, a railway line cuts through, houses small, dust dust dust – but lively and proud too. Jony bounces out of a seemingly deserted concrete shell to greet us. Such enthusiasm and that smile! No wonder he's taking on the world. Jony's success finds him building a house that, while no mansion, will be a spacious, comfortable dwelling. If ever completed: at the moment it resembles a bunker. And when Jony leads us inside I can't believe he's living here, the structure being completely open to the elements. Not quite: Jony, his wife and son are living in the one finished room, a habitable (plush sofas and mod-cons) if congested space. Jony gives a guided tour of what he hopes the bunker will be transformed into – guest bedrooms, recording studio et al. Which means he's either going to have to sell a lot more chalga in Bulgaria, a scene he's hoping to turn his back upon, or break into the Western world music market, something that's close, so close, yet still so far away.

I first became aware of Jony Iliev in early 2003 when his album *Ma Maren Ma* was released on Asphalt Tango Records. Being signed and produced by the good people who had brought Fanfare Ciocărlia to the world signalled quality and, f'sure, *Ma Maren Ma* is a gorgeous disc, mixing wailing ballads with frisky Balkan rockers. Jony's big ache of a voice, his lyrical directness and driving band suggest he's heir apparent to Šaban Bajramović. And with the godfather of Gypsy song living directly north-west of Sofia – Niš is the first Serb city you hit when crossing the Bulgarian–Serbian border – this is understandable. 'Šaban's great,' says the Prince of the King, 'always an inspiration. I've often sung with him at Gypsy gatherings.'

Khaled. Whitney Houston. Mariah Carey. Joe Cocker. Lots of Turkish singers. Arabic rhythms. These are Jony's favourite non-Gypsy singers and sounds. Cocker's a surprise as the Balkan states hold little interest in Western artists beyond superstars – Whitney and Mariah can be heard in every mahala, their elastic vowel-strangling appealing to the Romas' love of 'ornamented' voices – although I can find shared qualities in Joe and Jony's voices (sing soft, sing rough, sing soulful). Khaled, the King of Algerian rai, is an eclectic and expressive singer while Arabic music has existed in the Roma psyche for untold centuries – Gypsy musicians once were hired to play in the great courts of the Middle East and North Africa.

Jony's wife Naza looks to have stepped out of a nineteenth-century painting of Gypsies: electric black hair, honey-coloured skin, liquid eyes, cowboy mouth…a fierce beauty and smart with it too. She's always at Jony's side, participating in interviews, helping him write songs, adding steel to Jony's gentleness.

Jony says he can't remember ever having problems with Bulgarians, communist or capitalist. Maybe he's being diplomatic but as his birth name, Stefan Iliev, is thoroughly Bulgar there was never pressure to change. Also, his family are Christians so escaped the anti-Muslim edicts. Not Naza. Her family were forced to change their names. She became 'Natalie'. And her eyes, eyes as black and potent as in a Picasso painting, fabulous Gypsy eyes, blaze when she speaks.

'This society has always thought that the Gypsies are uncultured, lazy, don't want to work but maybe we weren't given a chance – you don't give us jobs so Gypsies are forced to do things to feed their family. Don't allow us to work then say "we are lazy". If we steal because we are hungry we are accused of being thieves but how else can a man feed a family? And then if there is a rich Gypsy they are hated for being rich. Jony is welcome in Bulgarian society because he's an artist and, also, he's a very good man. We have Bulgarian friends who understand as well but this is not the rule.'

The Iliev family have always been musicians and Jony accepts music was his destiny. Singing with the radio, beating out rhythms, these are his memories of early childhood. Jony married as a teenager in Kyustendil, the last Bulgarian city before the Macedonian border, and fathered two children. But something, perhaps the lure of Sofia's bright lights, the temptations that surround a rising star, split the coupling. Yet in Naza he's met his match, a determined, articulate woman who wants – expects – to see her husband succeed.

Rockin'
Mahalas from
city to city

Photo: Garth Cartwright

'Being a singer in Bulgaria, it's not so easy as it looks,' says Jony.
'Long, long nights, sleeping during the day, often travelling to play
a wedding or, now, a concert in Europe. Thank God my wife has
the patience to wait for me and a love of the music. Making music
is a tradition in the family of many generations. My father had me
learning the tambura aged two. He died when I was nine years old
and Chico [the second oldest of eight brothers] raised me and made
such a discipline for me and my brothers. I hated him! Now I realise
this has really helped us. Boril is Bulgaria's leading saxophone player.
He can walk into a session and read the music. This really surprises
some music people here, that Gypsies can read music.'

Growing up, Jony was surrounded by music: his brothers all
earned a living either playing weddings or in military brass bands.
Jony's childhood came to an abrupt end as a pre-teen when the
family called on him to sing.

'Four of my older brothers had married so those of us at home
wanted to help our mother and earn some money and the only

way was with music. I was taken to a big Turkish Gypsy wedding, I was twelve, and I sang for twelve hours. I remember it well, it was in Pazardzhik, a small city, and the response from the guests at the wedding was so good from then on I was the singer. I couldn't manage to go to school any more because I had to go to sing with my brothers. I couldn't go and play football with other boys because I had to sing.

'From 1981 to 1982 I was singing professionally with another small guy. We'd go to Sofia to play in the mahala and Gypsies from all around would come to listen to us! We'd sing for eight to twelve hours. We sang songs we'd learned in the mahala and our own original songs – right from the start this was special to us. We'd have an idea for a song and my brothers would do the arrangement. Then my friend did his army service and he went crazy. He's living in the Kyustendil mahala but mentally ill.'

As Naza noted, Bulgarians like Jony. Good? Uh-huh. Except when the Mafia are amongst Jony's fans. This makes him wince. Bulgaria's close ties with Russia and corrupt post-communist governments have made life easy for the Moscow Mafia and their local associates, larceny permeating the nation. Even in mahalas talk surrounds Roma criminals intent on exploiting their own. Check it: Sudahan, the master Macedonian clarinet player, told me he turned down invitations to play at Bulgarian weddings simply because he feared the criminals who move amongst Bulgarian Roma society.

'At fifteen I became guitarist in the band and backing vocalist,' notes Jony. 'It was a very dangerous time in Bulgaria. There were a lot of criminals who wanted to take the money and control the music and my brothers were scared I would be attacked so they moved me to backing vocalist to protect me from these aggressive people. Sometimes these Mafia would demand I sing so I was recognised as a good singer even then. Some of the bosses of the Mafia created problems for my colleagues but somehow I managed to know how to deal with them so I became their favourite.'

Bulgaria's dons – jowls and jewellery, Jeeps and babes – represent the gory glory of the nouveau riche. Their thugs, known as 'bortsi' (fighters), are crop-headed, muscle-bound, often ex-soldiers or athletes. Ever wondered what happened to those Olympic-intimidating Bulgarian weightlifters? Here's your answer. Drug- and people-smuggling, prostitution, protection rackets, siphoning off government contracts and foreign funds…there's a lot of money at stake and extreme acts of violence are commonplace. In January 2004 a bomb in central Sofia killed a don and his three bortsi.

'I've seen people arrive with twenty bodyguards,' says Jony of his patrons. 'Then you know it's a big Mafia boss. It's not a comfortable feeling to be performing to these people in the club. The boss of the Mafia always says to me "Hello, how are you?" and that saves me a lot of problems. One night one of the bosses was at the Casbah and I had to sing for him until 4am. Then he went for breakfast and at 11am, man, they shot him!'

The Jamaican Yardie saying 'step on leather, kiss it better' is, thus, wise advice in Sofia's clubland. Jony's initial Bulgarian fame came through recording three chalga albums for Sofia's ARA label. These presented him in a slick electronic setting and while popular in Bulgaria nothing on them suggests he would appeal to a Western audience. The chalga industry is a tough one and although Jony remains tight-lipped about his experiences I get the feeling he might not have received the fairest of treatment. Returning to his roots, he found an international audience.

'An accordion player who I'd played with years ago returned from Vienna where he now lives and he said "Listen, Jony, I'm not interested in this chalga but I know that there are people in Vienna who would listen to real Gypsy music. Let's make an album." So we sat down with Boril and made a demo of what would become *Ma Maren Ma*. It ended up getting passed to Henry and Helmut at Asphalt Tango.

'Henry and Helmut came to Sofia and we played for thirty minutes and then the next day Henry and Helmut accompanied us to a restaurant we were playing to see how the people responded. It was a big success, people knew my songs, made requests. One guy made a request and said "I have no money but if you sing this song I will give you my mobile phone!" They saw how it was for me and we made the album.'

Jony sings a line from *Ma Maren Ma* that translates as 'don't beat me, I'm just a poor Gypsy boy'. As ever, the Balkan blues.

'That song is telling of a small Gypsy boy walking in the world, proud to be a Gypsy, acknowledging the ground is his mother, the sky is his father. And he's saying to the people he meets as he wanders "don't beat me just because I'm an orphan".'

'A Gypsy orphan,' offers Naza.

'In the second verse I sing "everywhere I go people beat me/I run away but, tell me God, where shall I go?" This is the Gypsies' fate. And I sing, "I've had enough/I want us to be friends". OK, this situation of being beaten has not happened to me but it's a real Gypsy story. Most Gypsies are normally treated like this. The song "Arizona", it's coming from my dream of Arizona. In the song I sing of how I'm looking for the wife and child that I've lost so I'm travelling the world until I'm in Arizona and even there I can't find them. The song "Godzilla" isn't about the movie, it's that many Gypsy women find themselves with nicknames such as this—'

'He's singing a story for the Gypsy people,' adds Naza.

'My Godzilla is a woman, one who has stayed in America. She didn't like the way of living in Bulgaria so she went to America, so I go there to get her back because I want her back so much.'

Is there a big difference between *Ma Maren Ma* and your chalga albums?

'A very big difference! Chalga is the opposite side; there I sing in Bulgarian and it's electronic instruments, 2/4 rhythm, overdubbed voices. Chalga is music made for money, for fame, for restaurants. I enjoy singing it because people like it but I prefer to work with the band where we can improvise. *Ma Maren Ma* is sung in

Romani and played by real musicians. The melodies come from old Gypsy songs but it's a new kind of style, a mix with elements of pop, Bulgarian folk, some difficult Bulgarian rhythms...the Jony Iliev style.'

A few mornings later Rumi and I gather at Sofia's central coach station. Here Boril, Camen and several other Kyustendil musicians prepare to board a coach for Belgium. 'We're going to Europe,' says Vasil, the keyboardist, proudly. 'Europe where people will pay us in euros to play music.' No point in suggesting that Bulgaria is part of the European continent; for many citizens across this peninsula they live in the Balkans while Europe is 'over there', geographically close but psychically removed, a land representing civilisation, wealth, equality, opportunity, stable government. All the things they find lacking in their Balkan states. Standing in the Sofia sunshine this concept seems almost comical – the low-rent violence that spills across my South London 'hood and the government sanctioned violence as practised on Iraq removing the UK from utopia lists – but to a group of raggle-taggle Gypsy musicians who know poverty's stale smell only too well 'Europe' exists as a dream state. Just as America does in Jony's songs. Somewhere to escape to.

Camen's organised a residency in an Antwerp Yugoslav restaurant, Belgium allowing Bulgarians to enter for six months without a visa. Jony's unhappy about losing two of his band. But there's no argument to be had: they will make more playing Balkan folk standards and sleeping six to a room in Antwerp than he can offer them on Sofia's restaurant and club circuit. 'What can I do?' says Camen. 'There's not enough work for me in Bulgaria. I have to go to other countries.' Equipment's loaded aboard the bus. Hugs and kisses exchanged with wives and children. Final puffs taken on cigarettes. The coach crawls into thick Sofia traffic, Boril's broad brown face pressed against the window, eyes glazed, ancestors adjacent, on the road again...

Azis:
The Brightest Smile in Town

He was afraid lest some light, emanating from the innermost depths of his soul, might not be illuminating him, might not, in some way from inside his scaly carapace, be giving off a reflection of his true being and rendering it visible to those who would be constrained to give him chase.

Jean Genet, *Querelle of Brest*

'…You don't count Azis's press cuttings, you weigh them. Azis has proved there is a Bulgarian Dream, one which emphasises it's not important, your ethnicity or family, but how big your dreams are. He has proved that if you trust yourself nothing can stop you. "One day I will be like Madonna!" These words of little Vasko made his friends laugh. But the times show he has the qualities of many world superstars. Mostly they compare him to Madonna and Michael Jackson – and he agrees he's influenced by them – but now he is not like anyone else. At least under the Bulgarian sun. What is sure, Azis will go down in the history of Bulgarian showbiz as a phenomenon. And he still didn't say his last word. His life is maybe like the story of the ugly duckling. He never hid that he was Gypsy. He was never ashamed to do any kind of job to earn some money. He walked dogs of rich people. Cleaned offices. Barman and waiter. But thanks to God that in all that time he continued to do what he could do best – sing and perform. Wise men have said that luck goes to courageous individuals. That means Azis…'

Azis

Photo © Krum Krumov

The overheated prose continues like this for several thousand words. Understandably so, it comes from a fan magazine issued to coincide with Azis's concert at Sofia's National Stadium in October 2003. Thing is, I'd normally never quote such stuff but with Azis… well, there's a ring of truth to it.

Azis…where to start? I first bore witness while on Bulgaria's Black Sea coast in early '03. It was early in the season and the bars were shut so my evening entertainment revolved around demolishing a bottle of the local Cab Sav in front of TV Planeta. Beginning to nod when a chiaroscuro video featuring the most extreme-looking Gypsy I'd ever seen (bleached hair, eyebrows, beard, moustache, Satanic gaze) unfurled across the screen. It was one of those TV moments worthy of Japanese horror flick *The Ring*:

this creature, leering and teasing, revelled in a nightmare of latent sadism and sexual insinuation. Double lock the door and resolve to quit drinking. 'Who was that?' I asked everyone I encountered. All knew the answer: Azis.

What is Azis? He's a Gypsy chalga singer. And then some. Check it: nothing (and no one) else in Bulgaria has quite so brazenly rejected the numbing greyness of official Bulgarian 'culture'. Not that Azis is a political activist. Indeed, I doubt if older he would have actively opposed Zhivkov's regime. Laughed at it? Sure. Winked at it too: I imagine he appreciates a man in uniform.

Initially Azis resembled a chubby, youthful André Agassi (big hair and stubble) and was viewed as just another Gypsy chalga singer, albeit one with a beguiling vocal style, his voice pitched high and keening. His metamorphosis into the most controversial entertainer in Bulgarian history involved a demonic appearance-shift and videos so lurid, so hallucinated with desire, they leave efforts by The Prodigy and Marilyn Manson gathering MTV dust. For the *AZIS 2002* album he was appearing in saris and belly-dance costumes, high heels on his feet, bleach in his hair, chest and armpits shaved. As were melodies from Greek, Serbian, Turkish, Egyptian and Bollywood songs, Azis adding lyrics (in Bulgarian and Romani) and a twisted eroticism: the beefy Gypsy boy transgressed into a symbol of the new Balkan night.

Indeed, Azis's concert at Sofia's Palace of Culture (in February 2003) was a near-perfect distillation of how Ottoman/Gypsy values have outlived Stalinism's attempt to crush such. The POC's a concrete haemorrhoid, 17,000 square metres of crap communist architecture. Opened in 1981 for the '1300 Years Of Bulgarian Nationhood' celebrations, the POC was once named after Todor Zhivkov's daughter, Lyudmila Zhivkova, who ruthlessly ran the Culture Ministry. 1981 was a big year for Bulgarian mythmaking and Lyudmila ensured daddy's nationalist fantasies were turned into epic, banal festivities; history got rewritten and state funds squandered.

Appropriately, when the POC hosted Azis he offered his own epic and beautifully banal fantasies. Taking the stage on a Harley accompanied by leather boys, his performance included simulating sex with men and women, marrying a body-builder then discarding said Muscle Mary so to gaze into a mirror and marry himself. Along the way he sang his hits, shook his tush and had a very good time. Parents, who'd somehow managed to overlook the blatant S&M tendencies in Azis's videos, declared themselves shocked and dragged little Boris and Dora away.

The POC was a warm-up: in October 2003 he attracted 15,000 fans to Sofia's National Stadium for an epic performance. Fronting a hot Gypsy band and flanked by a female body-builder and a local *Playboy* model wearing little more than body paint, Azis sang duets with several comely chalga stars, was groped by leather boys, surrounded by belly- and fire-dancers and even introduced his mother – a beautiful woman who grabbed the mic' and gave thanks to God for her son. Beyond spectacle, Azis possesses the brightest smile in town and sings in a voice charged with eerie, erotic beauty, quite unlike all I've heard before. The arrangements are strong, the band – led by Boril Iliev – cook up the chalga and the audience, dancing and holding lighters aloft, gets Thracian. It's Stadium Gypsy, good, unclean fun and I'd lay down lev to see him again.

For the nation's hottest singer Azis is remarkably easy to contact. Rumi rang his manager, who guaranteed an interview. In contrast, when Rumi contacted the ARA label who represent Sofi Marinova – Bulgaria's most popular female Gypsy singer – she was told 'Sofi only talks if she gets paid'. Explaining she'd get paid in ink didn't help and I ended up being offered an interview with her PR, who dropped such pearls as Sofi named her son Lorenzo after a Latin soap actor and how she has 'a Gypsy character distinct from our Bulgarian character'.

Shame I never got to meet Sofi, her albums are horribly overproduced but she can wail with the best of them. I once caught a wedding video featuring Sofi singing with Jony Iliev, their voices weaving and teasing, coiled and sensual. And she was easily the best duet partner for Azis at his National Stadium gig, the pair of them tossing off lines in Bulgarian and Romani as Sofi wiggled across the stage in leather hot-pants. Sofi's nicknamed 'Romska Perla' (the Gypsy Pearl) and Roma communities across the Balkans love her. But in Sofia the answer remains the same: no cash, no Sofi.

Arriving at Azis's management offices in central Sofia we're informed Azis is running late: he's filming a spot on the nation's leading light-entertainment TV show and shooting is delayed. Which makes me wonder: Azis as light entertainment…damn, Bulgaria really is one weird nation. His manager, Krum Krumov, crop-headed and heavily muscled, provides coffee and cigarettes, fires questions at me ('how' and 'why' does London know of and want to talk to his charge) and recalls Azis coming to him wanting to succeed. 'I'd had an idea to make a movie about the Gypsies so I knew something of them. In Bulgaria there's three groups of Gypsies. The Kalderash, who are the businessmen and are the highest class. The second group are the Yerlii, singers and dancers and shoe-makers. They're middle class. And then there's the Rudara who work with bears and make spoons and beg. They're the poor Gypsies.' As potted ethnography it's not exactly accurate but Krum's point is this: 'Azis is Kalderash so I knew we could do business.' Azis's career took off after they made the first scandal video that showed him and 'the Negro' together with a boa constrictor. 'That drove everyone crazy.'

Krum then plays the new Azis video for 'Nikoi Ne Mozhe' (Nobody Can). The clip begins in silence. Sitting in a nightclub, a body-builder and his female companion stare into one another's eyes. Then Azis enters and BB's eyes are all over Azis. Who pays no attention. BB rises. Girl tries to hold him back. BB rushes to touch Azis. Bodyguards pound BB. Girl screams. Cut to Azis in a spangly Hindu Love God outfit and outrageously fake fingernails standing in a fountain surrounded by white swans. He's wailing Bollywood style. Cut to Azis and body-builder bonding on pink satin sheets. Swans. Satin. Manly hugs. It goes on like this until the song finishes and the video cuts back to the nightclub's silence. Azis enters the toilets, where discarded amongst the urinals is BB with a needle hanging out of his arm. Azis brushes a tear away. Fini. As a performer Azis is one of those rare artists who's beyond embarrassment, no matter how tacky or kitsch his efforts. Krum asks: what do I make of the video? Uh, well, more fun than *Trainspotting*. The video was shot in O'Azis, the Sofia club Azis owns, says Krum. Boy's done well.

And then the boy is in the room. Smiling, eyes twinkling (beautiful eyes), gossiping and giggly about his TV appearance, checking me out, puffing on a cigarette, wearing leather pants, black T-shirt, denim jacket, eyeliner, tattooed neck. First impressions: he's big for a Gypsy, tall, huge thighs, strong shoulders, already carrying the belly that signals success on the Indian subcontinent. And dark, caramel skin glowing. The baleful Azis has been left on set; today he's more Liberace than Lucifer, his aura one of intrigue, mischief, of…Little Richard. Their impish sense of outrage, ability to blend musical forms and camp affectations suggest spiritual kin: Azis's chants and yearning wail as distinctive as Little Richard's shrieks and roaring 'AWOPBOPALOOBOP ALOPBAMBOOM'.

Introductions are made. Azis starts to talk.

'I was born Vasil Troyanov Boyanov in 1978 in Sliven [a central Bulgarian city that hosts the nation's largest Roma community]. Vasko's always been my nickname and even as a child I knew I could sing. My parents were always feeding me and always afraid to let me go out by myself. When I wanted to go alone they would follow me, hidden! One time I went to see *Indiana Jones*. There was a horrible moment when they pull out the heart of a man. I screamed. You know how high my voice is now, imagine it then in the cinema! Suddenly I heard my father call out, "Vasko, I'm here. Don't be afraid!" As a child I always liked dolls and sometimes I would dress up in my mother's clothes and do theatre for my grandmother. And I'd make her promise not to tell my mother! Although my father was a professional accordion-player he didn't like the idea of me being a musician at all. I started singing in the church choir, singing in Romani, but this was not enough for me.

'We shifted to Banishora [a working-class part of Sofia] and when I was eleven we formed a family ensemble and travelled all over Bulgaria and I would perform every night impersonating Michael Jackson. I took my school books with me but I never liked school, I always wanted to be at home watching my Madonna videos. A friend of my father gave me a cassette of Indian music and it impressed me very much, I listened to it day and night. My father saw my voice was not too different from Indian voices. The women of India impressed me very much and whenever they showed Bollywood movies at the cinema hundreds of Gypsies would be waiting and when the movie started we would all begin to cry.

'When I was thirteen my family shifted to Germany. In Stuttgart my mother gave birth to my little sister. My parents love one another very much. When my father sings love songs in restaurants he would think of my mother and cry. And my mother is very beautiful. In Germany people would think she was Whitney Houston. Every time I see Whitney Houston on TV I cry and call my mother. I didn't like the people in Germany at all. They weren't from my blood group. Cold, grey, tense. It's different in Bulgaria. I wanted to come home to my granny. I cried my eyes out. My mother wouldn't let me go for a year and a half but finally agreed. At least I learned perfect German. When I came back to Bulgaria

Sofi Marinova

Photo ©APA

all my relatives were at the airport, collapsing, crying. We, the Gypsies, are more temperamental, we cry for the smallest thing. I started living with my granny in Kostinbrod.

'I promised my mother that I would go to school when I returned to Bulgaria but I had totally different plans. I remember how everyone in the classroom was reading some books but that wasn't interesting to me. When they asked me why I wasn't reading I told them that I would be a star. The whole class was laughing at me, they constantly made jokes about me, but I knew I'd show them. I didn't want my mother or granny to give me money. They were worried what the people would think, that I would work and they would not support me, but I wanted to be self-sufficient.

'I started singing in my cousin's bar where I worked as a waiter. When the band left the bar they asked me to come with them as their singer. I had lots of jobs, did anything, I was determined to make it as a singer. Sure, I did weddings and traditional Gypsy things like that. But not for long. It's too small for me. I know Jony and Sofi but I've never been interested in doing that traditional Gypsy music thing. I'm for the big stage with professional sound and lighting. The small party, the small business, it doesn't interest me. So in that way I'm not the typical Roma performer. My parents did not make a big deal about being Gypsy and while I don't hide my Gypsy heritage I wouldn't say I was very proud of it.'

OK, bait the liberal Gadje time. But I'm not biting. Azis sings in Romani, employs Gypsy musicians, has supported Roma organisations. He might not confess such but word gets about. Bulgaria's Roma love him for this, for his success, for his fearless personality, for his freedom and fame. And for his music – no one anywhere in contemporary music has quite so much fun as Azis; he creates, to paraphrase Phil Spector, little Gypsy symphonies for the kids. Songs lurch into being, tablas bang out rhythms, cheesy synths boil, clarinets shriek, Azis chants before drifting into his lovely effete vocal, then the tune explodes – abrupt rhythmic changes, snippets of English ('Have mercy!' 'Eat this!') are dropped in – Azis squeals 'wey-hey!' and it's lush and crazy and camp and slick and trashy and ridiculous and funny and engaging and magical and senseless and vivid, yeah, extremely vivid…the mad Balkan Bollywood experience packed into four fabulous minutes. Where the 1990s' dance music boom produced a sound bereft of wit and rhythmic ingenuity, bland on bland, Azis offers a musical rollercoaster, the sound of surprise. 'I really like your songs,' I say.

'Thank you,' says Azis and wiggles his head, a very Indian gesture given a camp cowboy's twist. Considering the word 'bugger' is a distortion of Bulgar – the British once considered the nation full of sodomites – one could make a case for historic lineage out of Azis. Not here, not now. Still, it's worth noting that Bulgaria under Zhivkov was straighter than straight – homosexuality was outlawed in the Soviet states – and only the carrot of EU membership has recently forced a reversal of blatantly homophobic laws in Bulgaria and Romania (Yugoslavia having decriminalised homosexuality in 1932). I'm unaware of any research into Roma sexuality. Most likely a community of outsiders value their own shadow dwellers; the 'putzka' (gays) have always played a subterranean role in Hindu and Turkish society. And with the cult of virginity still a determinant for bride price then where do young Roma men turn for sexual release? Celibacy? In Bulgaria? Hmmmm. OK, time for the money shot: Azis, tick a box – gay–straight–bisexual?

Azis smiles. A smile bright enough to illuminate Sofia. Eyes twinkle. Says nothing. Not that I expected an answer. Krum had warned me earlier, 'No one knows if he is or isn't. The mystery keeps them guessing.' And those explicitly homoerotic pop videos? Keep 'em guessing. Sure.

'Azis's last album sold 68,000 copies,' says Krum. 'That is phenomenal for Bulgaria.'

Considering the majority of the nation don't own CD players and live in effective poverty that is, sure, phenomenal. Are they buying the music or the outrage? The decadence is as calculated as Madonna's efforts, sure, but the sound of Azis – yearning, playful, engaged – is light years removed from Madonna's icy corporate moves. Azis, has the explicit erotic content of your songs and videos ever brought about censorship problems?

'There was a time when some of the TV channels tried to stop showing my videos. But the people protested and no one is bigger than the people and the people love me.'

Azis blags another cigarette off Krum and starts messing with his hair. As, so far, nothing is written in English on Azis I'm unsure how long he's been recording for. Could he provide a brief career overview? Azis laughs and says something to Krum, who searches through his desk and comes up with a cassette that's passed to me. It shows a smartly dressed family on the cover and its Bulgarian title translates as Christian Roma Songs. 'That's my first recording,' says Azis with glee. It's hard to see the connection between the handsome, stocky youth standing behind his parents and the exotic peacock in front of me. 'Your parents must be very proud of you?' Azis cocks an eyebrow. 'I suppose you could say that.'

It was in 1999 that Vasko Boyanov signed a contract with Marathon Records and Azis was born. 'I was watching a Turkish movie on TV when I was eighteen and a character was called Azis. I wrote the name on the wall because I knew immediately here was my name.'

Azis's propensity for outrage came from looking East not West, his immediate spiritual ancestors being Zeki Müren and Bülent Ersoy. Zeki was Turkey's cross-dressing crooner, once a very pretty boy and forever loved by Turkish housewives. He ran to fat and tired of touring in the late 1980s but, unable to resist the spotlight, attempted a comeback tour in '96. Bad idea: presented with a four-kilo award for his contribution to Turkish culture the excitement was too much and Zeki had a heart attack. A trooper to the end, Zeki died with his makeup on.

Bülent is Turkey's transsexual superstar. Banned from re-entering Turkey in 1980 after a sex change – the then military government saw Bülent as a threat to public morals – he settled in Germany and played to the Turkish community there. Invited back in 1987 (the President was a fan and missed having Bulent around), she's not opted for a respectable middle age: singing the call to prayer on a recording, parading a variety of boyfriends (average age: nineteen) in front of the nation and, recently, announcing she wants to marry her current man. As imams and military figures howled in outrage and right-wing organisations issued death threats, Bülent raised a false eyelash and winked at Turkey's moral guardians, revelling in controversy. While Bülent and Zeki aren't of Roma origin much Turkish music and dance are informed by Gypsy culture. In turn, Balkan Roma recall the

Ottomans with some affection; Bulgarian communism smothered, but never extinguished, this cultural link.

Azis's first songs were included in the compilation *DJ Folk Marathon*. His 1999 debut album *Pain* opens with the lead song sung in Romani. He then won Singer of the Year at the Stara Zagora Roma Festival in Central Bulgaria.

'My music is addressed to the party people but my power is in the ballads,' he says when I ask him to describe his sound. 'That's where I spill my soul out.'

His second album, *Muzhete Sushto Plachat* (Men Also Cry), was released in February 2000 and a video featuring Azis and a stripper raised eyebrows. 'That's when the visual change started in me – I would appear on stage in makeup and started bleaching my hair. I don't know why I shouldn't put makeup on when my female colleagues can go on stage only in bra and knickers. And for those who criticise me I only say, "Hate me, that makes me live".'

In August 2000 Azis announced he was going to bleach his face. Just like Michael Jackson. He didn't but the media were excited and Azis's star kept rising. He scored a huge hit with 'Sulzi' (Tears) and won the Best Live Artist award at The Golden Mustang festival in September 2000. In 2001 the 'Hvani Me De' (Come On, Catch Me) video found him dressed in Bollywood drag, playing with a python and licking milk off the chests of two underdressed black men. The ensuring hysteria guaranteed household-name status.

'I touched many themes that are taboo in Bulgaria. I was in a hurry to do it as, one way or another, someone was going to do it. I either do something truly or I don't do it at all.'

In 2001 Azis met Lili Ivanova and declared her his idol; Lily's the grand old diva of Bulgarian pop, having built her career singing estrada (Russian-style pop). Once the nation's darling, Lili still sings, though she's now more famous for copious plastic surgery than her bland songs. In the 1960s Lili played Shirley Bassey to Emil Dimitrov's Tom Jones; his big number – commissioned by the communists and still hugely popular – is 'Moia Strana, Moia Bulgaria' (My Country, My Bulgaria). Emil's still singing and, having never married, is assumed by most Bulgarians to be gay. All of which suggests Azis should enjoy a long and profitable homeland career.

The *AZIS 2002* album found him perfecting his sound (hits 'Obicham Te' and 'Niama') and image – bleached hair, eyebrows, facial hair and contact lenses against chocolate skin made him resemble a Gypsy android. 2003's very fine *Na Golo* (Naked) album finds Azis looking as if he may have, with the help of surgeons (or Photoshop), crossed genders. Rumours abounded that he was now a transsexual. On the back cover he's fetching in a bright sari and stilettos. *Na Golo* is fabulous, the best Balkan pop album ever. 2004's *Kraliat* (King) finds him mimicking Madonna's *True Blue* album cover and singing several epic Balkan ballads. The chalga numbers are less inspired, lacking the madcap bhangra exuberance of *Na Golo*. Azis is flash and hype, sure, but so are, say, Outkast and Prince, both of whom he bears a certain resemblance to. And when he sings a ballad it's as if Smokey Robinson's ethereal spirit was enticing the listener on, hand against heart, condoms and KY jelly on show.

Back in the office the slow pace of questions being fed into Bulgarian and answers translated back into English finds Azis distracted, flicking through a magazine. Does he enjoy meeting fans? 'No, no. It bores me.' What made him open a club? 'Sofia needed a club like you see in movies where you can see naked women and naked men walking around.' What does he do when not working? 'Watch TV, videos. I'm very lazy, I shift from this sofa to that sofa. Most of my friends are gay, very funny people, so we're sitting, laughing, talking.'

OK. Thanks for your time. 'Thank you very much,' he says in bubbly English. And flashes that smile. Waiting outside Krum's office is the body-builder who featured as the doomed love interest in the *Nobody Can* video. Rumi, who'd been reluctant to do the interview ('why do you want to talk to him? He's so vulgar!'), is impressed. 'Well, I'm surprised,' she says. 'He speaks very good Bulgarian. Unlike all the other musicians you interview who speak rough Bulgarian because they spend all their lives speaking Romani. But he, wow, he speaks it without any accent, as beautifully as a politician.'

Out on the street I start chuckling. Rumi gives me one of her 'crazy foreigner' looks. But I can't help this happy mirth, seeing Azis as emblematic of all the eccentric possibilities the Balkan future holds. And with Rumi now on side, Rumi who until this evening dismissed chalga out of hand and felt a strong nostalgia for the Zhivkov era, well, Bulgaria looks bright. Now the world can only be Azis's aphrodisiac…What's that sound? AWOPBOPALOOBOP ALOPBAMBOOM!

Mahala Blues 4:
The Saddest Place On Earth

Bill went on, 'See all those things go into the same word.
The fact of the business, back in those days a Negro
didn't mean no more to a white man than a mule'.
                                        Blues In The Mississippi Night

I love the Balkan night, dark shadows and a lingering sense of mystery. And no night is more tangible than that of Ederlezi, the night of the Gypsies. Soon we will be deep in the Kyustendil mahala, watching the evening explode. Fire. Fire will be everywhere. Tongues of flame licking across buildings, beautiful and incandescent.

Leaving Sofia we pass, while crawling up a mountain road, a huge blond stone statue of a haidouk, those nineteenth-century Che Guevaras of Balkan myth. I do my usual 'who is it?' and Rumi shakes her head and mutters about being force-fed lies about the 'heroic liberators' for decades. Rumi guns the Peugeot, up, up we go and round and round we twist. Suddenly we're crossing Vitosha Planina and Bulgaria is beautiful. Let me emphasise that: Bulgaria is beautiful. Many are surprised when I tell them this. Which is understandable if all you've seen is Sofia. Cos Sofia's mutt ugly. And as we start to descend the mountain the land opens and rolls forth, gentle, golden terrain spreading like a fertile wave pattern, earth that's fed countless generations, resplendent Balkan beauty. After a week in Sofia, living on the fourteenth floor of a dilapidated tower block, wandering the city's concrete basins and crumbly

Photo: Garth Cartwright

Dirt poor…Kyustendil mahala

mahalas, I start babbling, nature boy himself. Rumi sucks on a cigarette, gives me the arched eyebrow look I'm becoming familiar with across the Balkans and balls the jack. Vrrrrrooooooooom! Vrrrrrrooooooooooom!

This highway used to be decorated with communist propaganda billboards, huge socialist–realist rectangles advertising the Warsaw Pact's ever smiling, always sunny face. A popular image involved virtuous Bulgarian and Russian workers advertising 'solidarity'. Another often found was of peasants celebrating bumper harvests and the 'eternal friendship' between Mama Russia and baby Bulgaria. Then there were billboards with 'Peace' written in many languages. In the early 90s these billboards still stood, wonderfully anachronistic, mementoes of a vanished society. Finest of all was a mural featuring a peasant girl painted on the side of a building in one village. Today the mural is buried beneath Coca-Cola ads. Shame – communist art was naff, sure, but entertainingly so, and if still standing would provide a welcome respite from the crap tobacco and soft drink billboards now littering the highway.

Pernik, which rises in front of us, could sure use a few billboards celebrating proletarian spirit. Once powered by coal and iron production, Pernik's now primarily infamous as home to Kati, chalga's most fabulously slutty singer (theme tune: 'I Like it Best with a Few Men'). Today the city's beginning to resemble a Soviet-era ghost town, all crumbling factories, seriously dilapidated housing estates, rusty machinery, swastika graffiti, men sitting on benches staring into a distance further than I ever want to see. Rumi sighs like she's stumbled on a bad memory, fixes eyes on the highway, urging the Peugeot south. Smooth shoulders, dangerous curves, a true Balkan highway unfolds as we roll through poor, poisoned Pernik. I lean out the window, catch the breeze, sense Macedonia in the distance, calling my name.

Travelling with Rumi allows for no dull moments; leaving Sofia, she, having missed the exit, slammed the car into reverse on the motorway – 'It might take me half an hour to find another exit' – so zig-zagging amongst oncoming traffic…From this moment on I knew nothing, sweet nothing, could go wrong and Dean Moriarty's spirit was cruising, yeah, cruising alongside us. Appropriate company as we're heading towards a destination where sleep will be unknown. We talk local politics; I'm intrigued that, at present, Bulgaria's king is the elected Prime Minister. Especially considering Bulgaria's a republic. Never underestimate the Balkans' ability to deliver the absurd.

'He's a good man but when he was elected [in June, 2001] he made so many promises about how he was going to raise the standard of living for Bulgarians and now, a few years later on, that's not come true. So people are discontented. I believe he's honest but those around him…the corruption continues. Maybe for people in Poland, the Czech Republic, Hungary, life is better now communism has ended. But in Bulgaria we have never had good government and life is so much more difficult. OK, we have more freedom and it's much easier to buy things. You used to have to have contacts to get certain things. But beyond that, everything is worse. Before, Sofia was a clean city. They had lots of people employed to keep the city clean. Now, well, someone has a contract to keep the city clean but the money vanishes rather than is spent on employing cleaners. And before you never worried if you could feed your children, what you would provide for dinner that night. Now, it can be so tough. Before, life was very easy. We used to take two holidays a year. One on the Black Sea and one in the mountains. Now we can't afford to take holidays.'

Tsar Simeon II is a populist who rode to power due to his not being a career politician. Exiled in Madrid for fifty years – the communists held a 1946 referendum (of sorts) that found overwhelming support for Bulgaria to become a republic – he began returning to Bulgaria in the mid-1990s. His leap into politics is very recent and appears motivated more by a desire to try and save the nation than simply regaining the throne. Good luck to him; Bulgaria is 57th on the UN Development Programme's human development report (based on the wealth and life expectancy of its citizens and the government's commitment to education), ranking above Romania, Albania, Bosnia but behind most other East European states. The Tsar's got his hands more than full with economic and social problems. And nowhere are these problems more evident than the mahalas.

Last time I arrived in Kyustendil I leaped off the bus from Skopje, landing without lev. Or much idea of where I was. Kyustendil, sure, but nothing around me appeared familiar. Sunday evening so even the forlorn exchange office opposite the bus and train stations was solidly shut. Through sign language and much waving of a bank-card I persuaded a taxi to take me to what appeared to be the city's one operating ATM. Laden with lev, I informed the driver 'mahala'. 'Mahala?' 'Da. Kyustendil mahala.' 'Mahala? Tsigane?' 'Da, da. Jony Iliev.' 'Ah! Jony Iliev! OK!'

Today we sweep through fields of sun-ripened maize before turning off the highway into the mahala's narrow streets. An ambient world unfolds in front of us. Not much traffic noise (not many inhabitants own cars) but everywhere motion, sound, people, horses, carts, dogs, music…kinetic community stuff. In one corner of the mahala's square a wedding's taking place. The bride's tiny and stout, the groom tall and lanky; hand in hand with guests they dance, swaying in a semicircle motion, a gigantic amoeba, dogs and drunks slipping amongst them whilst accordion, clarinet and drum open up and bleed, reedy and weird, calling the children home. There's maybe two dozen guests, tiny compared to Elvis's event, but the affair is charged with emotion. Back and forth they move, dancing the horo (a constant, loving rhythm), bride in white, groom wearing sports jacket and trilby, walking on sunshine.

Chico Iliev greets us. He's proprietor of the café on the south side of the square and one of the most decent and thorough human beings I've ever had the good fortune to meet. He's also Jony Iliev's older brother and mentor, having taken on the patriarch's responsibilities when his father died. We embrace; Chico's a huggy bear type of guy, someone so overflowing with good will a squeeze from him is a dose of vitamin C for the soul. Kyustendil: it's good to be back.

There's lots of catching up to do: deliver a Beckham Real Madrid football top as requested by Yulian, Chico's oldest son; a chat with Alex, Chico's younger son who speaks English following an extended sabbatical in the UK; and kisses on both cheeks for Lubka, Chico's beaming wife. Dump our bags at the family house, a spacious abode in the north of the mahala. Jony and Naza are here, Ederlezi reuniting families. The mahala's squeezed into the arse-end of the city, past crumbly apartment blocks and crusty factories. Streets aren't so much potholed as cratered and although the concentration of people and housing is extremely urban the detritus of rural existence – horses, pigs, chickens, produce drying in the sun – remains visible. Patjival o manus an' la vi anda gav xaljardo? Let's hope, for there are many righteous men and women in Kyustendil's mahala.

Rumi and I leave everyone to get on with family affairs and head for central Kyustendil. The contrast between the city's mahala and its centre is such the term 'underdevelopment' – as opposed to simply saying 'poor part of town' – springs to mind. Famous since Thracian times for thermal springs, on a blazing Balkan afternoon Kyustendil's wide, tree-lined avenues and café-dominated squares are mighty appealing.

Trawling the main pedestrian boulevard I find it hard to believe two things: firstly, that Bulgaria's in such shabby economic shape – the well-dressed, well-fed people at leisure here could be Austrians – and, secondly, the Third-World poverty so defining the existence of many mahala residents is allowed to exist only a couple of kilometres away. The Black Eyed Peas are MTV regulars while I wander the Balkans and I think, yes, where is the love?

Rumi and I do the white thing – take a table in the sun, order drinks – and watch Bulgaria stroll. Spring, idyllic weather, delicious beer. Yet this all only serves to heighten my slow, weary blues. *Mingra manus.* My people. That's how Jony describes the mahala dwellers. I've stayed there often enough, spent considerable time amongst Balkan Roma, begin to sense they're my people too. Crazy, I know, this Kiwi goof who can't even communicate without Rumi translating, trying to suggest kin. Yet...Yet great affection and empathy, we share it. Oh, gosh. Yes. So, in some crazy mixed-up way, these are my people.

Returning, we physically sense the mahala before seeing it: tarmac disintegrates, grass verges haven't been trimmed, garbage gathers in piles. To be a mahala resident involves something less than being a citizen – living like a refugee in the nation of your birth – marginalised by local and national government and all the powers that be. Them belly full but we hungry. I'm amazed the mahalas don't occasionally erupt, hordes of ragged Gypsies raging towards the town hall, sharing their love of fire with government buildings, too much of nothing making people burn. Of course, tomorrow the mahala will erupt. In celebration. And maybe this contains and cools the fuel that feeds riots. Or perhaps it's the inherent gentleness of the Roma. Throughout my many visits to Kyustendil I'm yet to attract any hostility, this Gadje who wanders amongst them, yet these people are amongst the poorest in Europe. Or maybe booze and glue strip spirit, asbestos for the soul.

Back at Chico's Jony and Naza want to stroll. Chico joins us. All right, this should be interesting. I start telling Jony about my misadventures with Sofi Marinova, 'she's a good person but lately getting a swollen head', and my encounter with Azis. 'He's a little vulgar but a good singer and performer. I'm happy for his success as it reflects well on all of us.'

Mahala life is lived on the streets: these are social people, quick to smile, always wanting to share a word, a gesture. Our part of the mahala is comfortable, broken tarmac and dusty, sure, but the houses have been built by individuals who managed to earn hard currency – Chico spent three years labouring and playing music in Germany to build his house. There's none of the extravagant architecture of Shutka here, perhaps because this mahala is smaller, poorer, and Bulgarian communism was so severe it squeezed the juice out of everyone. Edelweiss, the alpine flower, appears to be the mahala's emblem, its outline patterned into walls and terraces. As we drift across the central square, houses get smaller, streets narrow, until we arrive in what Jony and Chico refer to as 'the ghetto'.

Here houses become shacks constructed out of concrete, brick, wood and canvas. Windows lack glass – not a concern in today's heat but the snow-capped Osogovo and Rila mountains loom close; in winter these people surely freeze. Rubbish is dumped, a confetti of plastic bags clutter the stream, there's no sewerage or running water for the shanties, country living remains the principle – horses tethered in front of houses, mangy dogs, pigs and chickens in the yard (of better-off ghetto dwellers), electricity's siphoned from power lines and the streets are dirt.

Now I comprehend Jony's statement, 'If it rains in Kyustendil it is the saddest place on earth.'

This extreme poverty, closer to the shanty towns encircling Kathmandu and Delhi than the barren concrete estates looming across much of urban Eastern Europe, means time passes slowly here. Not in the leisurely manner one expects of rural idylls. And Kyustendil's mahala is anything but rural, being surrounded by derelict factories and a traffic artery. Instead, time grinds, minute by minute, no work and little hope lending an air of emptiness and frustration. People sit on door stoops, idling over cigarettes, brushing away flies. TVs are watched with blank attention. Nothing happens and for most nothing ever will. Here souls are harvested, hung up and left out to rust. Men look through me: jailhouse tattoos, hollow cheeks, tombstone eyes. Children, golden-brown and coated in dust, surround Jony, the Gypsy pied piper, shrieking with excitement and palpable joy. In Chico's section of the mahala the children are smartly dressed, black hair shiny, clean. Here they wear rags, play amongst trash. We live on, from and upon garbage. Again and again, these same mahala blues.

'A lot of the children have talent,' says Jony as he pats heads, 'but what is killing me is that the talent will never get the opportunity to come out.'

Wandering amongst us are youths sniffing from plastic bags, blunted on reality: numb smiles and sightless eyes. Chico observes, a man of constant sorrow, then states that in recent years he has adopted two boys, both wrecked on glue. The older now has a job outside the mahala. The younger, Ivolo, I've met as he helps in Chico's café. Whether from glue or birth I'm unsure but Ivolo's clearly mentally handicapped, a man-child, constantly smiling, his eyes giddy, mind sated. 'When I found him he was in a very bad way,' says Chico. 'He is one of eight children whose father is a drunk and sends them out to beg. Now he is off glue and learning tasks.'

The sight of Jony ensures a traffic jam of humanity soon engulfs us. Old friends call out, shake hands, exchange kisses. 'Jony, you have forgotten us but we haven't forgotten you,' shouts a woman. Jony smiles a sad smile and nods (indicating 'no'). Not forgotten but this isn't home any more. 'I feel good to meet my own people in the place where I grew up,' he says. 'At the same time I feel bad because I see they live a very hard life, very poor, and I can't really help them except with my music. They say they want me to be mayor because they trust me but I'm not a political man.'

Mahala survival involves a desperate hustle: begging charity scavenging petty crime poor housing no legal title. Chico takes us to a series of solid huts built by an Austrian charity. They resemble those used by the military or mountaineers. We enter one. It consists of a large room – four bunk beds, stove, sink, running water. A photo of Azis, ripped from a magazine, is decoration. 'We are very happy to have this,' says the hut's hostess. 'Before we lived so badly.'

Walking back, we stop at Mama Iliev's house on the border of the ghetto. Naidenka Ivanova Ilieva remains a formidable matriarch – as you would expect, having raised eight boys and one girl, survived fascism and communism and seen the mahala collapse into what she calls 'these bad times.' Mama Iliev is sixty-seven although her weathered features – black eyes, silver hair, fierce presence – suggest she's as old as the earth itself. Her tone is gentle, reflective, happy for Jony and Boril's success yet sad for the Romas' plight.

'We've always been from this mahala. My grandparents were from here so I never heard stories of our ancestors being nomadic. My husband and I worked in the tobacco factory and he played music. I was very young when the Germans were here but I remember them coming to the mahala and bombs going off and my mother taking me to hide in the fields. There was a man from Kyustendil called Dimitar Peshev and he was the man who saved

the Gypsies and the Jews. After the communists came to power
they put him in jail for fifteen years. Ten years ago his name was
rehabilitated and his house is now a museum.

'Maybe the only people who could be happy under communism
were the Gypsies because things became better and they took
houses from the rich and gave to the poor. And they built up
factories so there were more jobs. Now Gypsies don't have homes,
jobs; everything is difficult and we wonder why all these changes
yet things are worse than before.'

Chico adds that under communism it was obligatory to work.

'The police would check your papers and if you said your job
was "musician" and didn't have the stamp in your papers [stating
exactly where you were working] they would beat you.'

Retreat to Chico's café. It's a simple structure offering local
newspapers, soft drinks and scalding coffee in plastic cups. Don't
try and order a decaf latte here. Yanis, Jony's teenage son from his
first marriage, arrives and embraces dad. 'Football and education
are, I think, his real passions,' says Jony. 'But I also know blood is
thicker than water and maybe he will be a singer.'

Alex helps Chico run the café. Tomorrow he gets engaged. His
bride-to-be, Macarena, is a pale-skinned, henna-haired beauty with
a wise, wry look in her eye. Alex's year in the UK came about through
him gaining a visa to see Bulgaria play Northern Ireland at football.
Game over, he applied for asylum, citing anti-Roma sentiment at
home. He laboured and learned English. To the British tabloids Alex
is their worst nightmare, an asylum-seeking Gypsy.

'People helped me. One man would make me repeat the things
he said. "What is your name?" "Wha es yer nom?"' He laughs at
the memory. 'But that is how I learned English. And then I went to
England and lived in Southampton. I liked the English, very polite,
always saying "sorry". I got a job laying paving and the people who
we were working for would always come around and offer us coffee,
tea, lunch. Nice people, nice houses.' Alex was interviewed three

Mama Iliev

Photo: Garth cartwright

times about his application during the year he was living in the UK. 'Always so many questions,' he remembers. 'Were you really persecuted?' I ask, as if an undercover Home Office agent. 'Some. But not so much. Gypsies have problems here but I have never suffered the way some have.' And the British decided? 'I decided that I missed my family and friends so I returned here,' says Alex. 'I would like to go back for six months to see people I met there and save some money because it is so difficult here to earn any money. But I don't think I need to live in Britain again.'

That evening Lubka serves lamb stew, peppers fried in egg and a spicy salad. If anyone intends to open a Roma restaurant, hire this woman. Chico introduces Stefan Lazarov, schoolteacher and head of New Morning, the local Roma organisation. Lazarov offers a mahala history lesson: in 1890 the Roma of Kyustendil were forced from the centre of the city to its outskirts. 10,000 Roma live here with up to 95 per cent unemployment. Bulgaria's Roma once identified themselves by the work their specific communities specialised in and Kyustendil is largely home to Christian Yerli Roma (as opposed to Muslim Horohane Roma), especially the Dassihane caste, the basket-weavers. There is little demand for weavers these days – cheap imports from China having wiped out much of Eastern Europe's traditional Roma manufacturing base – so only a few manage to eke out a living weaving baskets and brooms. Lazarov claims the Roma people were originally made up of four different tribes who left west India two thousand years ago and the inhabitants of Kyustendil's mahala are descended from those of the noblest tribe. Wish fulfilment? Sure, but one that displays itself in community pride.

After the fall of communism the Roma began organising: they have their own school that teaches in Romani and Bulgarian. Lazarov proudly notes in recent years the mahala school has seen two hundred people graduate – it is thought as few as 50 per cent of Roma children in Bulgaria attend school – producing five university graduates, four students currently at university and other students going on to higher education. Finance comes from an American development organisation, entrepreneur George Soros, Dutch and UN human rights organisations. And from the Seventh Day Adventist Church, which, over the last decade, has gathered a considerable following amongst Bulgarian Roma. This mahala is, he says, the best organised in Bulgaria because 'no one steals the money'.

On my initial visit to Kyustendil I found Rom@net, the only mahala internet café I've ever encountered. Set up by Ilcho Dimitrov, Rom@net was a giant step forward, offering computer skills to mahala youth. Yet now Rom@net's no more. The financing ended and Ilcho couldn't cover costs. Unbowed, he teaches from his home. Still, a defeat for the mahala and, considering the funds wasted on EU and NATO projects, a tiny cash injection could surely have kept Rom@net going.

Anti-Pun, a four-man Roma theatre troupe, arrive. They talk of how in 1999 the government introduced a specific programme of eight directives to help Roma (health, education, women, development). Yet the directives remain 'a programme that was written but remains only written. It stayed on the books, you understand me? It was never implemented within the mahalas. The programme was important for Bulgaria's candidacy for the EU. After Bulgaria was put on the list for EU entry in 2007 the programme was conveniently forgotten.' They also mention a tale I've heard before: when President Clinton was booked to visit Bulgaria the US Embassy emphasised the government had to be pro-active towards the Roma populace or his visit would be cancelled. The government issued new legislation. Clinton visited. Nothing changed. Perfect realpolitik. Lazarov and Anti-Pun leave. Chico broods, full of sorrow and anger.

'I can discipline my dog but many of the Gypsies here, they know no discipline, have no respect. They're not proud of being Roma, don't know their history and of people like Esma [Redžepova] who have discipline, work hard. Communism was good for Gypsies. They were like sheep and this suited them – Baaa! Baaaa! – they didn't have to learn to read or write or to think for themselves. Everyone was forced to do a job – if you refused they put you in a labour camp – but the work never really was too hard nor did much have to be done. It was a corrupt time. I'll give you an example. I was in the military band and it was my birthday and my wife was working in a factory and so I wanted to take her out but my commanding officer wouldn't give me the evening off. So I went and brought him a bottle of brandy and suddenly I had the evening free. That's how everything worked.

'This mahala needs more people like me. But I'm alone. The schools aren't good. Even if they can't read they go on to the next class. People play and dance but they don't learn. Basically, all the teachers are Bulgarian and some of the children have bad parents who don't make them go to school and the teachers don't care. I'm like an immigrant here – I've lived in Stuttgart and know the need for discipline and organisation. But many parents don't. And then you get outsiders coming here and saying "the roads are terrible", "the poverty is terrible", but they get nothing done. The Gypsies need their own boss to make improvements. And the children need to go to school with Bulgarian children so they get a real education. They have good minds but they need to be opened. They need a bit of Hitler's discipline.'

'Hitler murdered lots of Gypsies.'

'No, Hitler never hurt the Gypsies.'

'He did. C'mon, Chico, he was a bad guy.'

A long pause follows as Chico thinks.

'Hitler made it very bad for everybody, yes. But his discipline and punctuality are good for people. If a Gypsy makes something bad they make it bad for every Gypsy.'

Stuttgart's obviously made quite an impression on Chico. As have the Seventh Day Adventists: Chico and family joined the Adventists, finding the American Evangelists very welcoming. Gimme salvation? Step this way. Chico suggests many in the mahala have turned Adventist. A proportion remain Orthodox, some Muslim, others atheists. Balkan Islam is notoriously lax and, recently, Saudi Arabia's begun pouring money into mosque construction in mahalas, aiming at converting Muslim Roma and Evangelical strays to their strict Wahhabi sect form of Sunni Islam. In Bosnia, where bitterness and a sense of betrayal pervade, this may work. But I doubt the Wahhabis will catch on elsewhere. I mean, how can you praise Allah without rakija?

Chico and Yuli

Yuli Iliev's taken the night off from playing Sofia's restaurants with his band Red Bull in preparation for tomorrow's festivities. Why, he asks, isn't Jony's German manager interested in his chalga? Europe's full of modern music, I say, which is why it hungers after traditional Balkan Gypsy music. Yuli plays me new tunes on a large Korg keyboard. Tough jazz funk. A thumping chalga track. TV theme music. How can I help him get these instrumental tracks heard by someone in London? Get a great singer, Yuli. Get Jony or Sofi and have them sing on the tracks and then people may listen. What about, he asks, with a rapper? Well, I reply, he would have to be a very good rapper who raps in English. 'What about Panjabi MC then?' *Touché*: the only music I heard emanating from Britain during my Balkan sojourns was Panjabi MC, his blend of India-greets-hip-hop being embraced by all ethnicities. Go for it, Yuli, create Balkan bhangra.

Yuli plays sessions, restaurants, weddings, is part of Azis's live band. But things are still not easy, there's too much scrabbling, and the stress is damaging his marriage, his wife Slavka having gone to 'visit' her mother in Sofia. At least Yuli's still in Kyustendil, many mahala men having left for Sofia or international pastures, their wives and children remaining here. Alexandria, Yuli's busty, bottle-blonde cousin, lives next door to Chico and is raising infant daughter Cicelia alone. 'Princess', it reads on Cicelia's shorts, and the way her mother and relatives indulge Cicelia it certainly appears this beautiful child is being raised as mahala royalty. Yet Alexandria's eyes have a sad, faraway look, one common to solo parents who recognise the huge struggle before them. Her husband? An economic migrant. And Alexandria's tired of waiting. First Ireland, she tells me, now for a long time he's in Holland. The lack of employment prospects chasing many young Roma men into the EU, their women become economic widows resigned to prolonged absences.

Chico's house is a comfortable place to sleep but a passing lightning storm sets the mahala's canines howling. A dawn chorus of crowing roosters welcomes the new day. Not long after the shimmy of horse and cart begins to resonate down potholed streets. Hooves, bell-decorated bridles and large rubber wheels create a warm dissonance as the mahala's rural workers take to the fields. Drums containing warm mineral water from a local spring are delivered by cart to the many houses in the mahala that lack hot water. A kiosk sells shots of intestine-scouring coffee alongside soft drinks, prepared foods and cosmetics. Several shots later and Lubka's prepared a breakfast of fry bread. She smiles and wiggles her head. Good morning, sunshine.

The mahala may play home to different religious congregations but all celebrate Ederlezi – the Romani name for the Balkan Festival of St George. The various Balkan spellings (Herdeljez, Erdelezi) are merely variants on the Turkish Hidirellez, a celebration occurring approximately forty days after the spring equinox so signalling the beginning of summer. The word itself is the combination of Hizir and Ilyas, two Anatolian prophets who drank from the spring of eternal life and thus promised to meet on this night, May 5th, every year to give rebirth to nature. Hizir is the protector of plants and the poor. Ilyas is the protector of waters and animals. Together they spread abundance and good health. The tradition dates back to pagan times with Christian and Muslim overtones added. For the Roma, wishes made on Ederlezi come true, the sick are healed, misfortune ends. According to Jony a cruel Tsar once sent a dragon to kill all the Roma – St George slew the dragon. Considering the dragons of Europe who have tried to enslave and exterminate the Roma these people require a strong saint.

Preparation for Ederlezi begins with New Morning, presenting awards for poems, essays, dancing – all are won by girls under fifteen. A poem is read saying Romas pray for better health/houses/work and until they get this they must keep singing the praises of God. Jony is asked to sing the anthem 'Ederlezi'. He requests everyone sing with him. Across the square there's a surge of pride as hundreds of voices rise.

Late afternoon: Jony and band set up on a makeshift stage built in front of Chico's café. The crowd is large and respectful, letting the smallest children gather at the front. The young women here possess a luminous, green-eyed beauty, Balkan-flavoured yet dappled by Asia. Yuli catches me eyeing the talent. 'Shukar?' he asks. 'Shu-kar,' I reply. Shukar being Romani for 'very good'. It would take someone with a trained eye to be able to select what ethnicity these girls were. But as the skin game's embedded deep in the East European psyche it appears locals can pick Roma, Turkish and Albanian origins from twenty paces. Beneath a bright Bulgarian sun all eyes are on Jony as he grabs the mic', grins at his assembled neighbours and leads the band into 'Ma Maren Ma'. Huge roar of appreciation. Jony's sound is a chilled balm, his voice curling and threading Romani phrases that all who are listening comprehend. The band – double bass, drums, percussion, saxophone, accordion, lead and rhythm guitar – cook up a gorgeous Gypsy soul gumbo, rolling the rhythm, stroking every note.

Jony takes a break and Anti-Pun soon have the crowd in stitches with a performance that finds Rambo sniffing glue while dad's on the run and mum bargains with a bill collector. Another skit pokes fun at Roma leaders who grow fat from playing at politics. Even with the language barrier this is good stuff. Jony returns and the performance is now one of collective joy – local men jump on stage and launch sky rockets, female singer Cherina duets and belly dances, people form lines and dance through the crowd, babies are held aloft, girls shake it, glowing gold and myrrh in the late afternoon light.

As the concert finishes the wail of a clarinet in the distance announces Alex's engagement party is heading towards the square. I venture out and get swept into a twisting horo, snaking around musicians (clarinet, accordion, bass drum), forming circles, swinging in a ragged anti-clockwise motion. The trio join Jony's band on stage so creating an epic wedding band. Trays of biscuits and cakes are held high by Lubka and friends, a sugar fix for dancers, whilst Macarena spins amongst the crowds, a blur of henna beauty. As night settles the engagement party retires to Chico's café. Next to me sits Rashid.

'It's good to be a nigga,' he says.

'Say what?'

'Look at USA. Best singers – niggas. Best boxers – niggas. Best athletes – niggas.'

OK, comprendo. For centuries the Roma have been referred to as 'blacks' by their paler neighbours. Via hip-hop this curse of blackness is sonically transformed into 'nigga power'. Liberation via MTV, hey? Rashid and friends have a limited understanding of New Zealand and a cynical one of the West. David Beckham is the most famous British citizen here. Blair and Bush are held in general contempt although it's hard to imagine the Roma viewing many politicians with respect.

A screen is set up on a rooftop to show Anti-Pun's feature-length video. The entire mahala ebbs and flows with people. Some watch the video, others wander in large merry groups. Girls dance across the square, men stand on rooftops, the atmosphere is relaxed, easy, festive. And then the fires start. A tractor tyre's soaked in gasoline. Snap. Crackle. Pop. Booooooooooom. Dense flame. Harsh fumes. Toxic smoke. On they come, the Gypsy zombies, wired on glue and rakija – *Here we are now, entertain us!* – feeling their way into the night, occupying a corner of the square, creating the Ederlezi apocalypse.

Look at them, these once golden youths stepping out of the shanties, carrying personal stereos – *ghetto blasters? Hey yah!* – pumping chalga, ripped and scary, toxic avengers, so high they're blind, bodies bent in the urban nihilist shuffle. Not that this distracts the vast mahala from street and house parties: as the witching hour strikes and May 6th begins tides of people dance down the street, alive to all the magical possibilities of Ederlezi, morphing through the darkness, communicating with old St George, sending out signals to ancient Asia, laughing hard, loose and rolling, all wild Gypsy joy. Another latex eruption while a clarinet shrieks into the night air. This mahala, its Roma, these Gypsies, oh, how they dance! On and on and on and on. Forcing themselves into an endless night, running through the urban jungle, dancing and singing until exhaustion topples, dancing and singing as a celebration of their very survival, the rattling drum, wheezy accordion and reedy clarinet being, for the righteous in a poor town, a triple-pronged sonic crown, a statement of how special you are and what you're worth. So let's just dance…

Epilogue:

Sometimes the Bear Gets You…

'You know the Gypsy cookbook? Every recipe starts the same. Say it's a chicken dish. The instructions read, "First, you steal a chicken…"' Much laughter. Yeah, we are merry, a little messy, I'm feeling ragged but then that's par for the course. The evening's comedian is Buca, a Serb Roma and Gypsy musician exiled in London. And our venue is the Polish Club, a west London restaurant complex housed in a gloriously faded modernist building. The Polish Club provides a meeting point for Slavs and a de facto centre for London's Balkan community. In the last year, notes Buca, he's backed Serbia's Olivera Katarina and Macedonia's Usnija Redžepova here. Belgrade's Kal made their 2004 London debut here.

Amongst the joking and singing Buca and I swap Balkan news: Kosovar Albanian thugs once again burning out and murdering the remaining Serb and Roma populace. Churches aflame in Kosovo. Mosques aflame in Serbia. Still Serbia, after four attempts at choosing a President to replace the assassinated Zoran Djindjić, gave reformist Boris Tadić the nod over an extreme nationalist. Šaban, Buca's old employer, is recovering from a heart bypass and has scored with 'Geljan Dade', a song he recorded with Croatia's leading salsa band Cubismo. After playing a triumphant concert in Zagreb, Šaban took his earnings and blew them at the local casino. As ever, a great consumer of life. Esma's currently without a Western recording deal so has recorded an album singing her songs in Serbian and has been touring as a guest of Boban Marković. She also held down a month's residency at Barcelona's Forum arts fair. Elvis and Perihan have separated. Yuli and Slavka

Photo: archive Asphalt Tango

Every picture tells a story…the young Ioan Ivaneca

reunited. Azis mimed and minced outrageously in front of three hundred barmy Bulgarians at Walthamstow's The Pavilion (his first UK date) and recorded three of Yuli Iliev's tunes on his 2004 album *The King*. The Taraf and Fanfare continue their international conquests. Macedonia, shaken by an earthquake in Skopje, census results showing Albanians make up 25 per cent of the population and the death of President Boris Trajkovski in a plane crash, holds its breath as bad news (terror real and fabricated) hovers over this fragile, soulful nation. Balkan life…never a calm moment.

'You know what they call a Gypsy who sells CDs? CD-Rom!' I heard that one when last in Belgrade. Got another? 'What do you call a Gypsy who smells nice? A Roma!' That's so corny. C'mon, Buca, something funny. He shrugs then asks, 'How do you know when you've finished your book?' No punch line I can offer. Still, a simple answer: Transylvanian flu (i.e. pneumonia) and chronic asthma provided the required coda.

The Balkans offer many things, including the ability to stomp an unwary traveller into absolute submission – old

Europe showing no mercy for the unprepared. Balkan hospitals aren't something I'd advise the casual traveller to check out; no matter how much people complain about Britain's National Health Service it remains free and welcoming. To the young doctor who received me at King's College A&E, many thanks for helping me breathe again. So. There. Not an easy way to end an assignment but, hey, at least I got to hear the bands play. And did they ever play: music isn't exclusive to the Roma; instead, they generate an energy field and welcome all to share it. For these are generous people.

Back in the early 90s I chose the Taraf over techno, Esma over Oasis. No regrets: if music is the soul of human culture then the Roma should be celebrated for constantly fertilising Europe's soul, for keeping the continent's culture fresh when so many are involved in marketing its more dehumanising elements. They've received little praise over the past thousand years, remaining – to some degree – 'the only group about which anything could be said without challenge or demurral'; that quote comes from the late Palestinian writer Edward Said, a man who knew too much about a people being demonised and exiled.

For now, I can only give thanks to all whom I encountered, their generosity and musical eloquence suggesting the Roma remain natural aristocrats. Maybe one day ethnicity won't be important and those we call Gypsies will exist and be judged as all others are. And maybe one day peace on earth will break out. Till then, the Roma have a saying:

> *Sometimes you get the bear*
> *Sometimes the bear gets you*

SELECT BIBLIOGRAPHY

Books

Barany, Zoltan, *The East European Gypsies: Regime Change, Marginality, and Ethnopolitics*, Cambridge University Press, 2002

Bechet, Sidney, *Treat it Gentle*, Corgi, 1960

Bennett, Christopher, *Yugoslavia's Bloody Collapse*, Hurst & Company, 1995

Booth, Stanley *Rhythm Oil*, Jonathan Cape, 1991

Broughton, Simon, Ellingham, Mark and Trillo, Richard, *World Music: Africa, Europe and the Middle East*, Rough Guide, 1999

Clergue, Lucien, *Les Gitans* (introduction by Tony Gatlif), MarVal Collection, 1996

Clergue, Lucien, *Roots: The Gipsy Kings & Their Journey: A Photographic History* (introduction by Garth Cartwright), On-Stage, 2004

Drakulić, Slavenka, *Café Europe*, Abacus, 1995

Fonseca, Isabel, *Bury Me Standing*, Vintage, 1995

Fraser, Angus, *The Gypsies*, Blackwell, 1995

Glenny, Misha, *The Balkans 1804–1999: Nationalism, War and the Great Powers,* Granta, 1999

Guralnick, Peter, *Feel Like Going Home,* Penguin, 1970

Hancock, Ian, *We are the Romani People,* University of Hertfordshire Press, 1988

Hickey, Dave, *Air Guitar*, Art Issues Press, 1997

Interface 27, Gypsy Research Centre, 1997

James, Jeremy, *Vagabond*, Pelham Books, 1991

Keil, Charles and Vellou, Angeliki, *Bright Balkan Morning*, Wesleyan University Press, 2002

Kenrick, Donald and Puxon, Grattan, *Gypsies Under the Swastika*, University of Hertfordshire Press, 1995

Kenrick, Donald, *Gypsies: From the Ganges to the Thames*, University of Hertfordshire Press, 2004

Leblon, Bernard, *Gypsies and Flamenco*, University of Hertfordshire Press, 1994

Lomax, Alan, *Mister Jelly Roll*, Pan Books, 1959

Lomax, Alan, *The Land Where the Blues Began*, Minerva, 1993

Magris, Claudio, *Danube*, Collins Harvill, 1986

Manea, Norman, *On Clowns*, Faber and Faber, 1994

Marre, Jeremy and Charlton, Hannah, *Beats of the Heart: Popular Music of the World*, Pluto Press, 1985

Murphy, Dervla, *Through The Embers of Chaos: Balkan Journeys*, John Murray, 2002

Palmer, Robert, *Deep Blues*, Penguin, 1981

Rădulescu, Speranţa, *Chats About Gypsy Music*, Paideia, 2004

Ristić, Dušan and Leonora, Suzanne, *Romani Songs from Central Serbia and Beyond*, Galbeno, 2004

Thompson, Robert Farris, *Flash of the Spirit*, Vintage, 1983

Tong, D., *Gypsy Folk Tales*, Havest Books, 1989

Udovički, Jasminka and Ridgeway, James, eds., *Burn This House: the Making and Unmaking of Yugoslavia*, Duke, 1997

Ugrešić, Dubravka, *The Culture of Lies*, Phoenix House, 1998

Ventura, Michael, *Shadow Dancing in The USA*, Jeremy P. Tarcher, Inc., 1986

Academic and Human Rights Reports

Bandy, Alex, *The Forgotten Holocaust*, The Hungary Report, No. 305, July 1997

Cartwright, Garth, 'A Little Bit Special': Censorship and the Gypsy Musicians of Romania*, Freemuse, 2001

Haji, Amina, *Kosovar Refugees in the Republic of Macedonia: An Outsider's Perspective*, Center for Refugee and Forced Migration Studies, Institute for Sociological, Juridical, and Political Studies, Skopje, Republic of Macedonia, November 2002

Helsinki Watch, *Destroying Ethnic Identity: The Persecution of Gypsies in Romania*, September 1991

Index on Censorship, *Gypsies: Life on the Edge*, July/August 1998 (featuring writings by G. Grass, I. Hancock, D. Kenrick)

Pettan, Svanibor, 'Male, Female, and Beyond in Culture and Music of the Roma in Kosovo', *Music and Gender: Perspectives from the Mediterranean*, Chicago University Press

Pettan, Svanibor, 'Gypsy Musicians and Folk Music Research in the Territories of Former Yugoslavia', Mediterranean Ethnological Summer School, vol. 4, Bojan Baskar and Irena Weber, eds., 2002

Pettan, Svanibor, 'The Encounter with "the Other" from Within. The Roma at the Center of a Musical and Academic Debate', *The World of Music*, Bamberg, 43/2–3:119–137, 2001

Pettan, Svanibor, 'Gypsies, Music and Politics in the Balkans: A Case Study from Kosovo', *Music, Language, and Literature of the Roma and Sinti*, Intercultural Music Studies 11, Max Peter Baumann, ed., Berlin: VWB, 263–292, 2000

Pettan, Svanibor, 'Lambada in Kosovo: A Profile of Gypsy Creativity', *Journal of the Gypsy Lore Society*, Washington D.C., 2: 117–130, 1992

Save The Children, *Denied a Future? The Right to Education of Roma/ Gypsy and Traveller Children in Europe*, 2001

Silverman, Carol, 'Move Over Madonna: Gender, Representation, and The Mystery of Bulgarian Voices', *Over the Wall/After the Fall: Post-Communist Cultures Through an East–West Gaze*, Magda Zaborowska, Sibelan Forrester, and Elena Gapova, eds., Indiana University Press, 2004

Silverman, Carol, 'Researcher, Advocate, Friend: An American Fieldworker among Balkan Roma 1980–1996', *Fieldwork Dilemmas: Anthropologists in Postsocialist States*, Hermine De Soto and Nora Dudwick, eds., University of Wisconsin Press, 2000

Silverman, Carol, 'Music and Marginality: Roma (Gypsies) of Bulgaria and Macedonia', M. Slobin, ed., *Retuning Culture: Musical Changes in Central and Eastern Europe*, Duke University Press, 1996

Silverman, Carol, 'State, Market, and Gender Relationships among Bulgarian Roma, 1970s–1990s', *East European Anthropology Review* 14 (2), 4–15, 1996

Silverman, Carol, 'Music and Power: Gender and Performance among Roma (Gypsies) of Skopje, Macedonia', *The World of Music* (Journal of the International Institute for Traditional Music) 38(1), 1996

Silverman, Carol, 'Roma of Shuto Orizari, Macedonia: Class, Politics, and Community', *East–Central European Communities: The Struggle for Balance in Turbulent Times*, D. Kideckel, ed., Westview Press, 1996

Statman, Julia, *Why Have the Roma Not Been Represented in the Holocaust?* Dissertation, Camberwell College of Arts, 1998

Sweeney, John, *The Life and Evil Times of Nicolae Ceausescu*, Random House, 1991

Magazines, Newspapers, Internet Journals

Colors 42, February–March 2001

Daily Telegraph, Zenga Longmore, 'Robber Brides', T Travel, July 15 2000; Garth Cartwright, 'The Real Gypsy Kings', Telegraph Magazine, April 29 2000

Economist, 'Can Moldova Get Worse?' July 13 2000; 'The Land That Time Forgot', September 21 2000; 'A New Misery Curtain', May 31 2001; 'Outsiders Aren't Helping', February 13 2003; 'A Gypsy Awakening', September 9 1999

Evening Standard, Pete Clark, 'Hello Boys', June 7 2001

Financial Times, Stefan Wagstyl and Phelim McAleer, 'Survey: Romania', October 3 2001

Folk Roots, Garth Cartwright, 'Transylvania: Hora Time In Maramures', December 2001; Garth Cartwright, 'Šaban Bajramović', June 2002; Lemez Lovas, 'Guča Festival', April 2003

Guardian, Jonathan Romney 'The Gypsy King', G2, August 14 1997; Kate Connolly, 'Even When I'm Singing' G2, May 8 2000; Kate Connolly, 'New World, Old Struggle', Society, June 7 2000; Kate Connolly, 'Europe's Gypsies Lobby For Nation Status', July 28 2000; Jake Bowers, 'Gypsy Kings', Society, October 25 2000; John O'Mahony, 'In the Ghetto', Saturday Review, November 3 2001; Jake Bowers, 'No Room to Move', Society, June 5 2002; George Monbiot, 'Acceptable Hatred', November 4 2003; Robert Nurden, Robert Nurden @Letanovce, March 8 2004

Independent on Sunday, Cole Morton, 'The Secret Neglect of a Nation's Children', December 17 2000

National Geographic, Peter Godwin, 'Gypsies: The Outsiders', April 2001

New Zealand Herald, Dina Kyriakidou, 'Child Bride, 12, Bolts Wedding in Vain', October 1 2003

Observer Magazine, Adam Higginbotham, 'Arkan & Me', January 4 2004

Patrin Web Journal, Ian Hancock, 'Time of the Gypsies', November 1997; Harold Tanner, 'The Roma Persecution', March 1997; Ian Hancock, 'The Trend to Minimize the Romani Holocaust', September 2000

UNESCO Courier, July–August 1994

www.eurozine.com/article/004-02-05-ditchev-en.html, Ivaylo Ditchev, 'Monoculturalism as Prevailing Culture: The Peculiar Absence of Ethnic Minorities from Bulgaria's Public Life'

www.filmintezet.hu/magyar/filmint/ moveast/8/Contents.htm, Marian Tutui, 'Is There a Recipe for Success in Balkan Films?'

www.geocities.com./paris1521/genocide/htm, Ian Hancock, 'The Genocide of the Roma'

Internet Sites

Balkanalysis; rich in features on all Balkan issues. The Roma feature rarely but what's going down politically and economically in their nations is being discussed here. www.balkanalysis.com

European Roma Information Office Brussels; an activist outfit at the heart of the EU. www.erionet.org

European Roma Rights Center; Budapest-based activists who combat abuses of Roma human rights and challenge governments over their nations' failings in this area. http://www.errc.org

Eurozine; features from all over Europe, often focusing on the Balkans, by leading European thinkers. More fun than it sounds. www.eurozine.com

Freemuse, the Scandinavian anti-music censorship organisation have reports on Romanian Roma and break new cases where Gypsy musicians face persecution. www.Freemuse.org

JourneyswithGypsies; Photos, features, news, etc. www.journeyswithgypsies.com

Kathy, an American Gypsy enthusiast, has lots of pop culture Gypsy trivia at www.pe.net/kathys/gypsy.html

Patrin; the major site for news, debate and in-depth features. www.geocities.com/Paris/5121/patrin.htm

Romani–English Glossary; polish up your language skills here. www2.arnes.si/eusmith/Romany/glossary.html

RomNews Network Newletter; contemporary happenings amongst the Roma. http://www.romnews.com

Ronald Lee, Canadian Roma activist. www.rmani.org

Guide Books

The Rough Guide to Romania, 2001
The Rough Guide to Bulgaria, 2002
Lonely Planet Eastern Europe, 2003

SELECT DISCOGRAPHY

I've tried to list albums that are largely available in the West but in some cases even these may be difficult to come by. Solution? The UK's major Balkan stockist is Passion Discs (www.passiondiscs.com) who handle both locally released and imported CDs. Good selection, good service, make use of 'em.

Compilations: many exist, here's a few of the best

Journeys With Gypsy Musicians (Honest Jons). Yup, the CD soundtrack to this book and the only disc where you will find everyone from Esma to Azis.

Road of the Gypsies (Network). Superb double CD opens with Camaron de la Isla at his most potent and then offers Gypsy music from across Asia and Europe.

Balkan Blues (Network). Good double CD selection that draws from the Balkan nations featured in *Princes Among Men* as well as Greece, Albania and Bosnia.

The Incredible Music of the Gypsies (Manteca). 14-track CD offers a good intro' to many of the genre's major stars.

Latcho Drom (Caroline). Superb soundtrack, from Rajasthan to France, of the fine film.

World of Gypsies Vols. 1–3 (Arc). Haphazard compilations that are worth checking simply because they often have obscure tracks unavailable elsewhere.

Serbia

Golden Brass Summit (Network). Fine double CD compilation taken from the Guča archives. Features all the major Serb brass orkestars of recent decades.

Srbija: Sounds Global (B92). Strong sampler of traditional Serb music, Gypsy and other.

Kosovo Roma (Arhefon). Magnificent CD of 'field' recordings from Kosovo in the early 1990s by ethno-musicologist Svanibor Pettan.

From unaccompanied vocal performances to near-psychedelic tallava.

Šaban Bajramović, *A Gypsy Legend* (World Connection). Šaban, backed by Bosnia's Mostar Sevdah Reunion. Gorgeous.

Šaban Bajramović, *Gypsy King Of Serbia* (Arc). Seventeen 1970s performances. Essential.

Šaban Bajramović, *Ciganske Pesme* (Biveco). 1990s home recording. Aficionados only.

Ljiljana Buttler, *The Mother of Gypsy Soul* (Snail). Rediscovered and backed by Mostar Sevdah Reunion, the awesome former Ms Petrović sings with wild beauty.

Ceca, *Greatest Hits Vols 1, 2 & 3* (Hi-Fi Centar). Trashy turbo-folk anthems? In spades.

Earth-Wheel-Sky-Band, *Waltz Romano* (Asphalt Tango). Olah Vince creates ambient, lush soundscapes.

Ekrem and Gypsy Groovz, *Rivers of Happiness* (Enja). Melodic and jazz-flavoured Balkan brass.

Kal, *Kal* (Galbeno). A solid effort with a fine reading of 'Djelem, Djelem'.

Boris Kovač and Ladaaba Orchest, *The Last Balkan Tango* (Piranha). Uncompromising meditation on the Balkan apocalypse.

Boban Marković, *Live in Belgrade* (Piranha). Monster brass blowout.

Boban Marković, *Boban & Marko* (Piranha). 2003 studio effort finds 15-year-old Marko taking giant steps while Boban draws from ancient places.

Alexander Šišić, *Magična Violina* (B92/Ring Ring). The master returns in 2004!

Macedonia

Gypsy Queens (Network). This superb double CD also features Romanian (Gabi and Romica), Hungarian and Spanish singers yet its most potent moments are six tracks by Esma and four Džansever tunes: the only Džansever you will find in the West.

The Very Best of Macedonia (Arc). Esma, Naat and a variety of lesser artists, most non-Roma, in this solid introduction to Macedonia's sonic riches.

Kočani Orkestar, *L'Orient Est Rouge* (Crammed). A stone classic of Macedonian brass.

Kočani Orkestar, *Gypsy Mambo* (Plane). Homemade, eccentric Balkan music.

Ferus Mustafov, *King Ferus* (Globestyle). Fourteen killer tunes. Great sound, great grooves.

Ferus Mustafov, *The Heart of Balkan Gypsy Soul* (Tropical Records). Ferus in concert. Listen and hear a tiny giant roar.

Esma Redžepova, *Queen of the Gypsies* (World Connection). Double CD of Esma's 1960s/1970s recordings, one CD in Romani, one in Macedonian. Thin sound yet essential.

Esma Redžepova, *Chaje Shukarije* (World Connection). 1999 effort finds Esma recutting several classics. Powerful vocal performances, indifferent production.

Esma Redžepova, *Pomegju Dva Života* (KMP). Double CD (Romani and Macedonian) of 2002 recordings. Not often inspired but, for Esma watchers, a worthy effort.

Romania

Romania: Wild Sounds from Transylvania, Wallachia & Moldavia (Network). Good compilation of traditional Romanian Gypsy music that, beyond the Taraf and Fanfare, generously gathers artists I'm unaware of. Recommended.

Hungary & Romania – Descendants of The Itinerant Gypsies (Music of The Earth). Raw field recordings of village celebrations. This is it, music untreated for the Western ear.

Romania: Music for Strings from Transylvania (CNRS). Field recordings from north-eastern Transylvanian and Maramures. Ancient peasant music with some Gypsy input.

Suburban Bucharest: Mahala Sounds from Romania (Trikont). Eighteen urban tracks of largely Gypsy music recorded between 1936 and 2004. A secret city history on one CD!

Fanfare Ciocărlia, *Radio Pascani* (Piranha). Full-on debut offers the wildest brass blast you may hear in this life.

Fanfare Ciocărlia, *Baro Biao (World Wide Wedding)* (Asphalt Tango). Taking the Moldavian wedding party to the world: throw out your techno, this is the real funky shit.

Fanfare Ciocărlia, *Iag Bari* (Asphalt Tango) Third and most adventurous FC album. The horns are tempered for some soulful wailing.

Fulgerică, *Fulgerică & The Mahala Gypsies* (World Connection). The accordion virtuoso and his band and friends in full swing.

Nicolae Gutsa, *The Greatest Living Gypsy Voice* (Silex). Ignore the title and you still have a good CD powered by Gutsa's charged vocal.

Toni Iordache, *A Virtuoso of the Cimbalom* (Electrecord). Toni's best efforts available across two CDs. Music that sparkles like sunshine on water.

Mahala Rai Banda, *Mahala Rai Banda* (Crammed). Hot manele party band.

Muzsikás, *The Lost Jewish Music of Transylvania* (Hannibal). Hungary's Muzsikás recreate what was once the klezmer music of these beautiful, tragic lands.

Romica Puceanu, *Blestemat Sa Fii De Stele* (Electrecord). Nineteen perfect performances.

Dona Dumitru-Siminică, *Cine Are Fata Mare* (Electrecord). Haunted Gypsy soul.

Taraf de Haïdouks, *Musique des Tziganes de Roumanie* (Crammed). Seminal debut.

Taraf de Haïdouks, *Honourable Brigands, Magic Horses and Evil Eye* (Crammed). Highly entertaining second album.

Taraf de Haïdouks, *Dumbala Dumba* (Crammed). Balkan celebration time.

Taraf de Haïdouks, *Band of Gypsies* (Crammed). Live in Bucharest in 2001. Yup, better than Hendrix's *Band of Gypsies*.

Bulgaria

Folk Music of Bulgaria (Topic). Collected and edited by ethno-musicologist A. L. Lloyd, this gets the raw folk music of Bulgaria before communism distorted it.

Azis, *Azis 2002* (Sunny). Nasty disco-folk mutations, bhangra rips, epic ballads…it can only be Azis.

Azis, *Best* (Sunny). The hits up to early 2003 gathered. Worth it for the cover alone.

Azis, *Naked* (Sunny). Easily his finest, opening with a stomping bhangra chant and never letting up.

Azis, *King* (Sunny). 2004 effort finds him wailing alongside the obligatory chalga.

Jony Iliev, *Ma Marren Ma* (Asphalt Tango). Roaring Gypsy soul.

Sofi Marinova, *Studen Plamâk* (ARA). Sofi at her most potent on folk ballad 'Danniova Mama'.

Sofi Marinova, *Osudena Liubov* (ARA). Opens with Sofi and Azis duet. As ever, over-produced but her most consistent set.

Sofi Marinova, *The Best of Vols. 1 & 2* (ARA). All her Bulgarian hits are here.

Le Mystère des Voix Bulgare (4AD). Ethereal classic featuring the otherworldly voices of Bulgaria's village choirs.

Ivo Papazov, Panair (Kuker). Surprise: Papazov returns in 2004 with his best album yet. Artful, chilled, ECM-ish jazz mixed with fiery Oriental clarinet.

Yuri Yunakov, Balada (Traditional Crossroads). Sax' master and former Papazov sparring partner delivers solid album of slick wedding music.

Elsewhere

Ando Drom, Phari Mamo (Network). Superb Hungarian Gypsy band playing traditional music with Mitsou's distinctive vocals right up front.

Bebo and Cigala, Lagrimas Negras (Calle 54). Sublime pairing of Spanish Gitano singer Diego El Cigala and Cuban pianist Bebo Valdes.

Vera Bilá and Kale, Rovava (BMG Ariola). Vera mixes Czech Gypsy song with Latin flavours to fine effect.

Bratsch, Rien Dans Les Poches (Network). Eclectic French band draft in Ando Drom for fabulous results.

Gipsy Kings, Gipsy Kings (Columbia). Bamboleo & co'. Way cool.

Gipsy Kings, Roots (SINE). 2004 return to form. Their flamenco-flavoured, Gitano rumba retains undeniable charm.

Camaron de la Isla, Autoretrato (Phillips). Nineteen-track career overview. The rawness of the voice, the intensity of the delivery…only Camaron.

Istanbul Oriental Ensemble, Sultan's Secret Door (Network). Turkish Gypsy ensemble create glorious soundtrack for harems.

Mustafa Kandıralı and Ensemble, Caz Roman (Network). Turkish clarinet master M. Kandıralı blows beautifully.

Kanizsa Csillagai, The Boyash Gypsies of Hungary (Arc). Solid CD of traditional music from south-western Hungary.

Kalyi Jag, Gypsy Folk Songs from Hungary (Hungaroton, Hungary). Formed in 1978, this 1994 album is one of their best.

Loyko, Road of the Gypsies (Network). Named after violinist Loyko Zabar, this trio (two violins, classical guitar) create elegiac ballads with a rich Slavic flavour.

Jose Merce, Aire (Virgin). Fine 2000 album from the leather-lunged, mullet-headed icon of contemporary flamenco.

Mitsoura, *Mitsoura* (Mitsoura). High-tech remodelling of Ando Drom finds Mitsou's distinctive voice riding tabla breakbeats and ambient drift.

Mostar Sevdah Reunion, *MSR* (World Connection). Majestic album of traditional Sevdah music from the Bosnian traditional band. Esma Redžepova guests.

Parno Graszt, *Ravagok A Zongorara* (Fono). Very frantic and engaging debut from a village band in southern Hungary.

Django Reinhardt, *Retrospective 1934–53* (Saga). Thorough 3-CD compilation that covers DR's output from 1934 to 1953. Comes with a beautifully illustrated seventy-seven-page book.

Romano Drom, *Ande Lindri* (Daqui). Good 2003 album by leading Hungarian Gypsy band specialising in spicy vocal polyrhythms.

The Rough Guide To Gypsy Swing (World Music Network). Twenty-one-track compilation suggesting France's Manouche are busy keeping Django's legacy alive.

Russian Gypsy Soul (Network). Entertaining if overwrought (mucho restaurant emotions) double CD collection featuring Loyko, Lilya Erdenko and many others.

Various Artists, *Early Cante Flamenco* (Arhoolie). Recordings from the 1930s. A chance to observe how well cante jondo (deep song) stands against the US's country blues of the era. Features Gitano legends Manolo Caracol, Nina de los Peines and others..

SELECT FILMOGRAPHY

The Roma people have been the subject of documentary and feature films almost as soon as the medium was invented – a short of a travelling family was shot in Hungary in 1895 and another of Gypsy musicians and dancers in the US in 1906. Generally they're cast as thieves or mystical tricksters and played by anyone with a tan complexion. So beware when shopping for movies labelled 'Gypsy'.

Films listed are those generally available on video/DVD across Western Europe or, at least, in their home nations.

Serbia
I Even Met Happy Gypsies – director Aleksandar Petrović's 1967 film remains awfully brutal viewing.

Underground – Kustruica's 1995 epic comic fable about the rise and fall of Tito's Yugoslavia features brass bands galore and no little charm amongst the chaos.

Black Cat, White Cat (1998) – or Carry On Up The Balkans...Gypsy slapstick.

Cabaret Balkan (1998) – Misanthropic and misogynist satire of Milošević's Serbia.

Pretty Dyana – fine 2002 documentary on Kosovar Roma refugees surviving in Belgrade by reinventing old Dyana cars. Available www.dribblingpictures.com

Kosovo: Through the Eyes of Local Rom (Gypsy) Musicians – footage shot 1984–91 by Svanibor Pettan of Kosovar Gypsy musicians at work.

Macedonia
Time of the Gypsies – initially shot in Shutka, for the first hour this 1989 epic is a magnificent, magic/realist portrait of Balkan Roma.

Before the Rains – no Roma feature here, just the beauty and tragedy of Macedonia as Macedonian and Albanian citizens take to blood feuds in 1994.

Esma: The Fabulous Queen of The Gypsies (2005) – documentary focusing on Esma Redžepova. Features Elvis's wedding with rockin' footage of Sudahan's band. Produced and directed by yours truly and Michelle Rosaus.

Romania

Latcho Drom – Tony Gatlif's wonderful 1993 musical journey from India to Andalucia contains a great Clejani sequence with the Taraf and their neighbours.

Gadjo Dilo – superb 1995 film set in a traditional Roma community in rural Romania.

Iag Bari – 2001 documentary following Fanfare Ciocărlia as they venture from their village across the world.

Fanfare Ciocărlia: The Story of The Band (2004) – awesome DVD package featuring a live in Berlin concert, an edited version of Iag Bari, interviews, history, videos, Gypsy Caravan trailer. And more. Go buy!

Bulgaria

Azis: Live at the National Stadium October 2003 – big fella, big spectacle. More fun than anyone should rightly have.

Whose is This Song? – Adela Peeva's 2003 documentary finds her in search of the shared roots of a folksong all Balkan nations appear to claim as 'ours'. Travelling through Bulgaria, Turkey, Greece, Albania, Bosnia, Serbia and Macedonia she uncovers a feast of music and nationalism. Contains footage of Ederlezi and from the 1950s Yugoslav film *Ciganka*. Excellent if flawed: no Gypsy musicians are interviewed and Peeva fails to challenge a Serb nationalist's anti-Roma sentiments.

Elsewhere

Los Tanantos – Francisco Rovira Beleta's fabulous 1962 study of conflict between two Barcelona Roma families features a young Antonio Gades and Carmen Amaya. Filmed in the now vanished Somorrostro barrio, it's vivid with flamenco music and dance.

Angelo My Love – Robert Duvall directed this 1979 docudrama focusing on Angelo, a disco-dancing, street-hustling, Romani-speaking child of Balkan Roma origins in New York. A fixed kris and interracial puppy love keep things interesting.

Carmen (1983) – the second and best of Carlos Saura's flamenco triology. Antonio Gades is the dance instructor who falls for Laura Del Sol's Carmen during a flamenco staging of the Bizet opera. Paco de Lucia plays himself. The dance scenes sizzle.

Terra Gitano (1994) – PBS documentary on The Gipsy Kings and their community.

Seville South Side – offbeat 2003 flamenco documentary shot in Seville's Las Tres Mills, home to the city's Gitano community since the 1960s.

Mondo – Tony Gatlif's visually stunning, near-silent 1996 effort about a young Roma boy who wanders around a French town is a meditation on displacement.

Vengo – Gatlif's 2000 drama of conflict amongst Andalucian Gitano families opens with a musical collaboration between guitarist Tomatito and North African Sufi musicians led by Sheikh Ahmed Al Tuni. As ever, the master's at work.

Swing – Gatlif's 2002 feature focuses on French Manouche who keep Django Reinhardt's legacy alive.

Savršeni Krug/Perfect Circle (1997) – filmed in Sarajevo not long after the siege ended. A beautiful, excruciating film.

No Man's Land – Bosnian director Daniš Tanović's fine, blackly comic meditation on the absurdity of war won the 2002 Oscar for Best Foreign Film. Good choice.

Black & White in Colour (1999) – fine documentary chronicling Czech Gypsy singer Vera Bilá's life and music.